The Misfits

By the same author

Non-Fiction
The Outsider
Religion and the Rebel
The Age of Defeat
Encyclopaedia of Murder (with Pat Pitman)
The Strength to Dream
Rasputin and the Fall of the Romanovs
The Brandy of the Damned (Essays on Music)
Beyond the Outsider
Eagle and Earwig (Essays on Books and Writers)
Sex and the Intelligent Teenager
Introduction to the New Existentialism
Poetry Mysticism
A Casebook of Murder
Shaw – A Study of his Work
The Occult
New Pathways in Psychology
Order of Assassins
Mysteries
The Quest for Wilhelm Reich
A Criminal History of Mankind

Fiction
Ritual in the Dark
Adrift in Soho
The Schoolgirl Murder Case
The Philosopher's Stone
The Mind Parasites
The Killer
The God of the Labyrinth
The Glass Cage
The World of Violence
Necessary Doubt
Man Without a Shadow
The Black Room
The Space Vampires
The Janus Murder Case
Spider World: The Tower
Spider World: The Delta

Autobiography
Voyage to a Beginning

Colin Wilson

A STUDY OF SEXUAL OUTSIDERS

The Misfits

Carroll & Graf Publishers, Inc.
New York

HQ
71
.W525
1989

Copyright © 1988 by Colin Wilson

All rights reserved

First Carroll & Graf edition 1989

Carroll & Graf Publishers, Inc.
260 Fifth Avenue
New York, NY 10001

LIBRARY OF CONGRESS
Library of Congress Cataloging-in-Publication Data

Wilson, Colin, 1931–
  The misfits : a study of sexual outsiders / Colin Wilson.
    p.   cm.
  Bibliography: p.
  Includes index.
  ISBN 0-88184-420-9 : $19.95
  1. Sexual deviation.   2. Sexual deviation in literature.
I. Title.
HQ71.W525   1989
306.7—dc19   88-20979
                                                  CIP

Manufactured in the United States of America

CONTENTS

Acknowledgements
13

ONE
The Secret of Charlotte Bach
15

TWO
Charlotte and the Mysteries of Evolution
33

THREE
Anarchy Incarnate
47

FOUR
Romantic Agonies
71

FIVE
Rebel Angel
92

SIX
From Rebellion to Sex Crime
115

SEVEN
Victorian Misfits
143

EIGHT
Guilt and Defiance
172

NINE
Misfits or Mystics?
202

POSTSCRIPT
The Fifth Window
244

Bibliography
263

Index
266

ANALYTICAL TABLE
OF CONTENTS

————◆•◆————

One: *THE SECRET OF CHARLOTTE BACH*

Magnus Hirschfeld's *Sexual Anomalies and Perversions*. Case of musician who preferred schoolgirls. The problem of 'absurd good news'. Are 'moments of vision' an illusion? Why do so many sexual perversions date from the nineteenth century? George Selwyn, the necrophile. *The Outsider*. True case on which Barbusse's *Hell* is based. 'Criminal Outsiders'. *Origins of the Sexual Impulse*. How do we define sexual perversion? Opposing views of Tolstoy and Gide. A letter from Charlotte Bach. Her theory of 'emergent evolution'. The instability of great artists. Sexual perversion as the driving force behind evolution. Charlotte's account of herself. The transvestite professor. Charlotte becomes a cult figure. My article about her in *Time Out*. Bisexual behaviour of the ten-spined stickleback and zebra finch. Charlotte's eight sexual types. The eight-hour orgasm. 'That's what it's about – evolution!' What 'type' was Charlotte? Charlotte's *alter ego*, Carl Hajdu. How Carl Hajdu became a transvestite. Charlotte's novel *Fiona*. Hajdu's breakdown. Derrick Alexander discovers Hajdu's secret. Hajdu becomes Charlotte Bach.

Two: *CHARLOTTE AND THE MYSTERIES OF EVOLUTION*

Man and/or Woman. Carl Hajdu's sexual development. The desire of men and women to become *their opposite*. 'Displacement activities'. Social releasers. Man is a 'Peter Pan' species. Charlotte on alchemy. Her new vision of science. Why I rejected Charlotte's theory of evolution. Dr Johnson behaves like a pig. Charlotte versus Darwin. Charlotte and *Fiona*. Charlotte's murder. Charlotte's kleptomania. Charlotte's mendacity. The 'criminal streak' in

Dostoevsky. My account of Charlotte in *Mysteries*. Charlotte Bach and the Marquis de Sade.

Three: *ANARCHY INCARNATE*

'The most evil man who ever lived'. De Sade's kindliness. Must we burn de Sade? De Sade's childhood: 'The whole universe should humour my whims . . .' De Sade's love of flogging. His hatred of religion. His first arrest. De Sade's marriage. The Rose Keller incident. The Marseilles incident. De Sade's imprisonment. *Dialogue Between a Priest and a Dying Man. The 120 Days of Sodom. Aline and Valcour. Justine.* The misfortunes of incest. De Sade's lack of realism. The French Revolution. De Sade spares his in-laws. *Philosophy in the Bedroom.* De Sade as a 'violent man'. *Juliette.* De Sade's basic propositions. What is wrong with de Sade's philosophy? De Sade in the asylum at Charenton. De Sade versus Charlotte Bach.

Four: *ROMANTIC AGONIES*

Krafft-Ebing's *Psychopathia Sexualis*. Why were there so many perverts in the nineteenth century? What happened between 1740 and 1840? Sexual morals in the age of de Sade. De Sade's hatred of religion. Sex in fifteenth-century Venice. The meaning of fetishism. Samuel Richardson's *Pamela* – Europe learns to day-dream. Rousseau's *New Héloïse*. Its immense success. Goethe's *Werther*. The purpose of imagination: to improve on reality. Shelley. Novalis. Rape fantasies. Lewis's *The Monk*. Richardson as the father of pornography. Cleland's *Fanny Hill. The Story of Dom Bugger*. Anatomical precision of *Fanny Hill*: 'the power to conjure up reality in words'. Fielding, Smollett and Sterne. What is pornography *for*? The 'Barbusse phenomenon'. 'The Coolidge effect'. 'She is not my wife.' Sex and imagination. Masturbation is one of the highest human faculties. Evolution of the drama. 'Amplifying the emotions'. The creation of pornography.

Five: *REBEL ANGEL*

Byron wakes to find himself famous. Publication of *Childe Harold*. Byron's upbringing. His homosexuality. Sex life at Cambridge.

Pederasty on the Grand Tour. *Plenum et Optabilem Coitum.* Byron seduces Nicolo Giraud. The Byronic hero: combination of hero and villain. Lady Caroline Lamb. Byron seduces his sister. Byron's marriage. His separation. Social ostracism. His Italian mistresses. Death in Missolonghi. Byron's problem. The essence of sexual perversion. The quest for novelty. The 'reality function'. De Sade's illogicality. Byron as inspiration of the Romantic Movement.

Six: *FROM REBELLION TO SEX CRIME*

Sensation caused by Byron's death. Why Goethe was influenced by Byron. Byron as satanic rebel. 'Remove these curbs that keep me little.' Alexander Pushkin discovers Byron. *The Prisoner of the Caucasus*. Pushkin as Byronic hero. Pushkin's death. *Eugene Onegin*. Lermontov's *Death of a Poet*. *A Hero of Our Time*. What is an 'Outsider'? Imagination as a wonder-drug with dangerous side-effects. Gogol calls on Pushkin. His overnight fame. Gogol and 'solitary pleasures'. Gogol and the macabre. His romantic wanderlust. *Dead Souls*. Gogol as a 'man without qualities'. The problem of too much imagination. Gogol's death. The romantic reaction in western Europe. Victorian pornography. Little Miss Curious. Sexual fantasies of *The Pearl*. *The Power of Mesmerism*. Gurdjieff and Anglo-Saxon obscenities. Pornography as a special case of romanticism. The desire for 'the forbidden'. Blake and sexual fantasy. 'Focusing'. Lack of sex crime in the eighteenth century. The case of Andrew Bichel. Was Bichel a transvestite? The Frederick Baker case: 'Killed a young girl today. It was fine and hot.' Pieydagnelle and his murder rampage. Vincent Verzeni. Jesse Pomeroy. Sex crime and romanticism.

Seven: *VICTORIAN MISFITS*

Morley's review of Swinburne's *Poems and Ballads*. Swinburne's sado-masochism. His fascination with flogging. 'Glorious Eton beatings.' Meeting with Richard Monckton Milnes. Milnes' pornography collection. *Atalanta in Calydon*. Swinburne and Adah Mencken. The brothel in Circus Road. Swinburne's alcoholism. Retirement to Putney. Swinburne's admiration for de Sade. 'De Lautréamont' and *Maldoror*. 'The right to absolute selfishness'. Sergeant Bertrand, the necrophile. Arthur Munby and his obsession with working-class girls. Munby and Hannah. Why does the gorilla need a large brain? Nicholas Humphrey and his theory of 'social sensitivity'. 'Walter' and *My Secret Life*. 'The saint of sex'. Walter and cousin Fred. The joys of masturbation. Seduction of housemaids. Walter and Camille. Deliberate coarseness of Walter's language. His sexual obsession. His voyeurism. His experimentalism. Physical intimacy not natural to human beings. Scott Fitzgerald and *This Side of Paradise*. Inflation of language. The Jack the Ripper murders. Possible solution.

Eight: *GUILT AND DEFIANCE*

Sigmund Freud goes to Paris. Charcot and hysteria. 'Repeated doses of a normal penis'. Krafft-Ebing becomes Freud's ally. Moll's criticism of Freud. Moll's recognition of sexual energy. The Kipps Apparatus – 'reinforcement'. Havelock Ellis is troubled by seminal emissions. Ellis and Olive Schreiner. Ellis marries a lesbian. Ellis's *Studies in the Psychology of Sex*. Ellis meets Françoise. She urinates in Oxford Circus. Ellis and urolagnia. De Selincourt seduces Margaret Sanger. Ellis recognises that homosexuality is not a 'perversion'. Homosexuality as a legal offence. Tchaikovsky's suicide. The Wilde case. Biological basis of homosexuality. Theory of Dr Gunter Dorner. Magnus Hirschfeld and transvestism. The Institute for Sexual Science. Hirschfeld's view of perversion as emotional immaturity. Right-wing attacks on Hirschfeld. His escape from Germany. The Institute is closed. The sexual revolution. Ibsen and *Ghosts*. Zola and *Earth*. Shaw's *Mrs Warren's Profession*. Elinor Glyn's *Three Weeks*. Wells and *Ann Veronica*. Sudermann's *Song of Songs*. Suppression of *The Rainbow*. Proust: the Einstein of the novel. Proust and perversion. Joyce and *Ulysses*. Mrs Bloom's monologue. Lawrence and *Lady Chatterley*. Lawrence and censorship. Henry Miller and *Tropic of Cancer*. Orwell's assessment of Miller. Miller's *Opus Pistorum*. Miller's hatred of civilisation. D. H. Lawrence's hatred of intellect. The anti-intellectual cul-de-sac. Romantic freedom and intellectual anarchy.

Nine: *MISFITS OR MYSTICS?*

Ella Strom meets Percy Grainger. 'I am really not interested in anything but sex.' Grainger's sadism. Influence of Grainger's mother. Grainger's 'obsession with evil'. Grainger's 'Nazism'. Desire for incest. John Cowper Powys and sadism. *The Unforgivable Sin*. The 'mystical' aspect of sexual perversion. Lawrence and sodomy. Joyce and underwear fetishism. 'Superheated sex'. 'Cultivating the child' in ourselves. Jung and individuation. Jung's immaturity. The strange case of Paul Tillich. 'Screaming and kicking'. Was Tillich a fraud? Bertrand Russell. T. E. Lawrence and creative frustration. 'Professor Newcomer'. Revolt in a vacuum. Lawrence joins the RAF. The Deraa incident. Lawrence admits it is untrue. John Bruce's revelations about Lawrence's masochism. Ludwig Wittgenstein and sexual guilt. Wittgenstein at Cambridge. Wittgenstein's asceticism. The *Tractatus* as 'the solution of all problems of philosophy'. Russell and logical paradoxes. Wittgenstein's later philosophy. Wittgenstein trapped in the fly bottle. The compulsion to avoid boredom. The suicide of Yukio Mishima. Mishima's unstable childhood. Sadistic day-dreams. *Confessions of a Mask*. Mishima evades military service. Overnight fame. *Forbidden Colours*. Mishima's homosexuality. Financial success. Right-wing sympathies: the conversion to militaristic romanticism. 'Patriotism'. Mishima criticises the Emperor. *The Sailor Who Fell from Grace with the Sea*. *The Sea of Fertility*. Its ambiguity. Mishima's Shield Society. Mishima commits *seppuku*. 'Magical thinking'. 'The great romantic obsession'. 'Cutting adrift from reality'.

Postscript: *THE FIFTH WINDOW*

Lack of evidence for Charlotte's transsexual theory of evolution. Alternative theory based on the evolution of imagination. The history of imagination. The 'gap' between day-dreams and actuality. Maslow's hierarchy of needs. Sexual needs are halfway down the hierarchy. A wider view of evolution. The paradox: man's need for civilisation, and his tendency to become bored by security. The 'automatic gearbox'. The need to develop a 'manual gearbox'. Blake's 'fifth window' – the imagination. Disadvantages of sexual imagination – the rise of sex crime. 'Furnishing' the human mind. Do the lower animals possess imagination? The flatworm and boredom. Reinforcing the imagination. Faculty X. Proust and Toynbee. Koestler's experience in the Spanish jail. Julian Huxley's 'transhumanism'. Huxley's 'cultural' views of evolution. Rupert Sheldrake and his Hypothesis of Formative Causation. McDougal's experiment with white rats. How can crystals 'learn' from other crystals? 'Magnetic induction'. Does this explain the history of European culture since Richardson? Faculty X and its development. The Reality Function. Is man about to develop Faculty X?

ACKNOWLEDGEMENTS

I owe a considerable debt of gratitude to Bob Mellors for generously providing me with so much biographical information on Charlotte Bach, and to Della Aleksander for filling in some important gaps. I wish to thank the Percy Grainger Museum in Melbourne for providing information about Grainger. Geraint Jonathan drew my attention to the passage on James Joyce in Chapter Nine. I also owe a debt of gratitude to Kazue Kobata for insights into Mishima. The idea of this book originated in a conversation with my friend, Donald Seaman.

Colin Wilson
Gorran Haven, 1987

ONE

❖

The Secret of Charlotte Bach

I was in my early twenties when I first came upon Dr Magnus Hirschfeld's *Sexual Anomalies and Perversions*, subtitled 'A textbook for students, psychologists, criminologists, probation officers, judges, educationalists and all adults'. This impressive description was obviously an attempt to forestall a prosecution for pornography – the book was usually to be seen in the windows of shops that sold rupture trusses, sex aids and 'encyclopedias of sexual behaviour'. In those days before the permissive society, such works would never have been found in respectable bookshops.

Sexual Anomalies and Perversions was, in fact, compiled by Arthur Koestler, although his name does not figure on the title-page, and he never received any of the abundant royalties that the book must have earned over the years. There can be no doubt that most of its purchasers were not the judges, probation officers and educationalists envisaged by the publisher, but the kind of men who wear shabby mackintoshes and hang around playgrounds trying to peer up the skirts of schoolgirls on swings. After a few chapters describing the sexual organs and the biological foundations of sex, the book launches into the case-histories that are its real *raison d'être*. So on page 93, we encounter a twenty-nine-year-old musician who exclaims: 'How wonderful, how enthralling, how dainty are the figures of schoolgirls and how fat, plump and coarse are the figures of grown women. Are normal people blind?' And he goes on to admit: 'My urge for schoolgirls, which I am unable to satisfy on account of the law, I have hitherto tried to compensate in this way, that when I have a schoolgirl near me or walking with me, I take hold of her by the hand, or place a hand on her neck or leg, and masturbate without the girl noticing anything. After masturbating in the presence of the girl . . . I feel light, fresh, alert; there is something harmonious in my whole being.' As the book progresses, the cases become more bizarre: transvestism, sadism, masochism, necrophilia. A woman tells how she is tormented by an urge to bite her lovers and drink their blood; a young man describes how he achieves orgasm by swinging a chicken around so that its wings brush the tip of his penis . . .

I found it all scarcely credible. How on earth had people managed to develop such weird compulsions? Then, as I began to glimpse the answer, I experienced an excitement that was quite distinct from the inevitable sexual stimulation induced by the cases. The musician preferred schoolgirls because they were less complicated, in a sense less *real*, than adult women, as a dream is less complicated than reality. The basic paradox about sex is that it always seems to be offering more than it can deliver. A glimpse of a girl undressing through a lighted bedroom window induces a vision of ecstatic delight, but in the actual process of persuading the girl into bed, the vision somehow evaporates. Does this mean that the vision of ecstasy was a delusion? Not quite; for the real problem here is that of the *mechanics* of sexual intercourse. It could be compared to an unskilled pianist who knows that his rendering of the 'Liebestod' from *Tristan* is appalling, but who cannot do any better. So can a man be blamed if, instead of struggling with the complexities of real love-making, he enlists the help of his imagination to achieve satisfaction with a schoolgirl – particularly if the result is a sense of freshness, alertness and harmony?

What excited me was the recognition that this was simply another version of the problem that had obsessed me all my life – the problem of those moments when life seems entirely delightful, when we experience a sensation of what G. K. Chesterton called 'absurd good news'. Life normally strikes most of us as hard, dull and unsatisfying; but in these moments, consciousness seems to glow and expand, and all contradictions seem to be resolved. Which of the two visions is true? My own reflections had led me to conclude that the vision of 'absurd good news' is somehow broader and more comprehensive than the feeling that life is dull, boring and meaningless. Boredom is basically a feeling of *narrowness*, and surely a narrow vision is bound to be less true than a broad one?

My favourite poets and artists – the so-called 'romantics' of the nineteenth century – had been obsessed by the same problem. They had also experienced 'moments of vision', and then awakened the next morning to wonder if the whole thing was an illusion. They had also used their imaginations to compensate for the trivialities and frustrations of 'reality'. And this immediately led me to the interesting recognition that nearly every case in *Sexual Anomalies and Perversions* dated from the nineteenth century. Could that mean that sexual perversion and romanticism sprang from the same 'longing for distant horizons'? The Contents list of the book certainly seemed to support that conclusion; there were very few cases dating from earlier periods. One of the few exceptions was a comment on George Selwyn, an eighteenth-century gentleman who was obsessed by executions and never missed a hanging at Tyburn in many years. It was striking that Selwyn made no secret of his morbid fixation. When Lord Holland lay dying, he told his butler: 'If Mr Selwyn calls, show him in. If I am alive I shall be pleased to see him, and if I am dead he will be pleased to see me.' Selwyn's necrophilia was obviously talked about quite openly, as a rather amusing peculiarity. It was not until the nineteenth century that such little oddities became a matter for shame and concealment.

In the following year, 1954, I began to write a book about this problem of 'absurd good news' – about what Carlyle called the problem of 'Eternal Yes versus Eternal No'. My book was called *The Outsider*, and it opened with a paragraph about a man trying to look up women's skirts as they climb on buses. The character in question was the hero of Barbusse's novel *Hell*, a young man who finds a small hole in the wall of his hotel room, and spends his days peering through at the people who come and go in the next room. According to Hirschfeld, Barbusse had based the plot on the true case of a waiter who was prosecuted for boring a spy-hole in the communicating door between two hotel rooms, one of which was reserved for honeymoon couples. Barbusse's hero is obsessed by the problem of truth, and by his feeling that society conceals it under pretences. As he sits at dinner, he listens to a conversation about a man who has raped and strangled a little girl:

> A young mother, with her daughter at her side, has half got up to leave, but cannot drag herself away . . .
> And the men; one of them simple, placid, I heard distinctly panting. Another, with the neutral appearance of a bourgeois, talks commonplaces with difficulty to his young neighbour. But he looks at her as if he would pierce deeply into her, and deeper

yet. His piercing glance is stronger than himself, and he is ashamed of himself . . .

And when he listens to a novelist explaining that other writers deal in pretences while he stands for Truth, Barbusse's Outsider feels a weary disgust. Yet the paradox is that Barbusse himself does not dare to tell the truth. In the original case, the waiter masturbated as he looked through the hole, and often handled the penis of a boy who peered through another hole. Barbusse's hero also watches a young woman undressing in the next room, but the author is careful to avoid any suggestion of sexual excitement. There was no question of his telling the 'truth' about such a case. And, in *The Outsider*, I too was inclined to sidestep the sexual implications of the problem. I started to write a chapter called 'The Outsider as Criminal', dealing with sex killers like Jack the Ripper and the Düsseldorf murderer, Peter Kürten; but it struck me that it was out of place in a book that was mainly concerned with literature, and I abandoned it. (It was later printed as an appendix to my *Encyclopedia of Murder*.)

But in 1963, I decided to make another attempt to explore these sexual implications of 'Outsiderism', and wrote a book called *Origins of the Sexual Impulse*. It was not a success – most critics seemed to feel it was a disguised attempt to write soft pornography – but I felt that it came close to telling the truth about this problem that had fascinated me for so many years. I began by quoting the view of Tolstoy in *The Kreutzer Sonata*, that the modern world has created too much leisure, and that this has led to the sexual urge being exaggerated and distorted. In earlier centuries, says Tolstoy, most men worked so hard from dawn till dusk that they had little time for sexual indulgence. Now the upper classes have too much leisure, and they spend all their time thinking and dreaming about sex. According to Tolstoy, all this is a misuse of the sexual impulse. It was intended solely for reproduction, and should be practised for no other purpose. Even love-making between man and wife should be regarded as a 'perversion' unless it is aimed at producing children.

This view, I pointed out, at least has the merit of consistency. For how otherwise can we define that word 'perversion'? Most 'sexologists', from Krafft-Ebing to Hirschfeld, have defined sexual normality as 'any activity that leads ultimately to the act of reproduction'. So a man who wears a contraceptive is more 'abnormal' than a man who beats his wife to increase his sexual excitement, or a man who rapes a girl after knocking her unconscious. And this is plainly absurd. It defines normality in terms of the end rather than the means. The end of most sexual activity is to achieve orgasm. Surely it is the means by which it is achieved that define normality or abnormality?

André Gide took the opposite view from Tolstoy: that *no* form of sex is abnormal. In *Corydon*, a defence of homosexuality, he points out that animals are stimulated by the smell of oestrum released by a female on heat. Human beings have dispensed with the smell of oestrum. They have sex all the year round, and are stimulated by their individual sexual preferences – i.e. by *ideas*. So why should homosexuality or masochism be regarded as more 'abnormal' than sex between husband and wife?

In *Origins of the Sexual Impulse*, I examine various forms of sexual 'abnormality' and conclude that in human beings sexuality has evolved to a higher level, a 'symbolic' level. My conclusions parallel closely those of the philosopher Ernst Cassirer.

I had, apparently, at least one enthusiastic reader, although I was unaware of it at the time – a strange lady who called herself Dr Charlotte Bach, who had arrived in England soon after the Communist takeover in Hungary in 1948. She was obsessed by one particular sexual abnormality: transvestism, the tendency of men to dress up in women's clothes. She wrote to me for the first time in the autumn of 1971, sending me lengthy extracts from a work-in-progress called *Homo Mutans, Homo Luminens* (an almost untranslatable title, meaning 'Man the Changer, Man the Light-bringer'). Its 'Prolegomena' alone was more than 500 pages long, and began with the sentence: 'This book is an introduction to the introduction proper to human ethology and to a new theory of emergent evolution.' This was one of the few sentences in the book that was more or less comprehensible to me. The author explained that her ideas were practically unintelligible because they were so new, then went on to make them even more unintelligible by writing in an abstract jargon that made me feel dizzy. She was like a person who, asked to tell you what he did this morning, draws a deep breath and begins: 'I have to start with the birth of my great-grandfather . . .' Moreover, the work was full of jeers and sneers at all the people she disagreed with – and she seemed to disagree with just about everybody. She was obviously a highly abrasive and aggressive lady, and my first impression was that she was one of those paranoid nuts who place an absurdly high value on themselves, and lose their temper with anyone who seems even mildly sceptical.

But one October day, when I was confined to bed with a severe cold, I decided to make a determined onslaught on the vast type-script and see if I couldn't at least get some inkling of what she was talking about. And although I was not particularly successful on this first attempt, it soon became obvious to me that she was a woman of formidable intelligence, and that her reading had been very wide indeed – philosophers, alchemists, biologists, zoologists, psychologists, cosmologists . . . She obviously had difficulty ex-plaining herself in words of one syllable, but it was equally clear that she had something important to say. I wrote the same day to tell her so. And her reply, which came almost by return, began: 'Thankyou, thankyou, thankyou and thankyou again . . . Your reply was what I expected, but was afraid to hope for . . .' She told me later that when she read my letter, she burst into floods of tears.

As far as I could make out, her basic idea was this. There is in every man and woman a powerful element of the opposite sex, which attracts like a magnet. In other words, every male has a deep unconscious desire to *become* a woman, and every female has the same urge to become a man. This makes us sexually unstable and explains why there are so many sexual perversions. But it is pre-cisely this instability that makes human beings so creative and has led to the amazing growth of human culture and civilisation. Culture is not simply the outcome of man's craving for security and happi-ness; it is the outcome of his 'sickness'.

This view was obviously close to what I had been saying in *The Outsider*. Most of the great artists have been unstable characters – 'great wits are sure to madness near allied' – and it is obvious that their instability is closely linked to their talent. My friend Negley Farson, one of the great travel writers, was an alcoholic; when he went to see a specialist about a cure, the doctor told him that he could cure his alcoholism, but he would probably cure him of his writing talent at the same time. (Negley preferred to remain alcoholic and talented.)

All this I could understand. But was she talking sense when she said that this was the basic mechanism of evolution? How about Darwin and Mendel and the discovery of DNA? It all sounded just a little too far-fetched. But as she continued to send me enormous chunks of her typescript (mostly typed on bright yellow paper by a typewriter that had only capitals) I continued to wrestle with her elusive prose, and continued to be exasperated by her obscurity and impressed by the sheer extent of her reading. I also continued to be astonished by her assurance of her own greatness. Sending me the latest draft of one of her 'introductions', she wrote: 'I sincerely believe that it heralds an entirely new scientific and intellectual epoch in our history.' And in a letter to Professor Stafford Beer (of which she sent me a copy), she wrote: 'Compared to my discovery, the invention of the hydrogen bomb is like constructing a pop-gun.'

Some time that autumn I met her in London. She proved to be a broad-shouldered mammoth of a woman with a deep masculine voice and a heavy Hungarian accent. I was staying with a painter friend – Regis de Cachard – and we all went to dinner in a little restaurant in Old Brompton Road; afterwards we sat in Regis's flat and drank wine (she seemed capable of putting away an impressive quantity), and she told me about her background and how she came to create her theory. Both she and her husband had been lecturers in psychology at Budapest University until the Communists drove them out. In England, in 1965, her husband had died on the operating table after their son had been killed in a car crash, and she had a nervous breakdown. (She burst into tears as she told us all this.) Then, hoping to make money and perhaps to impress some university, she decided to compile a dictionary of psychological terms. It was when she came to write about 'perversions' that she realised that no one seemed to define exactly where normality ends and abnormality starts. She read my *Origins of the Sexual Impulse*, but ended by rejecting my own 'theory of symbolic response'. Then she decided to start asking the 'perverts' themselves; so she passed the word among her friends, and eventually succeeded in interviewing a large number of 'deviants'.

One of these was an Oxford professor, a tweedy, pipe-smoking man who certainly looked completely normal. Before they began the interview, he asked her: 'Do you mind if I behave normally?' When she said no, he stripped off his trousers and revealed a pair of black lace panties, and stockings held up by a suspender belt.

Then he sat in his armchair, his pipe in one hand, and told her to go ahead.

It struck her that he seemed to experience no kind of guilt or shame; he obviously felt completely normal dressed like a woman. In this he seemed totally unlike many homosexuals and lesbians she had interviewed, who were obviously unable to shake off a sense of guilt. Interviews with other transvestites confirmed this observation: they seemed to feel that it was perfectly normal to behave like a member of the opposite sex. Then what was the basic difference between transvestites and homosexuals that made one feel normal and the other abnormal? It was as she brooded on this subject that she began to think about 'instability' and evolution . . .

I was inclined to suspect that she was not telling the whole truth. Surely no one decides to write a dictionary of psychological terms in order to make money? I was simply unable to believe that her interest in sexual deviants was as 'academic' as she asserted. That argued that she herself was some kind of deviant – presumably lesbian. But that notion was exploded after Regis and I had seen her off in a taxi (for which I paid – she was apparently very poor). I gave her a kiss, and she also kissed Regis. As we went back indoors, he said: 'You know, as she kissed me, she stuck her tongue halfway down my throat.' We both laughed about it. That seemed to dispose of the lesbian theory.

The next time I was in London, I took her out to dinner again; this time I was staying with my friend Bill Hopkins, and once again Charlotte told us the story of the death of her husband, and burst into tears. I began to suspect there was something of the actress about Charlotte. Her manner was usually reserved, as if she re-garded most of the human race as fools; it was as if she was aware of this, and wanted to dispel the impression with a dramatic gesture.

By 1973 she was already beginning to acquire an army of disciples and admirers, even among academics; I was asked to write a letter to a businessman on her behalf – he apparently believed that her theories could be used in public relations, although I never under-stood quite what he had in mind. Soon after that, she wrote to tell me that the magazine *Time Out* intended to interview her, and had expressed interest in an article on her ideas to be written by me. I replied that I couldn't possibly write about them until I understood them myself, and suggested that next time we meet I should bring a tape recorder, and she should make a determined effort to explain herself in words of one syllable. In due course I gave her lunch at the Savage Club, then I took her into a quiet corner of the lounge and produced my tape recorder. This time I ruthlessly kept her to the point, interjecting questions every time she said something I didn't understand and interrupting her every time she showed a tendency to digress. In this way I finally managed to obtain a clear and simple outline of her theory.

The study of transvestites, she explained, was not the only thing that convinced her that we are all a balanced mixture of male and female. Someone had drawn her attention to a paper on the ten-spined stickleback by Desmond Morris, in which Morris had expressed his bafflement at its apparently 'homosexual' behaviour. In the mating season, the male stickleback turns black and selects an area of 'territory'. If other males approach this territory, they are driven off. But if a female approaches, her passive behaviour acts as a stimulant, and the male invites her into his parlour. There the female deposits her eggs, while the male swims up and down releasing his sperm into the water. Then the female swims away and the transaction is complete. But in some years there are so many males that they cannot all find territory; the less dominant ones swim around looking lost, and gradually lose their black colour. And now, if one of them pauses outside the territory of another male, the male may mistake it for a female and invite it inside. In that case, the pseudo-female pauses, just as if laying eggs, and the male swims up and down releasing his sperm. Then the pseudo-female swims away. Of course, no baby sticklebacks are born, so the next year, there is more than enough territory to go round. It looks as if nature has devised a rather less wasteful method of reproducing the species than allowing half of them to starve to death.

A little bird called the zebra finch behaves equally oddly. The male attracts the female with a song-and-dance routine. If she fails to respond or rejects him, the male begins to perform the female 'come and get me' display. If the mating is interrupted by some danger and the nervous female breaks off, the male again goes into the female display. And the female often begins to perform the male song-and-dance. They have reversed roles. Charlotte's explanation of this oddity is that when the male is thwarted, his excessive masculine drive spills over into the female pattern, like water splashing out of an over-full bucket.

These examples – and others taken from Desmond Morris, Konrad Lorenz, Niko Tinbergen and other zoologists – convinced Charlotte that this half-male/half-female pattern is normal in nature. (Jung had arrived at the same recognition in his notion of the *animus* – the male component in all women – and the *anima* – the female component in all men.) It is obviously a part of the basic blueprint of creation.

Now it struck her that a man or woman can react to this 'pull' to become the opposite sex in one of two ways: either resisting it or accepting and affirming it. So a man who dresses up in women's clothes is simply affirming his femininity – allowing his *anima* to hang out, so to speak. A woman who likes to look like a man, but who still prefers men to women as sexual partners, is affirming her *animus*. And this was one of Charlotte's most basic observations about transvestites: most are *not* homosexual or lesbian; they prefer the opposite sex.

There are some rather odd complications, however. Some males are really women in male bodies: they are psychologically female. And they can react to this situation in one of two ways: by either denying it or affirming it. (Charlotte called the resisters 'denialists' and the affirmers 'asseverationists'.) These *are* basically homosexuals. Such a man might deny his 'pull' towards becoming the opposite sex (which in this case is male, since he is really a woman) by wearing female clothes and becoming a 'drag queen' – a quite different thing from a transvestite. Or he might affirm it by wearing excessively male gear, like some leather-jacketed teddy boy. Such a person is a 'male negative asseverationist' – meaning that he is anatomically male, psychologically female, and he goes out of his way to show off his pseudo-maleness. He may, in fact, stop denying his femininity and become a straightforward homosexual, accepting that he is really a woman in a man's body.

Clearly there are eight possible 'types'. The normal man is a male positive denialist: a male soul in a male body, denying his femininity. The normal woman is a female positive denialist: a female soul in a female body, denying her masculinity. The 'femme' lesbian – who often seems excessively feminine – is a female negative asseverationist: a man in a woman's body, asserting her femininity. The 'butch' lesbian, oddly enough, is a female soul in a female body, asserting her desire to become male; she is the female equivalent of the transvestite. Then there is the female negative denialist – a man's soul in a woman's body, denying that she is feminine; she may be a slightly bossy female. There is the straight homosexual or drag queen, the male with a woman's soul who denies his maleness. There is the masculine negative asseverationist – the leather jacket rowdy who is really a pouf underneath. And, finally, there is the male positive asseverationist – basically a normal male who allows himself to express his feminine nature – the 'normal' transvestite. These are the eight types, which Charlotte also called the 'eight ritual streams'.

We can see that what we have here are four 'normal' types and four 'abnormal'. The normal types *include* the transvestite and the butch lesbian, and these tend to be quite stable. The four abnormal types are basically homosexuals, and they are unstable. Their instability may easily make them creative – Charlotte had observed a drag queen who became an artist, a lesbian who became a writer.

And it was this observation that led Charlotte on to her theory of evolution. A young man who was in the grip of religious obsessions told her one day that he had experienced a sexual orgasm that lasted for eight hours. She assumed, naturally, that he was lying. Then, reading a book by Mircea Eliade on shamanism, she read about the lengthy ecstasies often experienced by tribal shamans and religious mystics. Suddenly, like a flash of light, the solution dawned on her. She was so excited that she leapt to her feet and danced around the room, shouting: 'That's what it's about – evolution!'

What struck her is that the shaman has risen *above* sexuality, so he is neither male nor female. And the opposing tensions, which cause so much misery to 'sexual deviates', have built up to a strength that creates a glowing discharge of nervous energy that can go on for hours. To a lesser degree, this also applies to the great creative geniuses. A Beethoven was, to a large extent, 'asexual'; like a priest or shaman, he tried to do without sex. The result is great music. Michelangelo and Leonardo, like so many great creators, were homosexual, and their tensions and guilt contributed to their creativity. Instead of becoming some variant of the drag queen or the over-masculine rowdy, they transformed their tensions into great art.

All this fascinated me. Yet I must confess I had my doubts. Charlotte told me that I was a normal male – a male positive denialist. I felt flattered at the time; but when I came to think about it more carefully, I saw it was not quite the compliment it had looked. The normal male is stable and therefore non-creative. And, even leaning over backwards to be modest, it was fairly clear that I am not uncreative. I also felt doubtful about Charlotte's classification of the butch lesbian as a basically 'normal' transvestite. That would seem to deny that she *is* a lesbian. And what about Charlotte herself? She did not seem to fit into any of her own classifications. In spite of her powerful shoulders and deep voice, she seemed to enjoy asserting her femininity. When I chaired a scientific debate at the Royal Institution, she came and sat in the front row, wearing a large hat and fanning herself violently with an enormous fan, which thoroughly distracted the speakers (John Taylor and Lyall Watson). She was not a female negative denialist – a man's soul in a woman's body, denying her femininity (the slightly bossy woman type) – for she asserted her femininity. And she certainly wasn't a female negative asseverationist, for that is the femme lesbian. She looked like a butch lesbian, but obviously wasn't. Charlotte simply refused to fit into any of her own classifications.

I am, as I frequently admit, in some ways a rather stupid person. The answer was staring me in the face, and I simply failed to recognise it. I learned the truth on 17 June 1981. That was the day that one of Charlotte's disciples phoned me to say she was dead. A neighbour had noticed the accumulation of milk bottles on the doorstep of her flat in Highgate, north London. The police broke in and discovered her body. When it was undressed in the morgue, the ample breasts proved to be made of foam rubber, and the removal of her underwear revealed a penis. Charlotte was a male transvestite – one of those human beings who, according to Charlotte's own theory, had thrown away all possibility of being creative . . .

Over the next few months, as 'her' admirers and followers studied her papers, the true story of Charlotte Bach began to emerge.

Charlotte's real name was Carl Michael Blaise Augustine Hajdu*, and he was born in Budapest in 1920. According to his own account, he was the son of a high-ranking civil servant who had been a wealthy landowner but who lost his estates in the Paris Treaty after the First World War; he was also a baron, and Carl inherited the title after his death. Alas, this version of the truth proved as unreliable as Charlotte's other tales about herself; when her friend

* pronounced 'Hi-du'

Bob Mellors, in the course of researching a biography, succeeded in contacting Carl Hajdu's sister, he learned that their background had been fairly ordinary working-class, and that the title had been pure fantasy.

Carl taught himself to read at the age of four, and his sister verifies that he was a brilliant but wayward pupil at school. 'I loved putting my teachers through the hoop. In turn they loved proving at exam times that I wasn't so bloody clever.' He was also sexually precocious. 'I started masturbating at the age of ten, and haven't stopped since.' At fifteen, he lost his virginity with a prostitute, a kindly woman who made his first experience of real sex a pleasure. Watching her pull on her stockings afterwards, he wanted to begin all over again, but his friends were waiting outside – and, in any case, he didn't have the money. (A psychiatrist later told him that if he had been able to do so, he might never have become a transvestite.) He also tried to earn some money as a homosexual prostitute – a friend was 'an enthusiastic amateur procurer' – and spent an evening with a cultured elderly gentleman who gave him an excellent dinner with wine; but when the time came, he couldn't get an erection and left in disgrace. In later life, he went back to this earlier method of supplementing his income with more success, advertising himself in contact magazines as 'Daphne' and administering corporal punishment.

In his teens, Carl went to Budapest University, but wasted his time – he never seems to have had much application. When the war came, he became a junior lieutenant in the Hungarian army. In 1944, the Hungarians accepted collaboration with the Germans as an alternative to being occupied by them, and Carl was somehow attached to the SS. In a later autobiographical novel, *Fiona*, he mentions that he was a courier officer whose job was to find Hungarian soldiers in German field-hospitals and arrange for their transfer to Hungary. Suspected of aiding the escape of two Englishmen, he was arrested and held in detention for five months; although he was grilled he was not physically ill-treated. One of his fellow prisoners was executed, but Carl was saved by the bell – the end of the war. He returned to the university, and this time did well (Charlotte told me that she received her doctorate in psychology and become a junior lecturer). But in 1947, he landed in trouble again, this time with the Communist regime, and spent a few more months in jail. In 1948, he escaped to England via Austria, arriving in April.

He was already well into transvestism. It had developed slowly; it first appeared when he had been making love to a girlfriend, and was lying naked on her bed afterwards, covered by her satin dressing gown and watching her making coffee. Looking at the contours of his own thighs under the satin, he became excited and began caressing them. Then the coffee arrived and he forgot the incident. A year or two later, he bought several pairs of nylon stockings for another mistress – he seems to have been something of a Don Juan. She rang up at the last minute to cancel the date, and he went to bed with a book. Then, on impulse, he got up, put on the stockings and admired his legs in them; then he masturbated with 'a hitherto unexperienced intensity of personal involvement'. Upset and ashamed, he tore the stockings to pieces and vowed never to do it again. Analysing it later, he says that it all seemed as natural as an apple falling off a tree, and that what a psychiatrist later told him about 'substitutes' and 'displacement of affect' was like explaining the fall of an apple by saying that it is heavy. What bothered him was that the stockings on his legs seemed a more than adequate substitute for the girl herself.

When a friend happened to leave a suitcase full of his wife's clothes at Carl's apartment, he once again found himself unable to resist dressing up – this time in a complete women's outfit. He felt so ashamed that he rang his friend and asked him to remove the suitcase immediately. But after that, he began buying items of female clothing and dressing up. Periodically he experienced revulsion and had a 'purge', wrapping the clothes in parcels and 'losing' them on buses or in parks. When he left for England, he gave away the lot to the Hungarian equivalent of OXFAM.

In London, Carl found a job as a translator at the Harwich Labour Exchange and began an affair with a married woman called Julia. It was more convenient for her to leave some of her clothes and cosmetics at his flat. On days when she was unable to come, he began dressing up in her clothes and using her cosmetics. The affair lasted three years, and ended when her husband found out.

In the early 1950s he met Phyllis, a divorcee with a small son and a pleasant flat. He made a habit of spending weekends with her, and when she said she was pregnant he decided to marry her, convinced he was at last in love. He wanted to believe that the urge to transvestism had finally vanished. Nevertheless he kept the clothes for the first five years of his marriage, until he decided to

save the half-crown a week he was paying for storage by getting rid
of them. (The pregnancy proved a false alarm.)

For the next part of Carl's life, it is necessary to draw on the
autobiographical (and unpublished) novel *Fiona*. On all points
which I have been able to check, the story is an accurate account
of his own life, and he calls the hero Gregory Blaise – Blaise being
one of his own Christian names. In the ninth year of his marriage
– 1964 – Blaise has rented himself a room in Mayfair where he is
making some kind of a living as an estate agent. He spends weekends
with his wife in Hampstead, but keeps a great many affairs going
at the same time. On the whole, these affairs are not deeply
satisfying – although the descriptions of physical seduction make it
clear that Carl Hajdu had a powerful normal sexual impulse and
took a great deal of pleasure in his *savoir-faire* – he can spend as
much as three pages describing the details of seduction. It is equally
clear that all this Don Juanism leaves him basically unsatisfied; its
purpose is to bolster his ego, and it seldom succeeds for longer
than a few hours at a time – at least, until he meets a general's
daughter named Fiona (it is impossible to avoid noticing that the
author is obsessed by rank and social position), who finds him
fascinating and intriguing, and whose soft, gentle nature brings out
the best in him. The novel reads like a gloss on Rosenstock-Huessy's
remark: 'Even a man who believes in nothing needs a girl to believe
in him.' Blaise compares her to the fairy princess who kisses a toad
and turns it into a prince. But he adds that, after the affair breaks
up, he turns back into a toad again. But Fiona finally begins to find
him unsatisfying – perhaps because he cannot resist cheating on
her with other women – and leaves him. He returns to his wife,
but she dies shortly afterwards during an emergency operation. A
week later, his stepson is killed in a car crash as he returns to
school. The author gives the novel a happy ending, with Fiona
saying, 'Hello, darling . . . you should have known I would return
to you.' But the real-life Fiona never came back, and Carl Hajdu
had the severe mental breakdown which turned him into Charlotte
Bach.

In real life, Carl Hajdu was making a living as a flat-finding agent
in Paddington (not Mayfair). In 1957 he only just avoided a brush
with the law when he organised a Freedom Fighters' association to
help the Hungarians, and collected £2,000. A journalist on a London
evening newspaper pursued 'Baron' Carl Hajdu (the journalist puts

'baron' in quotes), and managed to wring from him the admission that he was going to have some difficulty in showing how the money had been spent. Soon after this, Hajdu changed his name to Michael Karoly, and became a lecturer and journalist. He took a job as an 'Agony Aunt' on a magazine called *Today*, writing articles with such titles as 'Should big girls be spanked?' and 'Why, oh why, do I steal?' In 1959 he lectured at the Stanislavsky Institute on the role of psychology in acting – he had given himself a string of bogus degrees – and in 1961 wrote a book about hypnosis. (I was later amused to realise I had had it on my shelf for years without realising that it was by Charlotte.) He also set himself up as a hypnotherapist – this time achieving a Mayfair address – and seems to have been reasonably successful. He was now making determined attempts to 'become known', and to acquire a few celebrated acquaintances – writing to, among others, Gian Carlo Menotti. The affair with 'Fiona' actually took place; so, of course, did the death of Phyllis and his stepson. And although he was Michael Karoly and not Charlotte Bach, the results were actually much the same as he described to me. He locked himself up in his flat in Highgate and allowed himself to disintegrate. He ran up debts, failed to pay bills, and spent two months in prison. During this time, he dressed continually as a woman, wearing his dead wife's clothes. Then, finally, he made an attempt to pull himself together and establish himself as an author – not with a dictionary of psychological terms, but with a book about transvestism called *Man and/or Woman*. Soon after this, he decided to widen his experience of transvestites and placed an advertisement in the *New Statesman*, announcing that he was a psychologist who wanted to interview transvestites.

Among those who answered the advertisement was a forty-four-year-old TV (the usual abbreviation for transvestite) called Derrick Alexander. Like Carl Hajdu, he was an apparently normal heterosexual male who had never had any difficulty finding girlfriends; but for the past fourteen years he had struggled with an increasingly powerful urge to dress up as a woman. He has described how, during his marriage, he would leave his wife watching television and sneak upstairs to dress up in her clothes. Derrick telephoned the 'doctor' and made his way to the flat at 52 Langbourne Mansions, Highgate. There he found he had already been preceded by another half-dozen TVs, all anxious to tell their life stories in exchange for coffee and sympathy. Carl Hajdu proved to be a tall, suave, bearded man, entirely without feminine mannerisms. Derrick Alexander also mentions that he felt rather repelled by other transvestites – they seemed rather silly and disgusting. Nevertheless he accepted an invitation to the home of a 'woman' in Wimbledon, where they all changed into women's clothes – with the exception of Hajdu – and chattered together like a lot of girls. There exists a colour photograph taken at this party. The 'women' all look perfectly normal, some of them even rather glamorous. Hajdu towers above them all. It was quite typical of 'Charlotte' that he had no wish to be 'one of the girls'; his certainty of his own uniqueness made him determined never to be part of any group.

As Derrick Alexander became a regular caller at Karoly's flat, he began to wonder why a psychiatrist should feel so obsessed by transvestism. When he commented on this one day, Karoly went to a drawer and took out several photographs. One of them showed Karoly sitting on the arm of a settee next to a woman whom he identified as his wife. For a moment Derrick was taken in; then he looked more closely. 'They're *both* you.' Karoly was pleased that it had taken such a close scrutiny to reveal that the photograph was a montage. It must have been a relief to him to know that there was one other person in whom he could confide. Derrick Alexander was intelligent and widely read, and the two soon became close friends.

Karoly, it seemed, had given a great deal of thought to the problem of how to appear in public without being 'read' (TV slang for rumbled). The first basic rule, he told Derrick, was never to speak unless you're in vision. Once someone takes it for granted that you're a woman, they will overlook the masculine voice. Next, observe women carefully and note the small 'feminine' things they do all the time. Derrick's self-confidence about appearing in public was low, since he had twice been arrested for 'disturbing the peace' (i.e. wearing drag in public). Karoly assumed the role of mentor, took Derrick out for an evening in the West End and made all kinds of comments on the mistakes he had made.

The following is a typical story of that period, told to me by Derrick (now Della Aleksander). One evening they were sitting in a wine bar in Camden Town when Charlotte went out to the Ladies – this was part of her ritual. Two old Cockney women at the next table were watching them, and one of them suddenly announced to her friend: 'That's a man!'

When Charlotte came back, Derrick murmured: 'You've been read.'

Charlotte eyed the two old ladies for a moment, then went over to their table. She announced courteously, with a strong Hungarian accent: 'It is my birthday and we are having a celebration. Would you two ladies care to join me in a glass of wine?'

The two old ladies looked taken aback, but said they'd love to. Charlotte then proceeded to tell them the story of the death of her husband and son in the same week, produced photographs of her tall, bearded husband, and became increasingly pleased with herself as the two old ladies obviously changed their minds about her sex.

Finally one of them asked sympathetically: 'Do you think you'll ever marry again, love?'

Charlotte did a little feminine *moue*. 'If I can find the right man.'

At this, one old dear remarked with Cockney spontaneity: "'E'd 'ave to be a giant.'

Della had to turn away to suppress hysterics.

At this period – the late Sixties – Karoly was actively considering a sex-change operation. He actually persuaded Derrick Alexander to take the plunge; Derrick went off to Spain, and returned as Della Aleksander. But Karoly never went ahead with the operation; the reason, I think, was that he had already become what he intended to become. He was Charlotte Bach, the greatest psychological discoverer of the twentieth century. All he had to do now was to persuade the rest of the world to acknowledge it.

TWO

Charlotte and the Mysteries of Evolution

Man and/or Woman was rejected by several publishers, but Charlotte was unperturbed. In 1969, she wrote to her literary agent, Michael Fenton, to tell him to withdraw the typescript from circulation, explaining that there had been 'important new developments'. At about the same time, she wrote to IBM explaining that 'she and her brother, another psychologist' had completed research on an important project about sexual deviation which might have considerable commercial possibilities – for example, in personnel selection. There is no record of their reply.

As I battled on through Charlotte's gargantuan typescript in 1971, I found it impossible to understand how she had made the transition from a theory about sexual perversion to an all-embracing theory about evolution. In fact, it is almost impossible to understand the leap without some knowledge of Carl Hajdu's sexual development. But once we know something of his history, the whole thing suddenly becomes clear.

Carl Hajdu was basically a normal male with an abnormally powerful sexual impulse. Women found him attractive, and his sexual conquests served an important function in bolstering his insecure ego. He was tormented by a sense of lack of purpose, lack of a real identity. He was brilliant, but he seemed to be a non-achiever. Admiring mistresses at least convinced him that he deserved to be admired.

On the day he pulled on his girlfriend's stockings and masturbated, he was confronted with another threat to his ego. Wearing women's underwear seemed to increase his sexual impulse, so he felt 'a hitherto unexperienced intensity of total involvement'. So it seemed that, apart from his other personality problems, he was also a woman in a male body. His immediate reaction was revulsion and a vow never to do it again.

Study of homosexuals and other transvestites finally led him to decide that this conclusion was unwarranted. Transvestites are actually male souls in male bodies. In that case, why the urge to dress as a woman? Desmond Morris's paper on sticklebacks and zebra finches seemed to provide the outline of an answer. If birds and fishes can 'switch' sex, then this same duality must be present in all living creatures. When frustrated, all of them experience a certain urge to 'let off steam' by giving in to the desire to *become their opposite*.

In zoology, letting off steam is known technically as 'displacement activity' or 'spillover activity'. When two male sticklebacks face one another at the edge of their respective territories, they look as if they are about to fight to the death; instead, each will suddenly stand on his head, and proceed to dig holes in the sand while making vigorous fanning motions with his tail. Two herring gulls in the same position will start to tear up grass. Two roebucks will attack the bark of nearby trees with their horns instead of each other. This is nature's way of preventing unnecessary bloodshed and, like the 'homosexual' activity of the unattached male stickle-back, it seems to demonstrate that Tennyson was doing nature a slight injustice when he described it as 'red in tooth and claw'. Among human beings, we can see displacement activity when impatient drivers begin to honk their horns, or a bored man drums his fingers on the table or whistles tunelessly.

Tinbergen observed – in *The Study of Instinct* – that, among birds and animals, displacement activities are often 'ritualised' into what he called 'social releasers'. When people are unsure of themselves they smile, and a smile is a social releaser; so is talking about the weather, another response to embarrassment. When cranes get aggressive, their fighting urge turns into displacement 'preening', and preening – like a boxer flexing his muscles – is also a warning 'keep off' gesture – another type of social releaser. The tail-fanning motion of the angry male sticklebacks is also used as a gesture of invitation to the female, inviting her to come into the nesting area.

Now Charlotte thought about the frustrated pseudo-female stickleback behaving like a female, or the frustrated zebra finches changing roles in the mating ritual – surely this was a displacement activity that was also a 'sexual deviation'? And when Carl Hajdu sat waiting for his mistress, and she phoned to say she couldn't make it, he tried to *defuse his frustration* by going to bed with a book, then put on the stockings and masturbated with an unprecedented sense of involvement. Frustration had 'spilled over' into sexual deviation. Suppose *all* sexual deviations were displacement activities? They certainly have the same illogical quality: a man becoming excited at the sight of a crutch or a black rubber apron, or dressing up as a baby and being spanked by a prostitute dressed as a nanny . . . In fact, there is something downright *childish* about most sexual deviations.

The word 'childish' provided Charlotte with another vital clue. There exists in zoology a curious phenomenon known as neotony, which means that members of the species *never reach adulthood*. We can imagine, for example, what would happen if, through some strange mutation, human beings began to reach sexual maturity at the age of two. They would begin to mate while still babies, and might well die at the age of ten, worn out by child rearing. Such species actually exist, one example being the variety of salamander called the axolotl lizard, which is actually a baby land-salamander.

In the late 1920s, a Dutch zoologist named Ludwig Bolk suggested that man may also be a neotonous species. At a certain stage, the embryo of an ape resembles a fully developed human embryo; but the ape goes *beyond* this, and develops brow ridges, body hair and specialised teeth. So it seems arguable that man is an undeveloped ape. Charlotte recognised that most of us remain emotionally immature all our lives. But a 'Peter Pan species' has one great advantage when compared to a species that goes on to full maturity – it has greater possibilities of development. The armour-plated dinosaurs reached a dead end because there was nowhere else they could go. The same is true of the turtle; its protective shell is also a prison from which it cannot escape. The more vulnerable and 'open' a creature is, the greater its possibilities. Man's immaturity means that he is still an 'emergent' species.

The young man who claimed to have had an eight-hour orgasm provided Charlotte with her final clue. *This*, she thought, is the reason that man lives in a state of emotional immaturity and nervous tension: because his 'opposing forces' were meant to build up into an explosion of creativity. At one point, she began writing a book trying to prove that Leonardo was a transvestite whose inner conflicts resulted in his paintings and scientific inventions. Charlotte's theory of evolution could be regarded as an elaboration of Nietzsche's comment that every man must have chaos within him to give birth to a dancing star. Her great original contribution, she felt, was to recognise that the basic cause of the chaos is that inner polarity of male and female in all of us.

We could say, then, that Charlotte's theory is in entire agreement with Goethe's statement that the eternal feminine draws us upward and on – or, rather, that the conflict between the eternal feminine and the eternal masculine draws us upward and on. Her theory of evolution could be compared to Newton's theory of gravitation. Newton accounted for the movements of the heavenly bodies by assuming the existence of a force called gravity. The earth and the planets are attracted by the sun's gravity but, because they are *in motion*, they do not fall into it, but revolve around it in elliptical orbits. In Charlotte's theory, the opposition of male and female is the force of gravity. And because we are alive and kicking – the kicking is especially important – the conflict produces evolution.

This was not all – not by a long way (although, for our present purposes, it will suffice). She came to believe that alchemy – with its basic emphasis on the male and female principles – was an ancient knowledge-system based on the same recognition; but since the ancients knew nothing about Newton or Einstein or cybernetics or displacement activities or neotony, they had to express their intuitive insights symbolically. Jung was correct, she believed, in seeing alchemy as the repository of an ancient wisdom (although he failed to grasp what it was all about). The 'philosopher's stone' is the capacity for the eight-hour orgasm and for even higher mystical experiences. When man learns to understand his own dual nature, he will also learn to *use* it to power his own evolution, exactly as he uses an electric current which alternates between positive and negative to light his cities. When he understands the cause of his self-division, he will learn to control his polarities to create intensities of mind which modern man only glimpses in the sexual orgasm.

Moreover, this new vision would free man from his present feeling of dependency on the physical world. Science, with its 'reductionist' tendencies, has trapped man in a static universe of space and time. Charlotte regarded the world as a pattern of information spread out in time. You could say that, since she thought of living beings as the heart of the world process, she believed that we should switch our view and try to see the world from behind their eyes, instead of attempting a kind of pseudo-objectivity. A human being is more like a symphony than a painting – he is a *process*, not a thing. And the universe itself is a process, not a thing. The scientist of the future will have to be time-oriented rather than space-oriented. When this happens, we shall realise that the universe is driven by living energies rather than physical forces, and that its essential processes are closer to magic than to science.

It was a noble and an impressive vision, and it is hardly surprising that Charlotte came to believe that she was one of the greatest intellects of the twentieth century. After studying relativity and quantum theory, she announced that she had found the fallacy built into both of them. 'I am now in a position to prove my theory from A to Z, incontrovertibly and beyond any reasonable doubt – it is, indeed, doubtful that my theory can be refuted within the foreseeable future . . .' Once she became convinced that this opposition of the male-female principles was the driving force of evolution, she began to see it everywhere – her last work is a vast typescript on the evolution of writing, in which she sets out to demonstrate that A and B are symbols of the male and female, and that all the other letters – particularly Chinese – can be interpreted as symbolic expressions of the male-female conflict. She even came to believe her theory proved that time is spherical and has ten dimensions.

Yet I must confess that, in spite of my admiration, I found myself unable to accept Charlotte's theory of evolution. When, in the mid-1970s, she decided to found an Institute of Human Ethology and to deliver lectures on the topic at the London Polytechnic, she asked me if she could use my name as a sponsor on her letterhead. I took a deep breath and told her that I felt that her central idea was simply untrue. I expected an explosion of rage and instant excommunication. In fact, she replied that she didn't mind me disagreeing with her ideas, provided I agreed that they deserved to be more widely known. Since I could safely assent to that proposition, I became a sponsor of the Institute of Human Ethology.

It seemed to me from the beginning that the weak point in Charlotte's theory was her emphasis on transvestism. My first recognition that she did not know what she was talking about came when she wrote to tell me she had read my novel, *Ritual in the*

Dark, and that she recognised an element of underwear fetishism that proved that I was basically a transvestite. I found this an absurdity. If I found women's underwear stimulating, it was not because I wanted to dress up in it, still less to become a woman. It was simply because it partook of the 'forbidden' nature of the 'eternal feminine'. I once asked a girlfriend why, in her opinion, I found her knickers stimulating, and she astounded me by the simplicity of her reply: 'Because they're associated with that part of the body.' For a moment I found myself wondering whether she was incredibly brilliant or I was incredibly stupid.

For Charlotte, clothes fetishism revealed a desire to become the opposite sex. To me the explanation seemed more straightforward. Under the unnatural conditions of civilisation, sexual desire is artificially heightened. (Monkeys in zoos engage in continual sex; in nature, they seem relatively indifferent to it.) Most young men are ready for sex long before they have the opportunity to try it, so the intensity of the desire 'spills over' on to objects associated with it. (In that respect Charlotte was right: deviations *are* displacement activities.) Dr Johnson always ate like a pig and spilled his food down his shirt-front; he told Mrs Thrale that this was because he was half-starved as a student, so that he now found it impossible to be moderate about food. But if Johnson had been told that his ravenous appetite was a desire to *become* a beefsteak, he would have snorted contemptuously.

Yet, in another sense, Dr Johnson *does* become the beefsteak – or at least the beefsteak becomes part of Dr Johnson. In the *Symposium*, Plato observes that men and women were originally halves of a single creature, which was divided in two by the gods to prevent it from becoming too powerful; now we all wander around searching for our 'other half'. As a man holds a woman in his arms he experiences a desire to absorb her, to blend with her, and the actual penetration of her body is only a token union. But absorbing and blending is quite a different matter from *becoming*, as we can see in the case of the beefsteak. It seemed to me that Charlotte had committed an elementary error in reasoning.

This insight led me to question other basic elements in her theory. Is it true that all displacement activities that have evolutionary significance are really aberrant sexual behaviour patterns, and that all social releasers in our species originated from these patterns? Think of a list of 'social releasers': a smile, a wink, a sigh, a groan of boredom, a look of confusion or bewilderment (which induces other people to ask if they can be of assistance), a comment about the weather . . . It is hard to see how these originated in sexual deviations. Is it even true that the male zebra finch is 'becoming' a female when he does the female courting dance? It seems more likely that he is simply trying to *remind her* of what she ought to be doing, and also trying to defuse his own frustration.

But this is not to say that these errors – if that is what they are – invalidate her theory. It seems to me that her insight into human evolution is fundamentally sound. According to Darwin, man has climbed the evolutionary ladder because of the pressure of circumstance; starvation and misery have prodded him on from below. This is obviously true to some extent. But Charlotte recognises that he has also been 'lured' on from above, by the pressure of a desire for what might be called 'the ideal sexual experience'. We all observe that the reality of sexual intercourse is far from perfect; yet that does not convince us that sex is a greatly overrated occupation. Every time a man glimpses a pretty girl pulling up her stocking, he catches a glimpse of what might be called the 'primal sexual vision'. It is unfortunate that there seems to be a certain disparity between this primal vision and most ordinary sexual experience. But it dances in front of us like a will-o'-the-wisp, luring us into tormented effort. It can lead novelists to write novels, poets to write poems, and musicians to write symphonies. (Charles Koechlin even devoted a symphony to his favourite Hollywood stars – an example of the influence of the 'sexual ideal' on music.) It certainly led Carl Hajdu into creating his evolutionary theory, as well as into dressing in women's clothes. So whether his 'transsexual' theory is correct may not be as important as it seems.

This theory of the 'primal sexual vision' and the problem of achieving it runs throughout the novel *Fiona*. In its first bedroom scene, Gregory Blaise is about to seduce a married woman called Norah (typically, she is a colonel's wife).

Not many minutes later, he was sitting on the carpeted floor . . . Norah sitting on a low chair beside him, a record player oozing out a sugary melody by Frank Sinatra and his hand up her skirt, feeling the warm yet cool flesh between the top of her stockings and her pants. The gap between the stocking and pants was narrow and his fingertips felt with an odd thrill the slippery nylon briefs. To all appearances he had made the conquest, yet there was no real communication between them . . .

He hammers home this point:

> Still holding his left arm under Norah's head, still holding the deep kiss, he unzipped the side of her dress, and pushed the skirt up above her waist.
>
> At this moment Norah said with a very sweet smile, which was just a shade too unselfconscious:
>
> 'Just a moment, please.'
>
> She reached out, picked off two more cushions from the settee, placed them under herself and, without standing up, slipped out of the dress with a lightning movement. Then, turning half over, she laid the dress on the floor, smoothed it, pulling the sleeves the right way out, making sure that it wouldn't crease badly . . .

A few paragraphs later:

> He lowered himself gently on top of Norah's body. Her legs came apart, her knees arched up. He felt his penis touching the blond pubic hairs, which a moment ago seemed obscene, but now were exciting. His body was driven by the desires of the flesh, everything else seemed of secondary importance. His weight rested on his left elbow, his left hand under Norah's shoulder-blades. His right hand slid down, past her hip, under her knee, intending to put his penis to and past the little pink spot amid the blond pubic hair. But Norah's hand was already there, doing it. At that moment he became terribly conscious of the moment in the restaurant [downstairs], as Norah was pulling her gloves off, revealing the housework-worn fingertips . . .

In a later love-making scene with Fiona, it is still clear that his hero is a man who is excited by underwear:

> Having divested herself of her dress, Fiona sat on the mattress, with only her bra, suspender-belt, pants and stockings. Gregory stood erect, looking down on her from his full height. He had a faint urge to help her undress further, as he had done in innumerable other cases with other women. His fetishistic inclination

usually gave him an additional thrill doing so. Or alternatively, ask her not to undress any further as the feel of the smooth slippery nylon with the living, moving flesh underneath aroused a greater sense of excitement than her bare body.

But although the description of love-making with Fiona is just as precise and clinical as with Norah ('In and out, in and out, in and out . . .'), Gregory now finds it perfectly satisfying. Why? Because 'she was in search of a Man. Man with a capital M . . . She had chosen him because she felt that he was a Man. It made him feel more of a Man.'

This sounds extraordinary, coming from someone who has chosen to dress and behave like a woman. What it reveals is that the obsessive Don Juanism was an attempt to bolster his self-esteem, to stabilise his sense of identity. But the failure of all his relations with women reveals that it was unsuccessful.

Fiona reveals another important aspect of Carl Hajdu's character: his criminal streak. Since Fiona is such an admiring audience, Blaise uses her as a mother confessor, assured of instant forgiveness. At one point he tells her how, at the end of the war, he was out after curfew, and was stopped by a teen-age soldier – a boy of about fifteen. The soldier proposed to take him to the guardhouse for a check. His papers were in order, and it was reasonably certain that he would be released in half an hour. But he was irritated by the way in which this peasant addressed him, a nobleman and an officer; so, as the boy walked a few steps in front of him – 'that shows what a stupid kid he was – he didn't even disarm me' – Blaise drew his pistol and shot him in the back of the head. 'Since then I have often wondered why I did it.' Fiona says tenderly that he must have suffered agonies of conscience, and he replies: 'No, it never troubled me that much.' Fiona feels confused; she knows him to be a kind and gentle person, and this fails to fit into the picture. This is almost certainly the reason that Hajdu tossed the anecdote into the novel – as one more illustration of what a complex and fascinating person he is. Charlotte told Della Aleksander that she'd shot a soldier who was about to 'shop' her, so it seems reasonable to assume that the anecdote is true.

Blaise has another confession that, in its way, is even more revealing. He shows Fiona a wallet, and confesses that he stole it. He had gone into the shop to buy one; this one, which he wanted, cost about a pound more than he intended to pay, so he slipped it into his pocket. He admits that the pound was a trifling sum, but says that he felt pleased with himself for stealing it so neatly. As he tells her about it, he bursts into tears, and Fiona again reflects what a strange and complex character he is . . .

So Carl Hajdu had a basic criminal streak. Like all true criminality, it arose out of a manic egoism, an obsession with himself that made other people seem relatively unimportant.

One day, when I took Charlotte out to lunch in Camden Town, we called at her printers and I was introduced to a pleasant man who obviously regarded her with a certain awe. After her death, one of her followers told me that she boasted that she never went into the printing shop without stealing some small item. Della Aleksander described how Charlotte would steal from big stores. But it was not straightforward shoplifting – that would not have been challenging enough. She would look through some items – let us say bras – and slip one of them – any one – under her coat. Later she would return to the store and explain to the shop assistant that she had bought it the day before, but found it to be the wrong size – could she change it? Asked for her receipt, she would explain that she had mislaid it, and put on such a show of being helpless and incompetent that the assistant invariably allowed her to choose the correct one.

In her letters, and in biographical accounts of 'Charlotte', she often seems to lie quite unnecessarily – in what one of Shaw's characters calls 'an ecstasy of mendacity'. In a letter to an expert on genetics, she describes how transvestites sometimes make inappropriate gestures learned from 'say, an actress on the screen, or a woman friend, or from somewhere else – perhaps even from me . . .', and one can almost hear Carl Hajdu snickering to himself.

The typical criminal lacks what David Riesman calls 'inner direction'; they tend to be weaklings who follow the path of least resistance, and who steal because it seems an obvious short-cut to obtaining something they want. But the problem with criminality is that relations with other people can never be healthily normal – except, perhaps, with other crooks. Other people are potential victims. The result, as Sartre points out in his book on Genet, is that a criminal is a criminal because he *feels* guilty. Since Charlotte seems to have been a lifelong kleptomaniac and petty crook, we are faced with the amazing contradiction between the arrogant, abrasive creator of the transsexual theory of evolution and the incorrigible thief. But then she triumphantly absorbs the contradiction into her own theory by pointing out that man is a neotonous (and therefore immature) species, and that this is his special glory. The guilt involved in sexual deviation is the motor of evolution. As to the objection that she was a transvestite and that, according to her theory, transvestites were an evolutionary dead end, she could reply that her creation of the sexual theory made her a special case; she had *used* her transvestism to achieve insight into her transvestism, then used the insight as the basis of a world-shaking theory. Like the founder of a religion, she was *sui generis*, unique.

But it would be a pity to let her get away with this piece of intellectual sleight-of-hand. For the criminal streak is the real key to Carl Hajdu's character. The obvious comparison is with Dostoevsky, whom his biographers suspect of lifelong guilt about the rape of an underage girl. Dostoevsky lays so much emphasis on shame and guilt that it is natural to suspect him of some carefully hidden sexual deviation, perhaps paedophilia. There is a chapter in *The Idiot* where, at a tea party, all the characters decide to confess to the most shameful thing they have ever done. In the suppressed chapter of *The Possessed* called 'Stavrogin's Confession', the Byronic playboy Stavrogin describes how he once stole money from a poverty-stricken clerk in an attempt to see if he could experience shame. Stavrogin also describes how he seduced a little girl, then made no attempt to stop her from hanging herself. Svidrigailov, a character in *Crime and Punishment*, has also raped a small girl who then committed suicide. Dostoevsky seems to positively revel in shame – his second wife has described how he would borrow her last few kopecks, then go and gamble them away. The hero of his novel *Notes from Underground* also makes a virtue of this tendency to weakness and self-contradiction; he declares that if one day science reduces the universe to a completely logical place, then man will go insane to turn his back on logic. 'I believe this because it appears that man's whole purpose is to prove that he is a man and not a cog-wheel.' So if expected to behave with gratitude or decency, he will deliberately behave with ingratitude and meanness to assert his own freedom. But at least Dostoevsky used all this guilt and shame and seething self-contradiction to produce masterpieces like *Crime and Punishment* and *The Brothers*

Karamazov. He seems to be the perfect illustration of Charlotte's theory of evolution through inner conflict.

Hajdu himself had his ready-made cause for lifelong shame in his kleptomania and his sexual deviance. Like Dostoevsky, he used his guilt and self-division as the materials of creation. Yet although he holds up the creator and shaman as the highest products of evolution, there is an element of absurdity in his major creation, Dr Charlotte Maria Beatrix Augusta Bach, Ph.D. He must have been aware of a certain element of absurdity as he prepared to receive his adoring disciples, who regarded him rather as the theosophists regarded Madame Blavatsky, by donning foam-rubber breasts and clambering into an outsize pair of knickers. He must have felt that he had lowered himself to the level of the 'chattering girls' party that he and Della Aleksander attended in Wimbledon . . . for the truth is that he had. Yet he would then proceed to lecture the disciples on the basic male-female duality of all creation, and reassure the inverts and deviants among them that sexual deviancy is the driving force of creation.

He was obviously wrong. But what *was* the real answer? That was the problem whose solution continued to elude me.

In 1978, I set down an account of Charlotte's theory of evolution in my book *Mysteries*. She was a little grumpy about it – she obviously felt that eight pages was not sufficient to do justice to her ideas – but was sufficiently pleased to have dozens of copies of it duplicated and bound in hard covers. *Mysteries* went into a dozen or so foreign editions and spread her reputation abroad, but I felt she was disappointed by the relatively mild response – she had hoped to be flooded with correspondence from all over the world. Charlotte was in a hurry. I think the lack of world-wide fame was a thorn in her side that she seldom forgot, and it may have contributed to the cancer of the liver that finally killed her. But in another sense, it was her 'secret' that really killed her. She must have known that, if she achieved the kind of fame she dreamed about, it would be impossible to go on fooling the world. And when she began to suspect she had a cancer, a few months before her death, she must have made a conscious decision not to allow any of her medical friends – of whom she had several – to examine her. So her death must be regarded as a kind of suicide.

When Della Aleksander read my chapter in *Mysteries* she commented: 'Colin Wilson will be *furious* when he finds out,' and Charlotte remarked casually: 'Oh, I don't think he'll mind.' She was right; I was merely *very* curious. And when one of her executors sent me the typescript of *Fiona*, and some autobiographical fragments, I read them voraciously, searching for the key to the mystery.

It was as I read *Fiona* that I became convinced that Hajdu's vision of the meaning of sex was not basically different from my own. There was a sentence in the love-making scene with Fiona: 'They were forcing their tongues deep into each other's mouths as if trying to reach all the way down inside each other.' It was obvious that this did not mean that Blaise wanted to become Fiona and vice versa; they wanted to remain themselves while *absorbing* some essential part of the other. Again, it was Dr Johnson and the beefsteak. Blake understood it: that what 'men in women do require' is 'the lineaments of gratified desire'. And as he lies on top of Fiona, 'moving slowly and in long strokes, raising and lowering his buttocks rhythmically, savouring every fraction of an inch of the movement', he is actually savouring his sexual conquest of her, not his desire to become her. Twenty-four hours earlier, she was a stranger in a bar; now she is naked underneath him, and her clothes are lying a few feet away on the carpet. He can tell himself that he is more of a Man than he thought, that he is not quite the purposeless drifter he has come to suspect. He can also tell himself that life itself is more rich and fascinating than he had given it credit for, that effort and vigilance and determination *are* worthwhile, and that the fates may yet have some important destiny in store for him.

It comes back to Dr Johnson's remark that when a man knows he is to be hanged in a fortnight, it concentrates his mind wonderfully. Sex also concentrates the mind wonderfully, and that is why civilised man is so obsessed by it. It enables him to 'savour every fraction of an inch', not merely of the act of sexual intercourse, but of living itself.

But that, of course, only underlines the basic problem: that, after coitus, 'man becomes sad', because he quickly returns to his unconcentrated and defocused state. In sexual excitement, it is as if the spirit itself becomes erect, and becomes capable of penetrating the meaning of life. Normal consciousness is limp and flaccid; its attitude towards reality is defensive. This is what Sartre called 'contingency', that feeling of being at the mercy of chance. And this is the problem that, in *The Outsider*, I had called 'original sin'. Blaise's endless sexual encounters are an attempt to escape his sense of contingency.

And the same thing, I realised, applied to his criminality. He had no idea what made him shoot a fifteen-year-old boy in the back of the head or steal a wallet when he could just as easily have paid for it. And Charlotte seemed to have no idea why she went shoplifting ('Why, oh why, do I steal?') or why she even stole from her printer, on whose goodwill she depended so much. It was because crime, like sex, caused a galvanic thrill of excitement that made her feel strong and purposeful.

These reflections had a flavour of familiarity; I had encountered them somewhere before. In Dostoevsky, perhaps? Or Genet? Then it came to me: not Dostoevsky or Genet, but in that one-man textbook of criminology, the Marquis de Sade. And the more I thought of it, the more it seemed to me that de Sade represented a challenge that Charlotte had deliberately avoided. No writer allows us to grasp more clearly the nature and aims of sexual perversion. And what he has to say, as we shall see, amounts to a flat contradiction of Charlotte Bach's theory of sexual deviation.

THREE

Anarchy Incarnate

Judged by his writings, the Marquis de Sade is undoubtedly the most evil man who ever lived; they are full of rape, torture, mutilation and murder, all performed solely for the gratification of his heroes. He is capable of describing children being flayed alive, the torments of a whole family forced to watch one another's sufferings, the death of a woman split in two by the sexual member of a donkey. There seems to be no excess of nauseating horror that he is not capable of describing with delight. So when the reader learns that he spent twenty-eight years of his life in prison, and died in a mental institution, the natural reaction is to murmur 'Serve him right'.

It comes as something of a surprise to learn that this incarnation of wickedness never actually committed a murder – or indeed any other kind of crime – and that his imprisonment was an outrageous injustice. This man whose imagination was capable of such abominations was liked by men, loved by women, and even respected by the officers of the law who came to arrest him. The phrenologist who examined his skull after his death said that it had a strong bump of benevolence and that, far from indicating criminal traits, it was 'in all respects similar to that of a father of the Church'.

As the facts of his life have begun to emerge, there has been a strong tendency to rehabilitate de Sade. Simone de Beauvoir wrote an essay entitled 'Must we burn de Sade?', and the answer was predictably no. A novel about him is entitled *Satan's Saint*. The poet Apollinaire described him as 'the freest spirit who ever lived'; but anyone who has ever laboured through *The 120 Days of Sodom* or *Juliette* will have to admit that this is nonsense. To get the measure of de Sade at his worst, it is only necessary to read the final orgy scenes of *Juliette*, in which a mother looks on while her lover rapes and sodomises her young daughter, then shouts approval and masturbates herself as he throws the child into a fire and watches her burn to death. 'Free spirit' or not, de Sade was undoubtedly an incredibly vicious and unpleasant character, and defenders who talk about his martyrdom are self-deluded sentimentalists.

Would it not, in that case, be better to ignore him? The answer must be no; de Sade's value lies in the sheer straightforwardness of his case-history. No one allows us a clearer insight into the cause and development of sexual deviations. To understand why de Sade became the worst 'mental criminal' of all time is to understand something fundamental about human nature and the sexual impulse.

Donatien Alphonse François de Sade was born on 2 June, 1740. His father was a count in the diplomatic service, his mother a lady-in-waiting to the Princesse de Condé; and de Sade spent his childhood in the palatial Hôtel de Condé. Here he was brought up virtually by servants, receiving little or no affection from either parent – a fact to which his biographers attribute the development of some of his nastier traits. He was undoubtedly a spoilt brat, admitting in one probably autobiographical passage: 'As soon as I could think, I believed that nature and fortune had joined hands to fill my lap with their gifts . . . It seemed to me that everything ought to give in to me, that the whole universe should humour my whims . . .' And by the time he was disabused of this notion – by being thrown into prison – he was too old to change, and went on creating a mental universe that should humour all his whims. At the age of nine he was sent to a Jesuit boarding school, where he learnt to detest religion. At fifteen he went into the army, where he spent an inordinate amount of his allowance on prostitutes, and in the pursuit of young actresses.

But no one knows where he acquired his chief mania, a lifelong obsession with the infliction and suffering of pain. It was, admittedly, common enough in the eighteenth century, where every brothel had its room lined with birch rods and instruments of bondage. In his *Sexual Life in England*, Ivan Bloch points out that the English were so enamoured of flogging that it was known on the Continent as 'le vice anglais'. Bloch explains, somewhat obscurely, that 'flagellation is the imitation and conscious synthesis of all physiological sadistic components of coitus' – by which he means that it is so like the sexual act that it can easily get mixed up with it. Hirschfeld seems to come closer to the point when he says that flagellation is simply an exaggerated version of normal male sexual aggression. And he supports his argument by citing the case of a man who acquired his taste for the rod when he was caught masturbating by a sadistic governess who then beat his bare buttocks with a cane. 'It burned my behind like fire, but at the same time prickled so pleasantly, so delightfully. And it was the blows that did it; it had never been so nice when we masturbated . . . Later, I noticed that the governess's hands, during my now regular chastisements, frequently strayed between my legs and stayed there.' It underlines the point that sex can become associated with anything that brings it repeatedly to mind – like a Pavlov dog salivating at the sound of a bell.

For whatever reason, the young de Sade came to associate whipping with sexual ecstasy and, whenever he went to brothels, was accustomed to ask the girls to allow him to whip their bare behinds, and to ask them to do the same for him. He also seems to have developed at an early stage a preference for sodomy with his sexual partners, no doubt because it was more 'forbidden' than vaginal intercourse. He was obviously a very highly sexed young man and, like most young men, would have been glad to deflower every virgin in the world. Long periods of barrack life meant that when he finally got into town he was ready for an orgy. And since he was a masochist as well as a sadist, the desire for sodomy was accompanied by a desire to be sodomised as well as beaten. He seems to have found the greatest pleasure of all in sodomising as he was being sodomised, a feat that must have required remarkable timing.

But his oddest 'perversion' – and the one that was the real root of his trouble – was his pathological hatred of religion. Again, we do not know why he hated it so much, but if we assume that his psychological starting-point was his feeling that 'everything ought to give in to me, and that the whole universe should humour my whims', we can also see that his strict Jesuit boarding school, where he had to rise at 5.30 AM, must have been the first and most violent shock to his sense of invulnerability. Whatever the cause, it is clear that something produced a burning resentment that turned him into one of the most consistently inventive blasphemers of all time.

De Sade had his first clash with the law when he was twenty-three; in fact, it was with the king himself. In October 1763, de Sade obtained through a procuress the services of a twenty-year-old fan-maker named Jeanne Testard. The pleasant-looking young man, only just over five feet tall, with a face marked with smallpox, began by asking if she believed in God and, when she said she was a Christian, he replied with 'insults and horrible blasphemies'. He declared that he had proved there was no God by committing sacrilegious acts, such as inserting a communion wafer into a girl's vagina before he had intercourse, then challenging God to avenge himself. After this, de Sade masturbated on a crucifix, then pointed a pistol at the girl and forced her to trample on a crucifix while uttering blasphemies. Then he spent the night reading her atheistic poems – she must have been almightily bored – and trying to persuade her to submit to sodomy. Finally, he made her promise to take communion with him the following Sunday, so they could pollute the hosts inside her. Then he left.

Jeanne immediately divulged what had happened to the procuress who came to collect her, and she in turn reported it to the police. Blasphemy at that time was punishable by death. De Sade was arrested and taken to Fontainebleau, where he was interrogated by the Minister of the Royal Household – Louis XV took an almost morbid interest in his subjects' goings-on – then he was imprisoned for two weeks in the state fortress at Vincennes. De Sade was young enough to believe that God had taken up his challenge, and he wrote penitent letters; when his father interceded on his behalf, he was freed, but banished to the country.

At the time of his imprisonment, de Sade had been married for six months. His bride, Renée-Pelagie de Montreuil, was the daughter of a recently ennobled tax-collector and therefore, strictly speaking, a member of the bourgeoisie. He had been forced to marry her by his father, whose bad management was causing his fortune to evaporate swiftly; de Sade resented it.

Six months after his imprisonment, Mme de Sade became pregnant. But as soon as the king withdrew his order of banishment, de Sade rushed to Paris and began an affair with an actress. When his mother-in-law, Marie-Madeleine de Montreuil, found out, she behaved with surprising moderation, allowed the young man to take her into his confidence, and broke up the affair by persuading him that the girl was deceiving him. Most of de Sade's biographers seem to agree that she was attracted by her son-in-law, or perhaps she was merely dazzled by his title. At all events, for many years she remained remarkably tolerant of his endless sexual escapades. De Sade soon found himself another actress from whom he borrowed a large sum of money to pay his debts, and rented a house in the Paris suburb of Arceuil where he could entertain prostitutes.

Inevitably, his tastes again brought him into conflict with the law. On Easter Sunday, 1768, he picked up a beggar woman named Rose Keller in Paris, and persuaded her to accompany him to his rented house, claiming that he wanted her to clean it. Once there, he ordered her to undress, tied her hands and feet, and proceeded to whip her. When she screamed – convinced she was about to be murdered – he threatened her with a knife. Finally, 'with loud and terrifying cries', he had an orgasm, and then untied her. Later she escaped by climbing out of a bedroom window with the aid of knotted sheets, and reported him to the law. Again, de Sade's mother-in-law intervened, sending a lawyer to buy off the girl at a cost of 2,400 *livres*, a huge sum. But the wheels of the law had been set in motion, and de Sade was arrested a few weeks later, and imprisoned in the castle at Saumur. This time it was six months before he was freed.

For the next three years, de Sade kept out of trouble; he rejoined his regiment and spent much time at his ancestral home, the Château de la Coste, near Avignon – his father had now died, and Sade inherited his title of Comte. He amused himself by writing and presenting plays, by trying to seduce his wife's attractive younger sister Anne – a canoness (apprentice nun) – and by hiring a manservant named Latour to sodomise him. But he longed for orgies and, in mid-June 1772, set out with his manservant for Marseilles, ostensibly to collect money, but in fact to have a brief fling with prostitutes. He took with him a jar of some aniseed sweets which he had doctored with Spanish Fly, an aphrodisiac. The day after he arrived, his manservant picked up four girls whose ages ranged between eighteen and twenty-three, and de Sade and Latour went to the house of one of them. There de Sade whipped the eighteen-year-old while he masturbated Latour; then he gave her sweets. Then he got one of the girls to flog him with a broom, after which he had vaginal intercourse with her while his manservant sodomised him. After this, the manservant had intercourse with another girl, after which de Sade whipped her. Finally, de Sade committed sodomy on one of the girls while his valet sodomised him. De Sade then paid them and left.

That evening, he made the mistake of visiting another prostitute and giving her sweets; she refused to allow him sodomy so he left. The following day de Sade and Latour returned home; by this time, however, the prostitute was being violently sick and vomiting blood and black bile. The doctor who examined her suspected arsenic poisoning and sent for the police. The other women were soon located; one of them had also suffered severe stomach pains after eating the sweets. She also admitted to sodomy, which was a hanging offence. And when de Sade heard that a warrant had been issued for his arrest, he fled from La Coste, taking his manservant and his wife's younger sister Anne, the apprentice nun.

For de Sade's mother-in-law this was the last straw; by eloping with his sister-in-law he had damaged the family honour beyond repair. So when de Sade came back from Italy and rented a house at Chambéry – then in the Italian duchy of Savoy – she applied to the king of Sardinia for a warrant for his arrest. (He had by now been sentenced to death in his absence.) De Sade and his manservant were taken into custody and imprisoned in the Fort Miolans prison. His long-suffering wife stood by him and, four months later, succeeded in arranging his escape. Eventually, de Sade was able to slip back into France and rejoin her at La Coste. As soon as his mother-in-law found out, she applied to the king of France for a *lettre de cachet*, an order for his imprisonment. But in spite of several raids, the police failed to find the fugitive.

Mme de Montreuil might possibly have decided to let bygones be bygones if it had not been for another scandal. This time de Sade hired five young servant girls, all in their mid-teens, and a young male secretary. He whipped some of them so badly that they needed hospital treatment. A maid named Nanon gave birth to his child. Incredibly, the Comtesse de Sade finally allowed herself to join in the orgies, perhaps in an effort to keep his love. When Mme de Montreuil learned that her daughter also had been debauched, she decided that it was time her son-in-law was permanently incarcerated. He was finally arrested in Paris in February 1777, and was to spend the next thirteen years in jail – in spite of the fact that the Marseilles 'poisoning' case had been re-tried and de Sade had been let off with a caution. The king's order of confinement overruled this verdict.

For an imperious man like de Sade, imprisonment at Vincennes was a nightmare. He was thrown into a small, airless cell whose ventilation ducts had been blocked, and where the floor was thick with dust; he was unable to sleep at night because rats and mice ran around the cell. He was forbidden exercise and even writing materials. He alternated between transports of fury and resentment, and attacks of despair and self-pity. It was three years before he was allowed to take daily exercise. And during this period the historic Marquis de Sade – the man whose name is equated with sadism – was born.

During his first years at Vincennes, de Sade wasted a great deal of energy on emotional explosions; his notes are full of denunciations of the governor, de Rougemont. Finally, he seems to have realised that hatred was a waste of time and, on Christmas Eve 1780, he began to sketch out a comedy. (He was always passionately fond of the stage.) In May 1881 his sister-in-law Anne died of smallpox. Two months later his wife was allowed to visit him for the first time. But de Sade became subject to such violent fits of jealousy that in October the visits were suspended. His emotional world was becoming increasingly barren. And in July of the following year, he completed the first of his typically 'Sadeian' works, the *Dialogue Between a Priest and a Dying Man*, his first – and in many ways his clearest – attempt to express his own philosophy of destruction.

Within its first few pages, it reveals the basic fallacies in de Sade's logic. The priest asks the dying man if he repents, and the dying man replies Yes, he repents of having been stupid enough to waste time on moral scruples when he was sent into the world to enjoy himself. Nature has given him his passions 'for her service', and he regrets having failed to use them to the utmost. He goes on to explain that he is an atheist, and refutes all the priest's arguments about the goodness of God. When he jeers at the idea that God has created him solely to punish him for desires over which he has no control, the priest replies reasonably: 'But you are free.' 'Only according to your prejudices, and these are soon demolished by the use of reason.' Would men commit crimes for which they know they will be executed if they had any freedom of choice? 'We are the pawns of an irresistible force, and never for a moment is it within our power to do anything but surrender to it.' The priest replies: 'In that case, we should not shrink from the worst of crimes', but – oddly enough – the dying man disagrees. Let crimes be punished by law – that will be a sufficient deterrent. After which he tells the priest that six beautiful girls are waiting in the next room to console his final hours, and offers to let him take his pick. Unbelievably, the priest accepts this offer, and 'in their arms became a man corrupted by nature because he had been unable to explain what corrupt nature was'.

So de Sade's argument can be summarised as follows. Nature has sent man into the world solely to satisfy his desires. There is no God and no freedom, so he has no choice. Yet this is plainly self-contradictory. If man has no choice, then why *do* most people restrain their desires? In later works, de Sade will attempt to answer this objection: because of fear. Those who hold the power in the world never attempt to restrain their desires: kings, judges, archbishops all indulge their vices to the full. But they preach religion to keep the poor in order. In de Sade's world there is no such thing as unselfishness or real goodness: only fear and self-delusion.

In February 1784, de Sade was removed from Vincennes to the Bastille. He occupied a room in the ironically named Liberty Tower, which was a great deal more comfortable than his quarters at Vincennes, and he was allowed to drape the walls with brightly coloured hangings. There were three meals a day, and the food was good. The Comtesse de Sade was again allowed to visit – she was now living in a convent to allay her husband's pathological jealousy. And it was in the Bastille that de Sade began to write his first work of 'criminal sexuality', *The 120 Days of Sodom*, which he completed in November 1785.

The *120 Days* is basically a sexual day-dream – the masturbation fantasy of a man who has been deprived of sex for a long time; it must be admitted that it is the ultimate sexual day-dream. The outline of the novel is simple: four libertines (including a duke, a bishop and a Lord Chief Justice) decide to spend four months systematically indulging in every form of sexual satisfaction. They have hired four brothel madams, whose job is to procure a small army of young men and girls – and a number of children – as well as to relate stories from their own lifelong experience of debauchery. Also present are the four daughters of the libertines, all of whom have been deflowered – anally – at an early age by their own fathers, and then married off to other members of the group, so everyone can continue to share their favours. By way of initiating his narrative, de Sade spends a few pages describing the habits and crimes of the libertines. The Duc de Blangis, for example, at one time practised highway robbery, during which he would rape all the attractive females – and males – then murder them all. His brother, the bishop, had once been appointed the executor of a rich man's will and guardian of his son and daughter; he had promptly embezzled the legacy, raped both children, then murdered them. The president of the court has a particularly sadistic sense of humour. He had once tried hard to procure a little girl whose parents had refused all his offers. So he had the husband convicted of an imaginary crime and sentenced to be broken on the wheel. To secure her husband's release, the mother brought her daughter to the president's house on the day of the execution, and the president so arranged it that he sodomised the child – held in her mother's arms – during the execution, achieving orgasm at the moment the husband expired. The shutters were then thrown open to reveal the execution scene, and mother and daughter sank down in a dead faint – never to awaken, for they had been given poison when they arrived. Variants on this particular scene were among de Sade's favourite sexual fantasies, and occur many times in his work.

What then follows, as de Sade's editor, Maurice Heine, has pointed out, is an extremely wide-ranging catalogue of sexual deviations, presented with manic precision and thoroughness and continuing for hundreds of pages. It starts mildly enough with a priest whose greatest pleasure is to masturbate in front of seven-year-old girls while he mutters obscenities, and another priest who likes little girls to urinate into his mouth. Another man wants to suck the milk from the breasts of a nursing mother while she masturbates him on her lap. A hundred or so pages later, de Sade is describing a man who reaches orgasm as he listens to the sound of hammer-blows as a naked girl is nailed into a coffin, and another who ties a girl to a corpse, 'knee to knee, mouth to mouth', and flogs her until he discharges. There follow assorted scenes of murder and mutilation: legs are torn off and eyes gouged out as the victims are violated. One pervert takes pleasure in having his victims buried alive, then lies with his ear close to the ground, listening to their screams. Children are flayed and roasted alive, fathers forced to rape their daughters, pregnant women disembowelled.

Interestingly enough, these latter scenes of the book are only sketched in rather than described in detail, evidence that even de Sade was unable to go through with all the horrors. The book was written on a forty-foot roll of paper in minute handwriting, and vanished after the storming of the Bastille, to reappear in Germany many years later.

What de Sade had done was to empty himself of every sexual fantasy until he was psychologically – and, no doubt, physically – exhausted. The catharsis turned him into an artist – not a very good artist, but an artist none the less. Having learned the trick of creation and rid himself of his darkest fantasies, he was now prepared to attempt something more conventional and make a bid for literary success. Obviously there could be no question of sadistic pornography. Instead, he borrowed the basic plot of Richardson's *Clarissa* – about a self-centred rake who lures a virtuous girl to a brothel, then rapes her – and transformed it into a lengthy work called *Aline and Valcour*. In de Sade's novel, Richardson's playboy, Lovelace, is transformed into a wicked father, the Magistrate de Blamont, who wishes to force his daughter Aline to marry a companion in debauchery, the financier Dolburg. The Magistrate de Blamont finally poisons his wife, then lures his daughter to a remote country property where he deflowers her, and she commits suicide in despair.

What de Sade is doing is playing a Machiavellian game. All his sympathies are obviously with the wicked father, but he does his best to convince his readers that Blamont horrifies him, and that he is firmly on the side of virtue. The book has an extraordinary profusion of incident – particularly in the account of Aline's amoral elder sister, Leonora – but it is obvious that de Sade's heart is not really in it.

The notion of adopting Richardson's moralising tone and writing with his tongue in his cheek, strongly appealed to de Sade's saturnine sense of humour. His next venture in this direction was a long short story called *The Misfortunes of Virtue*, originally conceived as part of a volume of *Tales and Fables*. It is the story of an innocent girl called Justine, who is thrown out upon the world after her father's bankruptcy and the death of her mother. Within a few pages, she is having her clothes torn off by a rich banker, and is only saved from rape when he has a premature orgasm. Condemned to death for a crime she did not commit, she escapes and falls into the hands of a band of robbers, who commit various perverted sex acts on her, but leave her virginity untouched. And so her misfortunes continue. She falls into the hands of a homosexual, de Bressac, who forces her to become the confidante of his plans to murder his mother and who finally lays the blame on her. She spends a period in a school where a rascally schoolmaster sexually abuses his pupils and commits incest with his daughter, finally branding Justine with a hot iron. She thinks she has found safety in a monastery, but the monks prove to be libertines; she is flogged, sodomised and made to perform fellatio. There also she finally loses her virginity – inevitably, with the maximum of pain. At the end of the story, after many sufferings, Justine is rescued from her miseries by her sister, Juliette – who has become a successful courtesan – but just as it looks as if she is on the point of living happily ever after, she tries to close a window during a storm and is killed by a flash of lightning.

De Sade was so pleased with this short novel that he decided it ought to be expanded and rewritten; it was later to become his most famous and popular work.

In the following year, 1788, de Sade wrote another short novel in his 'Machiavellian' manner. *Eugénie de Franval, or the Misfortunes of Incest* begins: 'To instruct man and correct his morals; such is the sole goal we set ourselves in this story . . .' It is about another wicked father, who conceives the design of corrupting his daughter and who brings her up without the slightest knowledge of religion or morals. On her fourteenth birthday, he commits incest with her. Eugénie soon becomes as corrupt as he is. When Eugénie's mother finds out – watching her husband and daughter make love through a crack in the door – she is frantic. Her husband persuades a young libertine to try and seduce her, but he fails. Eugénie also fails to seduce a virtuous priest named Clervil. Franval has him imprisoned on false accusations. When the young libertine tries to elope with Eugénie, Franval pursues them and kills him. Finally, as her mother dies, Eugénie repents, and dies of a broken heart. Franval also experiences belated remorse as he looks at his wife's corpse, and kills himself.

The chief interest of this preposterous farrago is that it makes the reader clearly aware of something that he has only suspected in reading the earlier books: that de Sade is creating a world of pure, unadulterated fantasy, and that he is totally incapable of even

a shred of realism. The circumstantial – almost Balzacian – openings
of many of his books produce a deceptive appearance of realism.
But de Sade is not remotely realistic. The books are long-drawn-out
masturbation fantasies, and all the characters are wooden dummies.
When Franval decides to seduce Eugénie, he sits beside her and
says: 'All those many charms, Eugénie, that Nature has lavished
on you – these you must sacrifice to me without a moment's delay.'
And Eugénie replies: 'But what is it you ask of me? Are you not
already master of everything? . . . Make Eugénie your victim;
immolated by your beloved hands, she will always be triumphant.'
So Franval becomes 'the ravisher of that virginity of which Nature
. . . had made him the trusted defender'. Then 'several days
passed in mutual intoxication . . . She would have wished to have
received him in a thousand temples simultaneously; she accused
her friend's imagination of being too timid, of not throwing all
caution to the winds.'

Obviously, no father is going to set out to seduce his daughter
in this way, and no daughter is going to react by crying, 'Make
Eugénie your victim,' and then reproach him for not having a
sufficiently dirty mind. De Sade is writing in a kind of vacuum.
And as soon as we see this, we also see that all his fantasies lack
realism. Would a bishop really be able to embezzle a dead man's
fortune and then rape and murder his children without anyone
noticing? Would it really be possible to force a father to sodomise
his daughter, or a brother his sister, at gunpoint? The truth is that
de Sade simply likes the idea, and makes no attempt to make it
sound plausible. That is to say, he simply lacks imagination. He
himself recognises this, in a passage in *The 120 Days of Sodom*,
when a prostitute describes how one client likes to eat the dirt from
between her toes. One of the libertines remarks: 'One need but be
mildly jaded, and all these infamies assume a richer meaning;
satiety inspires them . . . One grows tired of the commonplace,
the imagination becomes vexed, and the slenderness of our means,
the weakness of our faculties, the corruption of our souls leads us
to these abominations.'

Here de Sade has provided us with the key to his own sexual
deviancy. In human beings, sex is a response to ideas; and the
faculty that responds is the imagination – which is only another
name for the *sense of reality* – or what the psychologist Pierre Janet
called 'the reality function'. We acknowledge this when we say:

'He lacks imagination – he has no idea how much he hurts people', meaning that he has only a feeble sense of reality.

In most normal people, the imagination is fairly sensitive and responsive. In de Sade, it was curiously coarse and unresponsive, as if he had one layer of skin too many. Without imagination, all experience is oddly unsatisfying. When we are very tired, for example, it is difficult to appreciate a meal, or enjoy a television programme, or even read a newspaper. To appreciate any experience, we need to be *wide awake,* so the mind participates fully in the reality. De Sade's need to be flogged, to commit sodomy, to engage in multiple sex, all seem to indicate that his senses needed to be *jarred* into receptivity. He was like a man suffering from some nervous disease that makes him insensitive to pinpricks. In prison, without prostitutes to flog him or manservants to commit sodomy, de Sade tried to make the imagination a substitute for reality. But his imagination also needed to be flogged hard to produce any result. This is why his characters are never content just to have sexual intercourse; it has to be, at the very least, incest or the violent deflowering of virgins. Nothing less outrageous could make an impact on that extra layer of skin that covered his senses . . .

And then, quite suddenly, de Sade was free. The French Revolution overtook the king who was responsible for his imprisonment, Louis XVI. But, with typical bad luck, de Sade misjudged his chances, and left most of his manuscripts behind him in his cell. He had heard about the bread riots and about troops firing on crowds and, on 2 July 1789, using a funnel as a megaphone, he shouted from the window of his cell that prisoners were being murdered, and that the people should come to their aid. The authorities reacted swiftly; de Sade was dragged out of bed at 1 AM and transported to the Charenton asylum, outside Paris. Ten days later, crowds stormed the Bastille and slaughtered many of its garrison, including the governor, de Launay. Mme de Sade, who had been requested by her husband to collect his books and manuscripts, was a little slow off the mark, and they were pillaged by the looters; according to de Sade, fifteen books that were ready for the printer disappeared. Because he was in Charenton, de Sade had to wait another nine months for his imprisonment to end; he was finally released in April 1790. His wife refused to see him and, soon after, applied for a separation.

At first, all went well. As an ex-prisoner of the state he was in a good position to pose as a revolutionary, and became 'Citizen Sade'. He formed a liaison with a young actress, Marie-Constance Renelle, whose husband had deserted her, and it lasted the remainder of his life. He wrote comedies which were accepted by the Comédie-Française, and dreamed of becoming the Molière of the revolution. He rewrote *The Misfortunes of Virtue* in a longer version called *Justine*, which was a considerable – if scandalous – success when it appeared in 1791. In this version, Justine loses her virginity a great deal earlier. A handsome young traveller is captured by the robber-band and Justine saves his life and helps him to escape; he knocks her unconscious in a wood, rapes and sodomises her, then leaves her tied to a tree, taking her money. The revolution had evidently made de Sade feel that there was no longer any need for caution, and what had been a rather restrained book becomes an orgy of horror.

But he was permanently in need of money, and success as a playwright failed to materialise; only one play, *Count Oxtiern*, was performed – its hero-villain is another of de Sade's 'monsters', who has kidnapped and raped a virtuous girl – but members of the audience created a disturbance and it had to be taken off. The revolutionary Marat decided that de Sade was a typical aristocratic libertine of the old régime and ought to die; by accident, however, he denounced the Marquis de la Salle, who was executed. Marat discovered his mistake and was about to rectify it when he was murdered in his bath by Charlotte Corday. Unaware of how close he had been to the guillotine, de Sade delivered an address describing Marat as a great man.

De Sade soon became a judge on a revolutionary committee; it was within his power to destroy his mother-in-law and her husband; instead, he removed their names from the death list: 'That is the revenge I take!' As a member of the Hospitals Commission, he played an important part in improving conditions in the over-crowded wards. Appointed chairman of his revolutionary section, he resigned when asked to support a proposal he considered 'horrible . . . utterly inhuman'. Yet one of his revolutionary pamphlets was highly praised, and he was chosen as a delegate to appear before the national convention. He was, as he gleefully told his lawyer, Gaufridy, rising in the world.

In December 1793 his luck changed; he was arrested, charged

with having written a letter two years earlier, offering to join a regiment that hoped to rescue the king. But after the execution of Robespierre and other terrorists, de Sade was released in the following October. In 1795, *Aline and Valcour* appeared under de Sade's own name, and a straightforward pornographic work called *Philosophy in the Bedroom* appeared anonymously.

The latter is, in many ways, one of de Sade's most interesting and least revolting works. Written in the form of a dialogue, it describes the corruption of an innocent young girl named Eugénie by an incestuous brother and sister, and a libertine called Dolmancé. In fact, Eugénie is fairly easily corrupted. When Dolmancé first seizes her and kisses her, she struggles and objects; but when Madame de Saint-Ange tells her not to be a prude, and demonstrates a French kiss, she instantly allows Dolmancé to put his tongue in her mouth. After this, her mentors describe the sexual organs and their functions, and she is brought to orgasm as one inserts a tongue into her vagina and the other into her anus. She is told: 'In whatever circumstances, a woman . . . must never have any objective but to have herself fucked from morning till night; 'tis for this unique end Nature created her.' Then follow long speeches in which she is told that religion is a delusion, and that there is no such thing as crime – although a moment later the libertines are contradicting themselves by telling her that crime is the sweetest pleasure in the world. Then she is taught to suck Dolmancé's penis ('accomplished woman, never deny your lovers this pleasure; 'twill bind them to you forever'), and to sodomise him with a dildo while he sodomises Madame de Saint-Ange. She is then sodomised herself, and a country yokel with an enormous penis is brought in to deflower her. In de Sade, coitus is never succeeded by sadness or exhaustion; it is part of the myth he propagates that sex is infinitely delightful and that no one can ever get tired of it. The only 'Sadistic' part of the book is the ending, when Eugénie's bad-tempered and domineering mother arrives to order her daughter to return home immediately. Dolmancé seizes the opportunity to make a long speech proving that parents have no rights over their children. Eugénie then invites her mother to kiss her arse, and the indignant lady is stripped of her clothes and subjected to sodomy and flagellation, after which her daughter rapes her with a dildo ('. . . at one stroke, incestuous, adulteress and sodomite, and all that in a girl who only lost her maidenhead today'). After this, Eugénie sews up her mother's vagina, while the others indulge in a sexual orgy. The lady is then told: 'Your daughter is old enough to do what she likes; she likes to fuck, she loves to fuck, she was born to fuck – and if you don't want to be fucked yourself, the best thing is to let her do what she wants.' Eugénie's mother is then thrown out with a few hefty kicks.

A scene like this provides us with the key to de Sade. His hatred of any kind of authority is pathological, and he loves to portray it being deflated. But while most authors are content to show the authority figure losing his dignity and self-possession, de Sade has to go to insane extremes. Instead of merely expressing defiance, he falls into a frenzy resembling an epileptic fit.

Suddenly we can see precisely what is wrong with him. Van Vogt wrote of the type he calls 'the violent man': 'he makes the *decision* to lose control'. Most of us make this decision at some time, when something infuriates us; but most of us also recognise that it is not appropriate to react to *every* annoying situation by 'losing control'. For 'losing control' is subject to the law of diminishing returns. If irritation is expressed by a shout, anger with a scream, fury with a loud scream, then transports of rage are beyond the capacity of the human voice. De Sade never seems to recognise this simple truth; his reaction is always that of the spoilt brat who has never been taught self-control; he always wants to go further and further and further. Hence comments like: 'In whatever circumstances, a woman must never have any objective but to have herself fucked from morning till night', which carry a dubious half-truth to the point of absurdity.

Significantly, the chapter that de Sade thought most important in the book is not a description of a sexual orgy but a philosophical pamphlet called, 'Frenchmen, One More Effort if You Wish to Become Republicans'. Its thesis is that the French have dealt superstition a mighty blow by executing the king; now they should follow it to its logical conclusion by executing God – that is, overthrowing all religious superstition. As he calls for the reign of Reason, de Sade sounds like some idealistic social philosopher, a disciple of Rousseau and Voltaire. Instead of boring your children with 'deific stupidities', teach them ethical and social principles, 'and then true patriotism will shine out in every spirit'. There is only one minor objection to this hymn to reason. De Sade believed that all nature is permeated with evil, and that life is a panorama of 'cosmic criminality' and destruction; so it is difficult to see how reason can guarantee happiness . . . But de Sade never concerns himself about such trivial contradictions.

In 1797, his lack of self-control cost him dear when he went to Provence to try to collect some long-overdue rents; he lost his temper with a tax collector and accused him of stealing some of the money. The result was expensive legal proceedings and the humiliation of a public apology.

Money was a perpetual worry; he told his lawyer that the insecurity had done more damage to his health than his years in the Bastille.

It was also in 1797 that de Sade's publisher brought out his most substantial work to date: a vast novel (in ten volumes), combining the stories of the unfortunate Justine and her sister, Juliette. The author's aim is to go further than any human being has ever gone in conjuring up scenes of sexual violence and cruelty. The result is inevitable: within a few dozen pages, the reader has become so accustomed to scenes of rape and murder that they become merely dull and repetitive. Utterly typical is a scene in which a government minister is accosted by a beggarwoman who asks for alms; she takes him into a miserable hut where her two half-naked children are starving. The minister then reveals that he was responsible for having her husband thrown into jail, rapes her two children then sodomises her, blowing out her brains as he reaches orgasm. Scenes like these are interspersed with long discourses on atheism, crime, immorality, and any other subject that takes the author's fancy. The orgies also have a quality of repetitiveness: 'The girl of eighteen lies down upon the ottoman. I seat myself upon her face, Clairwil camps herself upon mine. I sucked and was sucked; above me the youngest girl gives her buttocks to be kissed by Clairwil whom another girl was embuggering with a dildo; the slenderest of the quartet, bending over, was fingering Clairwil's clitoris, which was established hard by my mouth, and in the meantime was presenting her cunt to my friend . . .' And so on, *ad infinitum*. Occasionally, de Sade manages to produce some new idea: an orgy in a graveyard, surrounded by rotting corpses; a cannibal banquet in which they eat roast breasts and buttocks; Juliette's murder of her own father after seducing him. All this is rather less horrible than it sounds, for the reader never ceases to be aware that this is merely a nightmare fantasy, a kind of Tom and Jerry cartoon in which no one is ever really hurt. Even so, the final scene, in which Juliette allows her lover to rape her own daughter then burn her alive, induces a certain queasiness in the stomach. In *Juliette*, Justine's death is saved for the end; after she has been struck by lightning, the libertines fling themselves on the body and have a necrophiliac orgy.

One thing is clear; it is pointless to condemn the book for being shocking, for that was de Sade's intention. As this gradually dawns on the reader, he begins to react with a certain half-amused resignation. De Sade is like some middle-aged hippie, or some rather old-fashioned member of the Dada-ist movement, convinced that he is still as shocking as ever, when he is in fact only slightly absurd. And once we have achieved this detachment, we are in a position to appreciate de Sade's 'argument', and to see through its fallacies.

That argument could be roughly summarised as follows.

1. The human body has an enormous capacity for pleasure, and most of us hardly begin to explore this capacity because we are inhibited by absurd religious and moral scruples.
2. Sex contains, in its very essence, an element of 'criminality'. Our own bodies do not excite us because they are 'familiar'. Other bodies excite us in so far as they are unfamiliar, alien, *forbidden*. This applies as much to married clergymen as to libertines. We have tried to domesticate sex, to remove this element of 'wickedness'. This is a mistake. We should recognise that the sex act itself is a form of symbolic rape, and that we wouldn't enjoy it if it were not.

So far we may be prepared to agree with him. These arguments are not dissimilar to those employed by D. H. Lawrence or Wilhelm Reich or various other 'sexual liberators'. In fact, the wide acceptance of the Freudian revolution has made this part of de Sade's argument almost superfluous. It is the next part that strikes us as dubious.

3. If all sex is a form of rape, why can we not accept this, and agree that every human being should be allowed to choose whatever form of 'rape' appeals to him – whether of children,

ANARCHY INCARNATE · 65

animals, nuns or even babies? These acts are not *morally wrong* in themselves, for we are all created by Nature, and Nature is indifferent to morality.

We ask: what about the social contract, our tacit agreement not to do unto others what we would object to them doing unto us?

De Sade replies: Nature is also indifferent to this notion. The law of nature is survival of the fittest. The strong may profess moral scruples, but in practice they plunder the weak.

And it is only at this point that we can suddenly grasp the central fallacy in de Sade's argument. He is arguing in favour of *total selfishness*. He is saying that, ideally, he would like to be a sultan with absolute power over the life and death of every human being; only then could he make full use of the capacity for pleasure with which Nature has furnished him. If we object: 'But surely the rest of the human race would have something to say about that?', he replies: 'Of course. But it is up to each individual to try to impose his will on the others – in fact, this is precisely how society operates, although no one is honest enough to admit it.' 'You mean there is no such thing as natural decency or goodness or generosity?' 'Precisely. At last you understand me!'

For most of us, such a statement is as absurd as claiming that black is white. We have all seen decency and generosity in operation, and know perfectly well that they are not really another name for self-interest. But then, we also have to take into account de Sade's claim to be a total materialist, to believe that man is a machine, and that free will is non-existent – we all do what our natures compel us to do. De Sade's whole philosophy of selfishness depends upon this assertion. Yet it is by far the weakest point of his argument, for he is telling us that the courageous choose crime rather than virtue; if we have no free will, such a choice is impossible.

It must also be acknowledged that de Sade was himself a living refutation of his arguments. He showed himself tender and affectionate towards his new mistress and her son, and went to some trouble to ensure that his mother-in-law was included on a list of those who were to survive rather than those who were to die. But then, Sade himself would undoubtedly have denied that this undermined his case. He would have replied that he made no claim to live up to his own principles of absolute selfishness and heartlessness – that all he wanted was to compel an intellectually dishonest society to agree that its religion and its morality were basically false. This is the view of de Sade that has been taken by modern defenders like Maurice Heine, Guillaume Apollinaire and Austryn Wainhouse, and is the basis of their view that de Sade is a profoundly misunderstood man. But if that is so, it is de Sade's own fault. He went to a great deal of trouble to declare himself an enemy of society and of the human race – one of his characters says that if he could snatch the sun out of the sky, he would use it to burn up the world – and if we take him at his word, he can hardly blame us.

Society certainly blamed him. By the year 1800, everyone was heaving a sigh of relief that the excesses of the revolution were behind them. Napoleon was apparently leading France back to greatness; rich and poor could once more feel proud and patriotic. De Sade had the reputation of being one of the spokesmen of the revolution. It was hardly deserved, for he was not a revolutionary by nature, but an old-fashioned aristocrat. At all events, *Justine and Juliette* excited precisely the kind of shock and horror that de Sade had intended. Memories of real bloodshed and cruelty were too recent for the new masters of France to feel tolerant about de Sade's imagined 'crimes of love'. On 6 March 1801, de Sade was visiting the office of his new publisher, Nicolas Massé – no doubt hoping to collect a few *livres*, for he was living in miserable poverty – when the police arrived. He and Massé were arrested, and Massé seems to have denounced de Sade as the author of *Justine* (de Sade continued to deny it strenuously) to save his own skin. It seems likely that the police had already put pressure on Massé, and that de Sade's arrest had been arranged beforehand. A thousand copies of *Justine and Juliette* were seized.

De Sade was to spend his remaining fourteen years of life in jail. He was apparently well-fed, for he became enormously fat – so fat that he could hardly walk. He was by nature self-indulgent, and if he was deprived of sex, he tried to make up for it with food. His conversation was so consistently filthy that young prisoners complained of constant attempts to corrupt them, and he was transferred to another prison. Eventually he was transferred back to Charenton asylum, where his family paid for his board and lodgings. He was treated extremely badly for most of the time, kept out of contact with other inmates, denied visits to church, and refused writing materials. In spite of this, he succeeded in completing another vast novel *The Memoirs of Emilie*, which was destroyed after his death, and several smaller works in the manner of the earlier *Crimes d'Amour*. One novel, *The Marquise de Grange*, even achieved publication during his lifetime. He wrote plays, which were presented with the inmates as actors. But when he died, at the age of seventy-four, in December 1814, he had virtually been forgotten. The French were certainly extremely anxious to forget him.

In spite of the advocacy of some able defenders, it is difficult for anyone who has actually read de Sade to feel much sympathy. There is an air of infantile nastiness about his works that makes it impossible to take him seriously. There is also a kind of stupidity. To believe that woman has no purpose but to get herself fucked from morning till night is simply unperceptive. Sex may be delightful, but we all have other things to get on with – many of them more rewarding, in the long term, than sexual enjoyment. We get rather tired of his assumption that sex is the most interesting thing in the world. De Sade's view of sex seems to be that of a dirty-minded schoolboy who has never experienced it.

But although his *œuvre* amounts to a literary curiosity rather than to genuine literature, at least it has the virtue of placing sex under the microscope and enabling us to disentangle the complex mixture of impulses that compose it. And, from *Eugénie de Franval* to *Justine and Juliette*, it makes us aware that the basis of the male sexual impulse is the will to power. Nature has programmed males to find woman erotically stimulating, which means that she is seen as 'forbidden territory'. In fact, one of the paradoxes of de Sade's work is that his heroines – Eugénie de Franval, Eugénie de Mistival, Juliette – cease to be erotically stimulating as soon as they acknowledge that they enjoy sex, and de Sade has to keep the pornography on the boil by deflowering more innocent virgins. He is stimulated by one thing and one thing only: the notion of the all-powerful male pursuing and ravishing his victims, like a wild animal hunting its prey. (It is no accident that food and sex were interlinked in de Sade's mind, so that one became a substitute for the other.)

Oddly enough, de Sade is not a pornographer. Pornography

enjoys gloating over the lascivious preliminaries and physical details of sex, trying to re-create in the reader's mind precisely what it is like to remove a girl's clothes, caress her body, establish genital contact, and so on. In de Sade, all this is perfunctory; de Franval merely 'ravishes' Eugénie's virginity, then teaches her 'all the mysteries' of love. A real pornographer would describe it with obsessive precision; this is not what interests de Sade – he is concerned only with the will to power: with making the father defy all religious and social conventions by seducing his own daughter. It is obvious that he enjoys writing his long atheistic monologues as much as describing orgies. His philosophy could be described as 'me-only-ism'; his daydream is to be Genghis Khan, Vlad the Impaler and Ivan the Terrible all rolled into one.

All of which brings us to the inevitable question: what light does de Sade's case-history shed on Carl Hajdu's theory of sexual deviation?

First of all, let us summarise Hajdu's theory once again. Each of us contains male and female polarities; each of us is powerfully drawn to that opposite pole. I am attracted to a girl because I wish to blend with her, to become her. Because human beings have learned the secret of 'symbolic responses', they may also respond powerfully to the girl's 'forbidden' underclothing. And since, in many ways, the imagination works better when there is no real girl to jar on its sensibilities, dressing up in female clothes may be an even more satisfactory way of achieving this identification.

'Normal' people resist this urge, to such an extent that they are not even aware of it. And great artists and religious mystics carry this resistance to a higher level, and somehow use its energy to produce more intense states of consciousness. In other words, the sexual energy becomes 'desexualised' and so becomes an evolutionary force.

De Sade would flatly contradict this. He would insist that the male's desire for the female is like a tiger's desire for its prey – not a desire to 'become' her, but to possess her, even to the point of destruction. The force behind evolution is not 'bisexuality' but the will to power. When a man makes love to a woman, his satisfaction springs from his feeling that he is imposing his will on hers; he is experiencing a 'god-like' sensation. Most of us prefer to ignore this basic fact of life – so that, for example, we speak of 'making love' rather than 'fucking'. But if we dared to face up to it, we would also recognise that sex can produce an intensity that approaches mystical ecstasy . . .

The central fallacy in de Sade lies in the second part of this argument. He has recognised that sexual excitement is based on the sense of 'forbiddenness', so he reasons that all we have to do to intensify that excitement is to look for increasingly forbidden pleasures – rape, incest, torture, murder . . . But the sense of 'forbiddenness' depends upon a *childish* element in ourselves, a defiance of adult authority. So in order to maintain the sense of the forbidden, we need to deliberately cultivate that sense of childishness, and refuse to grow into adulthood. It cannot be done. The adult part of us declines to be permanently suppressed, and 'wickedness' loses its flavour. So we have to look around for something more wicked still . . . and that, in turn, becomes boring. The sexual urge will simply not bear the weight de Sade tries to place on it; it buckles and crumbles. We *have* to recognise that real satisfaction lies in pursuing our inborn evolutionary purpose, and that, whether we like it or not, this involves outgrowing the notion that sex is the nicest and most important thing in the world.

But although the second part of de Sade's argument dissolves into absurdity, the first part has the ring of truth. Sexual excitement is basically a desire to *possess*. A male undressing a female is like a bear in search of honey. For de Sade, sex was the pursuit of forbidden honey. There is not the slightest trace in all his work of a desire to assume the woman's role or dress up as a woman. He saw sexual deviations more or less as misdirected efforts at possession, and would undoubtedly have regarded Hajdu's transvestism as a rather amusing attempt to possess all women through the medium of his imagination. How can the notion of dressing in women's clothes be reconciled with possession?

The very essence of perversion is 'forbiddenness'. The hero of Barbusse's *L'Enfer* says: 'It is not a woman I want – it is *all* women.' Yet when he picks up a prostitute, it is a boring anticlimax, for the element of the forbidden has been removed.

To understand the root of sexual deviation, we have to recognise that sex *does* have an unfortunate tendency to become anticlimactic, and that all de Sade's efforts were directed at preventing this from happening – an unending search for the forbidden. Hajdu was trying to sidestep the anticlimactic element in sex by dispensing with a real girl, and endowing female clothing with the magical aura of the forbidden; her clothes became a kind of decoy sexual stimulant. De Sade would say that he misunderstood his own motive, and reached the entirely erroneous conclusion that he wanted to *become* the woman.

In short, what de Sade and Hajdu have in common is an attempt to avoid the 'anticlimactic' element in sex through the use of imagination. This in turn suggests that the key to sexual deviation does not lie in the fundamental conflict between the male and female in all of us, but in the imagination itself.

The ten-spined stickleback provides an important clue to the way this works. When the female enters its nesting area, the male releases its sperm into the water. To human beings, this does not sound like a particularly satisfying way of achieving climax; but we have to understand that the stickleback is in a state of intense sexual excitement which is released by the mere sight of the female swimming up and down. Hirschfeld's musician who masturbated as he walked beside schoolgirls is behaving in much the same way. If sexual desire is powerful enough, it can be triggered by a 'Pavlovian' association, something which is merely linked to the sexual act. The deviant can even be excited by an association of an association – as de Sade was excited by crime, because crime, like sex, is 'forbidden'.

If these arguments are correct, then Hajdu's premises concerning the nature of sexual perversion were false, and the theory built upon those premises must also be false. In fact, a study of the history of sexual abnormality since de Sade reveals precisely why the premises are false. If perversion were really due to our innate male-female polarity, then it would have been the same down the ages. In fact, the nature of sexual perversion has changed and developed since the time of de Sade. What we would now label perversion is largely a product of the nineteenth century, and the factor behind its emergence is not transsexuality but a strange and morbid flowering of the imagination.

FOUR

————◆•◆————

Romantic Agonies

It was a century after de Sade had written *Justine* that the next
comprehensive study of sexual deviations was published in Europe.
This was not a novel but a medical textbook – *Psychopathia Sexualis*
by Richard von Krafft-Ebing – and it was in this work that Krafft-
Ebing coined the terms 'sadism' and 'masochism'. The book became
an immediate bestseller, with the result that the British Medico-
Psychological Association debated whether to cancel the author's
membership. The most striking thing about it is the sheer range of
sexual perversions it describes. After reading a dozen or so cases,
the reader begins to feel that the streets of nineteenth-century
Berlin or Vienna must have been packed with sadists, masochists,
voyeurs, fetishists and transvestites. We read of a man who placed
leeches in his girlfriend's vagina until she became anaemic, of one
who paid prostitutes to allow him to defecate in their mouths, of
one who could achieve orgasm only when drinking a girl's blood,
and of another who was sexually excited by old women's nightcaps.
Even de Sade would have blinked with astonishment at the remarkable inventiveness of some nineteenth-century perverts.

Krafft-Ebing was born in 1840, exactly a century after de Sade.
What had happened in that century to cause such an extraordinary
proliferation of sexual deviations? It is natural, of course, to assume
that they were as widespread in earlier centuries, but this proves
to be untrue. In *The Boundaries of Eros* (1985), Guido Ruggiero
examines sex crimes and sexuality in Venice during the fifteenth
century, and the record strikes us as astonishingly tame. Fornication
was regarded as a crime, and homosexuals could be burnt alive;
but there seems to be not the slightest sign of sadism, masochism,
exhibitionism and the rest. The reason becomes apparent in a
chapter called 'Sex Crimes against God', dealing with the sexual

misbehaviour of priests, monks and nuns, and people who committed fornication in church. A man who had made love to a girl under the organ was reproached with having 'too little considered the injury and offense which he occasioned to our supreme creator'. It becomes clear that, although the Venetians were far from prudish, they took sex crime seriously (i.e. incest, seduction of children, rape) *because it might land the perpetrator in Hell.* Sodomy was a sin because it was condemned in the Bible. But we also note that seduction was considered more grave if it took place between an aristocrat and a member of the lower orders. That is clearly why there was so little 'perverted' sex crime in Renaissance Venice: because both social and religious taboos were so powerful.

In his book on the Marquis de Sade, Ivan Bloch devotes a hundred or so pages to sexual morals in the age of de Sade. By this time religion was being seriously undermined by materialistic philosophy. Condillac virtually abolished the soul; La Mettrie wrote a book proving that man is a machine; Holbach's *System of Nature* was known as 'the Bible of Atheism'. Louis XV (who signed the original *lettre de cachet*) was famous for the immense number of his mistresses – one philosopher described the king's life as one of 'unwavering prostitution' – and he had his own private brothel, known as the Deer Park, stocked with young girls. Bloch presents page after page of police reports on the clergy which make it clear that most of them regarded their vows of chastity as a joke; father confessors in convents often took advantage of young nuns. Flogging had become commonplace in brothels. And one monk, quoted by Bloch, paid two prostitutes to dress him and paint him as a woman, 'a desire I have entertained for many years, but been unable to satisfy until today'. Nobles treated their servants as chattels, and sexual pleasure and the use of power sometimes became associated. The Prince de Condé enjoyed poisoning people, and his son, the Count de Charolais, once paused in the middle of love-making to shoot a thatcher off a rooftop. He and his brother, the Duke of Burgundy, liked to roast prostitutes in front of a fire – although only to the point of causing blisters and burns.

Once again, however, it is clear that there is a close connection between sexual deviation and the religious climate. In the famous 'Affair of the Poisons' – which occurred in the reign of Louis XIV – it was revealed that priests had performed black masses and sacrificed babies. The king's mistress, Mme de Montespan, had allowed her naked body to be used as an altar, with a chalice on her belly, and a baby's throat was cut over the chalice and the body thrown into an oven. Another of the king's mistresses came to make a charm, accompanied by a man; the officiating priest got the man to masturbate into a chalice, then mixed the sperm with the woman's menstrual blood. It is clear that the idea of blasphemy had come to play an important part in the orgies described at the trial in the 'Chambre Ardente' (candlelit chamber). Religion no longer commanded the awestruck respect it had enjoyed in the Middle Ages, but it still had enough power to make wickedness seem more deliciously sinful. So it became a kind of aid to orgiastic sexual behaviour.

All this supplies an important clue for understanding de Sade. Religion and sex were inextricably mingled in his mind – to an extent that is simply beyond the understanding of the modern secular mentality. The reader who fails to understand that is missing the whole point. 'My friends,' says Juliette, 'it is time I told you a little about myself and, above all, describe my opulence, fruit of the most determinedly dissolute living, in order that you will be able to contrast it with the state of indigence and adversity wherein my sister, who had chosen good behaviour, was languishing already. Your outlook and your philosophy will suggest to you what conclusions are to be drawn from these comparisons.' To the modern reader, that is merely a silly generalisation; de Sade's own observation of the world must have told him that the wicked often land in jail and that the good often make a fortune. But then, we can understand the paragraph (from *Juliette*, Part Three) only if we realise that it was not intended for our eyes, but for those of priests and prelates. The same applies to Juliette's conversation with the Pope, in which he admits to being a deceiver and a lecher, and she calls him an old ape. Only then can we understand what de Sade intended in a passage like the following:

The whole morning I was restive, gloomy, testy, I fidgeted. I flogged two of my female hirelings, I was cross; I teased a child that had been entrusted to the care of one of them, then lured it into tumbling out of a window; it died from the fall; this lifted my spirits somewhat, and I spent the remainder of the day at all sorts of little mischiefs . . .

Juliette is awaiting the arrival of her father, whom she plans to seduce then murder while being sodomised by her lover. And this scene, too, is intended for the eyes of the guardians of law and faith. Perhaps the most revealing parallel is with the confessions of the twentieth-century mass-murderer Carl Panzram,* a criminal of exceptionally high dominance whose reaction to a sense of injustice was to scream defiance and smash anything he could lay his hands on, even though he knew it meant being beaten unconscious by the prison guards. The more he was beaten, the more defiant he became; it was a point of honour not to allow himself to be broken. He formulated a philosophy of hatred very similar to de Sade's, based upon the proposition that life is brutal, meaningless and stupid; and he went on to commit twenty murders – many of children – simply as a defiant expression of this philosophy. The guilt for these murders, he believed, would somehow be visited upon those who had made him suffer – a notion that is obviously deficient in logic. De Sade wrote *The 120 Days of Sodom* and *Juliette* in precisely the same spirit that Panzram killed, and his logic will not bear examination either. But we are missing the whole meaning of *Juliette* if we do not understand that it was written in a century when man could still be executed for blasphemy. De Sade believed that the revolution had finally broken the power of the Church, and *Juliette* was intended to inflict a few hefty departing kicks, like those administered to Eugénie's mother by Dolmancé. De Sade failed to understand that Christian morality still had a powerful backlash.

What becomes clear from Bloch's study of de Sade is that there was far more sexual promiscuity and perversion in eighteenth-century France than in fifteenth-century Italy, and that this increase was due to the declining influence of the Church. (Bloch has a chapter on eighteenth-century Italy that leaves us in no doubt that the same applied to that country.) But there is still a world of difference between Bloch's dirty-minded prelates who 'lewdly fingered' and occasionally whipped the behinds of teenage nuns, and Krafft-Ebing's necrophiles, vampires, flagellants and crutch fetishists. Somehow, the world described by Krafft-Ebing – and by Havelock Ellis and Magnus Hirschfeld – is far more *fevered* than

* *Killer, a Journal of Murder*, edited by Thomas E. Gaddis and James O. Long, Macmillan, 1971

the world of de Sade. We feel that de Sade's characters simply need strong sensations to excite them to orgasm, while Krafft-Ebing's patients have made imagination a substitute for reality. He describes, for example, a man who could reach orgasm only while lathering and shaving a prostitute's face, a man who sneaked into the bedroom of a pretty maidservant to drink her urine from the chamberpot, a man who paid a prostitute to walk through horse manure in new shoes, then licked them clean. Among his most significant cases is one of a man who could make love to women only if they were fully clothed wearing a silk dress, petticoats and corsets; a naked woman, or a woman in a nightgown, left him cold. (Here we can see quite clearly that he was trying to carry into the bedroom the vision of walking along the street, staring at attractive women in crinolines and bonnets, so that, as he made love, he could feel the material of the dress and petticoats against his bare flesh. We might say that he was trying to be in two places at the same time.) Krafft-Ebing puts his finger on the essence of fetishism when he writes: 'The reason for this phenomenon is apparently to be found in the mental onanism of such individuals. In seeing innumerable clothed forms they have cultivated desires before seeing nudity.' That is to say, imagination and sexual frustration had combined together to 'imprint' their own idea of a sexually exciting female on the mind.

This, then, seems to provide a plausible answer to the question: what happened between 1740 and 1840 to cause such a proliferation of sexual deviations? The answer is that human beings learned to use the imagination far more than in previous centuries. *They learned to day-dream.*

In fact, it was in the year 1740 that a middle-aged printer named Samuel Richardson took the decisive step towards harnessing the power of day-dreams, and wrote what is now recognised as the first modern novel. It was called *Pamela*, and was the story of a young servant girl whose master makes every possible attempt to seduce or rape her, before capitulating to her virtue and leading her to the altar. He leaps on her out of a cupboard as she is undressing, and even places her in charge of a procuress who holds her hands while he tries to ravish her – he is only deterred when she has a kind of fit. For readers of the eighteenth century – accustomed only to picaresque novels and 'true narrations' like *Don Quixote* and *Robinson Crusoe* – the impact of this sexual realism must have been stunning. Until 1740, sermons had been the most popular form of reading, and many a clergyman became rich on the proceeds. After 1740, the public wanted stories about the kind of people they could recognise. The novel was a kind of magic carpet that could carry them away on long journeys into the world of imagination.

Within a year, Richardson was the most widely read writer in Europe, and hundreds of clergymen were preaching sermons on *Pamela*, which was taken for a kind of moral tract. Doubts began to arise with the publication of *Clarissa* in 1748, in which the heroine is finally drugged and raped in a brothel. But it was still only the realism that worried people; no one doubted that Richardson's intentions were highly moral. Two centuries later, V. S. Pritchett came altogether closer to the heart of the matter:

> Prurient and obsessed by sex, the prim Richardson creeps on tiptoe nearer and nearer, inch by inch . . . ; he beckons us on, pausing to make every kind of pious protestation, and then nearer and nearer he creeps again, delaying, arguing with us in whispers, working us up until we catch the obsession too . . . Nothing short of the rape of Clarissa Harlowe by a man determined on destroying her can satisfy Richardson's phenomenal daydream with its infinite delays.

And Richardson himself, embarrassed by the clamour, made sure that his next novel was about 'a good man', Sir Charles Grandison, and that it contained no scenes of rape or attempted seduction.

It is significant that the first two modern novels should be about attempted seduction. Richardson was the first novelist to learn the 'magic-carpet trick', and the magic was the magic of sex. Richardson was no aristocratic rake. He was the son of a joiner who became apprenticed to a printer and married the boss's daughter, and no breath of scandal ever touched his name. So the novels betray the ambivalence of a highly moral man who found sex fascinating. A century later, he might well have developed some peculiar perversion like shoe fetishism. Instead, he poured the fever of blocked – and largely unacknowledged – sexual impulses into these seduction fantasies. In doing so, he taught his contemporaries the trick of day-dreaming on paper.

I have pointed out elsewhere* that the most astonishing part of the story is that historians have failed to recognise the revolutionary significance of *Pamela*. They recognise it as a literary landmark, of course. They also observe that there was an immense psychological gulf between the age of Swift and the age of Dickens. But they are inclined to set it down to social causes: wars, upheavals and the Industrial Revolution. A glance at the history books shows this to be untrue; there was nothing very revolutionary happening in Europe around 1740. As to the Industrial Revolution and the French Revolution, they came fifty years later, when the imaginative revolution had already transformed Europe. They were the consequences, not the cause.

We can measure the full impact of Richardson's imaginative revolution in the influence of the most successful novel of the eighteenth century: Rousseau's *Julie, or the New Héloïse*, which appeared twenty-one years after *Pamela*. Jean-Jacques Rousseau had become famous a decade earlier with a *Discourse* on science and art in which he argued that civilisation has merely corrupted man, and that, if he wants to be free and happy, he has to go 'back to Nature'. In 1757, living quietly in the country and trying to write a novel, he fell in a love with a countess, Sophie d'Houdetot; but she was already in love with another man. Rousseau idealised her as the perfect woman, and put her into his novel as Julie d'Etanges. Julie's handsome young tutor, Saint-Preux, falls in love with her, and she soon admits that she reciprocates. They decide that, if they are in love, they are married in the eyes of God and, one night, Julie admits him to her bedroom.

This episode made *Julie* the most successful novel of the century. Rousseau believed that if Nature is good, then pleasure does not offend her, and men and women should give themselves without shame. This made *Julie* far more shocking than *Clarissa*, for the idea of a young girl willingly surrendering her virginity to a lover has always titillated readers even more than rape. (In the 1960s, the mere title *Sex and the Single Girl* was enough to make the book a bestseller.) That is why, when *Julie* appeared in February 1761, it made Rousseau the greatest literary celebrity in Europe. Libraries were able to lend it out *by the hour*. One contemporary records that women would kiss a scrap of paper on which Rousseau had written

* *The Craft of the Novel*, Chapter 2

his name, and would pay any price for a glass from which he had drunk. The novel went through seventy-two authorised editions before the end of the century, and was pirated in every country in Europe.

In fact, *Julie* has a moral ending. The lovers are tortured by remorse, and Saint-Preux goes off on a round-the-world voyage. Julie marries an older man who knows she is not a virgin. When Saint-Preux returns, the husband invites him to stay, and although he and Julie are still in love, they nobly decide not to betray the husband's trust. When Julie dies in an accident, Saint-Preux decides to devote his life to educating her children. In fact, the virtue and self-sacrifice were just as important a part of the book's success as the seduction scene, for they raised the affair from a coarse intrigue to an ideal love. Europe had been upset by the death of Clarissa Harlowe, but it shed rivers of tears at the death of Julie.

In the year following *Julie*, Rousseau's publisher brought out *The Social Contract*, the book that began with the controversial assertion that man is born free but is everywhere in chains. The French government immediately banned its importation into France, but this only made it an 'underground classic'. More than any other single work, *The Social Contract* was responsible for the French Revolution.

Works like *Pamela*, *Clarissa* and *Julie* taught Europe to dream; yet, oddly enough, other writers were slow to follow suit. In England, Fielding, Smollett and Sterne belonged to the old realistic tradition of *Dox Quixote* and *Robinson Crusoe*. The most remarkable French novel of the second half of the eighteenth century is Laclos's *Les Liaisons Dangereuses* (1782), which deals with the idea of seduction as an amusing pastime – its two chief characters, a male and a female libertine, exchange letters about their seduction of various virtuous innocents. The tone is very close to that of de Sade. It was in Germany that writers took the lessons of Richardson and Rousseau to heart. In his *Sorrows of Young Werther* (1774), the twenty-four-year-old Goethe succeeded in repeating the success of *Pamela* and *Julie*. Its hero, a young painter, falls in love at first sight with an attractive country girl, Charlotte, and his love takes on the character of a fever, an obsession, so that when she marries someone else, he commits suicide. The novel caused a wave of suicides. In the thirty-four years since *Pamela*, readers had learned to sympathise with ecstasies of love and transports of misery; Goethe provided these in a distilled form that was like high-proof liquor. If Richardson had taught Europe to day-dream, Goethe convinced it that it ought to let its feelings go. Suddenly, the Romantic Age had arrived; men and women were no longer ashamed to burst into tears. Novels of unhappy love-affairs poured from the presses, and Europe sobbed convulsively.

But the Germans soon took an important step further. What is the purpose of imagination if not to improve on reality? The German romantic school specialised in hazy landscapes with magnificent woods in the foreground and ancient castles on the horizon. The most popular novelist of the late eighteenth century was Jean Paul, whose novels are amusing and eccentric, but full of beautiful landscapes and powerful expressions of emotion; in his time, he was regarded as the equal of Shakespeare. The German romantic novelist loved nothing so much as setting his hero on the box of a stagecoach, flying along a winding country road in search of strange adventures. In the stories of Hoffmann, the hero is likely to walk through an ordinary doorway to find himself in a magical landscape, being addressed by a golden snake that has the voice of a charming girl.

The romantics also loved to write about unfulfilled longings. Shelley's *Alastor* is about a prince who dreams that he is embracing a beautiful girl who dissolves in his arms; he devotes his days to searching for her but meets only frustration, and dies in despair. Novalis's hero Heinrich von Ofterdingen sees a wonderful blue flower in a dream, and spends his life searching for it – but in this case, it was the author himself who died before he finished the novel. Novalis could conjure up marvellous sensations of sensual bliss:

An irresistible longing to bathe seized him; he undressed and stepped down into the basin. It seemed as if a sunset cloud was enveloping him; a heavenly sensation flowed through his soul; with voluptuous delight countless thoughts seemed to mingle within him. New images never seen before arose and interfused and became visible around him, and every wave of the element clung to him like a tender blossom. The waves appeared to be charming girls dissolved, which momentarily embodied themselves as they touched the youth . . .

The sexual imagery of the last sentence emphasises that the romantics associated their magical distant horizons with sexual bliss, the pleasure of feeling a girl's naked body against one's skin. Yet this in itself was one of the major causes of the deep pessimism that caused so many suicides and early deaths amongst the romantics. After all, some of them were attractive to women and had fully consummated love-affairs. But this still brought the ideal no closer. The girl was just an ordinary mortal, not an embodiment of the eternal feminine. So that romantics came to believe that the ideal was always unattainable – that there was a great gulf set between the real world and the world of imagination. And when they were feeling tired and depressed – or were suffering from tuberculosis – this was enough to tip the balance towards death.

In less idealistic writers, however, the longing for the eternal feminine overflowed into fantasies of seduction and rape. The 'Gothic novel' was invented by Horace Walpole in 1765; his *Castle of Otranto* is a weird compendium of pseudo-medieval horrors and mysteries: ghosts, giants, magic swords, underground passages . . . In most such fantasies, the heroine was held captive by the villain; so it was only a matter of time before she was forcibly deprived of her virtue, like the unfortunate Clarissa. This is what happens to Antonia, the heroine of Matthew Lewis's *The Monk* which became the literary sensation of 1795. The monk is the learned and virtuous Father Ambrosio, but his downfall begins when he learns that a young novice is actually a girl who has fallen in love with him; he surrenders to temptation and possesses her. Then he turns his attention to the lovely Antonia who wants him to help her sick mother. He is about to rape the drugged Antonia when her mother comes into the room; Ambrosio strangles her; then he carries Antonia off to a charnel house full of corpses, where he ravishes her, then stabs her to death. After being tortured by the Inquisition, Ambrosio is hurled to his death from a high precipice by the devil. After *The Monk*, most Gothic novels had heavy sexual overtones; Frédéric Soulié's *Memoirs of the Devil* (1837) is a typical example, full of adultery, incest and murder, and with a climax in which the devil causes the villain's castle to be swallowed up in an abyss. In *Champavert: Immoral Tales* (1833), Petrus Borel – who liked to call himself 'the Werewolf' (*le lycanthrope*) – fills his stories with rapes, murders and tortures. In one of them, an anatomist drugs his wife's lovers then uses their corpses in his experiments; when

his wife dies of horror, he uses her body for the same purpose. In
Dina, the Beautiful Jewess, the heroine, who spends her life in
quest of strong sensations, is finally raped by a boatman, then
hurled into the water with her hands tied behind her, and thrust
under with a pole. Borel steers deliberately close to the edge of
pornography.

The truth is that the virtuous Samuel Richardson may be regarded
as the father of pornography as well as the father of the modern
novel. Seven years after the publication of *Pamela*, a penniless
Bohemian named John Cleland who had spent much of his thirty-
eight years in debtors' jails decided to write his own tale of the
seduction of an innocent girl, and produced *Memoirs of a Woman
of Pleasure* (better known as *Fanny Hill*), which he sold outright
for twenty guineas; it made its publisher ten thousand pounds.
Cleland was heavily influenced by *Pamela*.

In earlier centuries, no one had drawn a clear line between
pornography – what a French writer called 'books that one reads
with one hand' – and literature, so Rabelais, Boccaccio, Aretino
and Margaret of Navarre were regarded as scandalous but amusing;
no one would have dreamed of calling them obscene (if only because
the word was not in use before the mid-sixteenth century). After
the death of Louis XIV in 1715, France heaved a sigh of relief, and
allowed its morals to relax; one result was the production of a
number of more-or-less pornographic works attacking the church
and the priesthood. One of the earliest, *Venus in the Cloister, or
the Intrigues of Sainfroid and Eulalie* by the Abbé Barrin, describes
the seduction of a nun by a Jesuit, and appeared during the lifetime
of Louis XIV. In 1745 there appeared one of the most famous
anti-clerical tales of seduction, *The Monastery Gate, or the Story
of Dom Bugger* by Charles Gervais de Latouche. (*Bougre* actually
meant a Bulgarian, because the Bulgars were supposed to be
addicted to sodomy.) A peasant lad named Saturnin peeps through
a hole in the wall and sees his mother having sexual intercourse
with her father confessor; he masturbates, then goes off to look for
his sister Susanna to try and rape her. She resists him, but tells
him that she has already learned the delights of lesbianism from a
nun – and she then tells her brother the sexual history of the nun
in some detail, in the course of which it becomes clear that the
lives of monks and nuns are one long sexual orgy. Both are now
sexually excited and, after peering through a hole at another scene

of fornication, Susanna yields to her brother. Saturnin then becomes a monk, and discovers that the pleasures of the monastic life have not been exaggerated; as a father confessor he is able to take advantage of his female penitents, and he even rapes the nun who initiated his sister into lesbianism. But he finally catches syphilis from his sister and has to be castrated; Susanna dies of sorrow. This is the result of the lives of sin they have learned from the monastery. Yet although the story itself sounds obscene enough, the intent is obviously satirical and anti-clerical, not specifically pornographic.

By comparison, *Fanny Hill* has only one purpose: to titillate. Fanny is an orphan who arrives penniless in London, and is engaged as a lady's maid in a brothel. On her first night there, another girl gets into bed with her and teaches her the secrets of love-making. But where Boccaccio or Brantôme or Latouche would merely have said they caressed one another, Cleland devotes two pages:

My breasts . . . amus'd her hands a-while, till, slipping down lower, over a smooth track, she could just feel the soft silky down that had but a few months before put forth and garnish'd the mount-pleasant of those parts, and promised to spread a grateful shelter over the seat of the most exquisite sensation, and which had been, till that instant, the seat of the most insensible inno-cence. Her fingers play'd and strove to twine in the young tendrils of that moss, which nature has contrived at once for use and ornament.

But, not contented with these outer posts, she now attempts the main spot, and began to twitch, to insinuate, and at length to force an introduction of a finger into the quick itself, in such a manner, that had she not proceeded by insensible gradations that inflamed me beyond the power of modesty to oppose its resistance to their progress, I should have jump'd out of bed and cried for help against such strange assaults.

Instead of which, her lascivious touches had lighted up a new fire that wanton'd through all my veins . . . [Finally,] . . . the cavity to which she guided my hand easily received it; and as soon as she felt it within her, she mov'd herself to and fro, with so rapid a friction that I presently withdrew it wet and clammy, when instantly Phoebe grew more composed . . .

This kind of anatomical precision had never been attempted before. In effect, a new use had been found for the vehicle of fiction: not merely to transport the reader into the feelings and sorrows of a young girl, but to enable him to share, in considerable detail, her first erotic sensations. In his way, Cleland deserves as much credit for breaking new ground as Richardson or Rousseau. When Fanny's first lover, Charles, takes her virginity, the process is described for three pages, again with considerable realism:

> . . . applying then the point of his machine to the slit, into which he sought entrance; it was so small he could scarce assure himself of its being rightly pointed. He looks, he feels, and satisfies himself; then driving forward with fury, its prodigious stiffness, thus impacted, wedge-like, breaks the union of those parts, and gain'd him just the insertion of the tip of it, lip-deep . . .

And so on until, half a page later: 'one violent merciless lunge sent it, imbrew'd and reeking with virgin blood, up to the very hilt in me.'

Throughout the book, Cleland exhibits this same ability to find the right word or phrase to conjure up the reality of sexual experience. If this constitutes pornography, then he is certainly a pornographer. But we have to read only half a page of *Fanny Hill* to realise there is more to it than that. It is obvious that Cleland is enjoying *his power to conjure up reality in words*. He is exactly like a travel-writer who enjoys trying to take the reader on a journey. Previous writers had made do with phrases like: 'Then they plunged into the delights of venery and lost no time in playing the game called the two-backed beast.' But Cleland has had his share of women, and he has an ambition to 'tell the truth'. So when Fanny sets out to seduce a youth who has a gigantic penis (to revenge herself upon her lover for his infidelity), he wants to make the reader share her experience:

> Oh then! the fiery touch of his fingers determines me, and my fears melting away before the glowing intolerable heat, my thighs disclose of themselves and yield all liberty to his hand; and now, a favourable movement giving my petticoats a toss, the avenue lay too fair, too open to be miss'd. He is now upon me; I had placed myself with a jet under him, as commodious and open as

possible to his attempts, which were untoward enough, for his machine, meeting with no inlet, bore and batter'd stiffly against me in random pushes, now above, now below, now beside his point; till, burning with impatience from its irritating touches, I guided gently, with my hand, this furious engine to where my young novice was now to be taught his first lesson of pleasure. Thus he nick'd, at length, the warm and insufficient orifice; but he was made to find no breach impracticable, and mine, tho' often enter'd, was still far from wide enough to take him easily in.

By my direction, however, the head of his unwieldy machine was so critically pointed that, feeling him foreright against the tender opening, a favourable motion from me met his timely thrust, by which the lips of it, strenuously dilated, gave way to his thus assisted impetuosity, so that we might both feel that he had gained a lodgement. Pursuing then his point, he soon, by violent, and, to me, most painful piercing thrusts, wedges himself at length so far in, as to be now tolerably secure of his entrance; here he stuck . . .

And the description continues for another three pages. In fact, the time it takes to read is obviously a great deal longer than the time it took to do. Cleland has *slowed down time*, in order to persuade the reader to share the imaginative experience. And this, of course, is precisely what Richardson had done in *Pamela*, and would do at even greater length in *Clarissa*. Dr Johnson went straight to the point when he said that if you read Richardson for the sake of the story, 'your impatience would be so much fretted you would hang yourself'. Richardson makes the assumption that Pamela and Clarissa become so real to the reader's imagination that we *want* to linger. A century and a half later, Marcel Proust will carry the same assumption to extraordinary lengths, virtually persuading the reader to abandon his normal sense of time. No writer before the time of Richardson would have dreamed of attempting such a feat: Cervantes, Lesage, Defoe, all relied on a profusion of incident to hold the reader's interest.

Fanny, like her creator, lived to enjoy the fruits of her libidinous labours; she ends happily married to her first lover, to whom she has confessed all and obtained forgiveness. Cleland, summoned before the Privy Council to explain why he had written an immoral book, pleaded poverty, and was awarded a pension of a hundred pounds a year on condition he wrote no more pornography. He lived on, free from debt, until shortly before his eightieth birthday, the year of the French Revolution.

Richardson's immediate successors did not make the slightest attempt to learn from his example. Henry Fielding and Tobias Smollett continued to write in the tradition of Cervantes and Lesage – in fact, both wrote novels (*Joseph Andrews* and *Sir Launcelot Greaves*) that were imitations of *Don Quixote*; Laurence Sterne looked even further back, to Rabelais. From our point of view, the most interesting thing about them is the attitude they shared towards sex. Although they all wrote about it with Homeric gusto, they were totally free of any element that we would now label pornography. The next generation deplored their coarseness and indecency, but no one could have accused them of being obsessed by sex. They simply took it for granted – together with eating, drinking and socialising – as one of the more important drives of human existence. What shocked the romantics was their realism. After pleading eternal fidelity to the girl he loves, Fielding's Tom Jones allows himself to be seduced by the first attractive woman he meets on the road to London. (Later on, it looks as if she was his long-lost mother, but this turns out to be a false alarm.) Smollett's Peregrine Pickle goes one stage further; as soon as he is absent from his true love, Emilia, he makes every effort to seduce a young lady he meets in the stagecoach – even to attempting rape – then elopes with the wife of a fellow traveller. He later comes into a fortune; but instead of offering his true love his hand, he offers her a large sum of money to go to bed with him (which she indignantly rejects).

Sterne's *Tristram Shandy* (1760) might be regarded as an extended bawdy joke. The humour depends on its endless digressions; the narrator seems constitutionally unable to get to the point. And the reason, we learn in the opening chapters, is that his father was suddenly interrupted on the point of orgasm. Mr Shandy used to wind the clock once a month, then make love to his wife. On the day his son was conceived, his wife interrupted his climax to ask, 'Have you wound the clock?', which put Mr Shandy off his stroke and prevented the vital fluids from doing their proper work. So his son Tristram also finds it difficult to carry anything through to its climax. (His problems are compounded by a childhood accident, when he was urinating out of a window which suddenly fell down . . .) Sterne will go to enormous lengths to make an indecent joke. In one chapter, he discusses at length the Catholic doctrine on the baptism of unborn children, and quotes a long document – in French – by an obstetrician, whose main point is that the surgeon has invented a kind of nozzle or squirter which can baptise the baby while it is still in the womb, 'without harm to the mother'. The joke lies in the fact that the French for nozzle – *canulle* – is also French slang for the male sexual organ. Sterne underlines the point by doubting whether the operation can be carried out 'without harm to the father' – that is, without making him a cuckold. So the whole point of *Tristram Shandy* is that, in its demure, tongue-in-cheek way, it is intended to shock – the joke being enhanced by the fact that its author is a clergyman. Yet there is obviously a basic community of sympathy between Sterne and his audience; he is like a favourite dinner guest who tells a risqué story in the full confidence that it will be appreciated. We feel the same thing as we read Fielding and Smollett; they place no distance between themselves and their audience. De Sade's desire to make his readers blench still lies thirty years in the future.

These observations also enable us to grasp the essence of pornography. Boccaccio and Rabelais are bawdy but not pornographic, for they treat sex as a *part* of life – a very important part, but a part nevertheless. Even Cleland is not truly pornographic, for the underlying feeling is a Rabelaisian delight in the grotesque ('. . . he gave her some hearty smacks, and thrusting his hands into her breasts, disengag'd them from her stays, in scorn of whose confinement they broke loose, and swagged down, navel-low at least . . .'). But in de Sade, sex is blown up out of all proportion until it has become the most important thing in the world – Fielding and Smollett would undoubtedly have regarded him as mildly insane. In pornography, sex has somehow become *detached from reality*, like a balloon that has drifted free from its moorings.

This in turn suggests an answer to our question: what happened between the birth of de Sade and the birth of Krafft-Ebing? The rise of the novel taught Europe to use its imagination. And when imagination was applied to sex, the result was the rise of pornography – and of 'sexual perversion'.

*

Let us, at this point, ask an apparently absurd question: what is pornography *for*? It sounds absurd because the answer seems self-evident: to arouse sexual desire. But if we try to put ourselves in the position of a Martian scientist who is studying human beings, we can see that it is not at all self-evident. The Martian would like to know: why do human beings want to *read about* a perfectly normal biological activity? They like food and drink, but there is no thriving industry describing gastronomic orgies.

Part of the answer lies in 'the Barbusse phenomenon' – that is, the observation of Barbusse's hero that although he wants 'all women', he finds that going to bed with a prostitute is an anticlimax. But what produces the 'anticlimactic effect'? This obviously leads us on to a far larger question: to what the psychiatrist Viktor Frankl called 'the law of reverse effort'. The harder a stutterer tries not to stutter, the worse he is likely to stutter. Oddly enough, the best way of not stuttering is to consciously *try* to stutter. Barbusse's hero lusts after a girl he sees on top of a tram because she is 'forbidden'. The prostitute is *too* available, and is therefore less exciting. Mark Twain enunciated a version of the same law in *Tom Sawyer*, in the chapter where Tom beguiles all his friends into painting the fence by whistling and looking as if he is enjoying himself. Twain says: 'Work is that which one is obliged to do; play is that which one is not obliged to do.' By that definition, having sex with a prostitute is 'work'.

The 'Barbusse phenomenon' seems to have a physiological basis. Animal breeders have discovered that a male can copulate with a female only two or three times before getting bored. If a male bull – or goat or sheep or horse – is placed in a pen with a female on heat, he may copulate once or twice, then loses interest. But this is not from sexual exhaustion. If the female is removed and another female on heat led into the pen, he will start all over again. And so on with a third, fourth or fifth – in fact with some animals the limit has not yet been discovered. But if one of the original females is reintroduced, the male declines to be fooled; he ignores her.

This phenomenon has been labelled 'the Coolidge effect', and the reason is explained in Donald Symons' study in human reproductory behaviour, *The Study of Human Sexuality* (1979). The story goes that Mr and Mrs Calvin Coolidge were inspecting a government farm, and were taken off on separate tours. As she passed the chicken pen, Mrs Coolidge asked the man in charge if the rooster copulated more than once a day.

'Dozens of times.'

'Please tell that to the President,' said Mrs Coolidge.

The man passed on the message when the President visited the pen.

'And does the rooster choose the same hen each time?'

'Oh no, Mr President – a different one each time.'

The President nodded slowly then said: 'Tell that to Mrs Coolidge.'

In human terms, it might be called the 'she-is-not-my-wife' effect. According to the old joke, a woman who suffered from migraines was furious when an expensive specialist told her to sit on the bed, press her hands to her forehead, and repeat over and over again, 'I have not got a headache.' Her husband advised her to try it and, to her amazement, the headache vanished instantly. A few months later, her husband began to suffer from sexual impotence, and visited the same doctor. He refused to tell his wife what the doctor had said, but his impotence vanished completely. Every night, before his wife came to bed, he insisted on having five minutes alone in the bedroom. One night, unable to bear it any longer, his wife tiptoed to the door and peered through the keyhole. He was sitting on the edge of the bed, his hands pressed against his forehead, repeating: 'She is not my wife, she is not my wife . . .'

So what we might call 'the Barbusse phenomenon' seems to have some biological foundation. The male has a fundamental desire for 'strangeness'. (Symons points out: 'A woman has nothing to gain reproductively, and a great deal to lose, by desiring sexual variety *per se*.') In human males, sexual desire is no longer triggered by the smell of the female on heat; this function has been assumed by visual stimuli, with the imagination playing an increasingly important part. It is imagination, as well as visual stimulus, that fills Barbusse's hero with desire for a woman whose skirt blows up on top of a tram. And the human actuality of the prostitute makes imagination superfluous, so he is in the position of a bull that has already serviced a cow three times and lost interest.

This is obviously the basis for most – if not all – sexual 'perversion'. If Barbusse's hero had had a preference for schoolgirls, he might have found the prostitute more satisfying if she had dressed in a school uniform.

Since human sex is regulated – to some extent – by the

imagination, then man has altogether more control over his sex impulse than a bull or a rat. They lose interest after the third copulation, and can only regain it if provided with another female on heat. When James Joyce was in London in 1902, he spent the night with a prostitute who told him that she had lost her virginity to her brother Fred, and that he had made love to her ten times in one night.* Fred was obviously stimulated to repeated activity by the thought that he was committing incest – the stimulus of the forbidden. But even imagination has its limits. Hence pornography, which stimulates the imagination with the well-chosen phrase ('he nick'd, at length, the warm and insufficient orifice') that brings the physical act to life.

All the same, our Martian scientist might still experience some bafflement about human sexuality. Why *should* humans want to read about sex rather than doing it, when a hungry man would far rather eat a meal than read about it? Here it is necessary to define another concept that is central to the understanding of human sexuality: what might be called 'the robot'. We all possess, in our unconscious minds, a kind of servant who performs certain automatic functions. When I learn to type or drive a car or learn a foreign language, I have to do it painfully and consciously; then, suddenly, my robot valet takes over and does it automatically; in fact, he does it far more quickly and efficiently than 'I' could. The main trouble with this mechanical valet is that he often takes over functions I would prefer to keep for myself – for example, when I am tired I eat 'automatically', and so do not enjoy my food. In fact, this is the reason that so much of our experience seems oddly 'unreal'; the robot has taken it over. When I am feeling low, I may live for whole days in a 'robotic' state, so that experience flows off me like water off a duck's back. And because I am not receiving any 'feedback' of pleasure or interest from my activities, I become duller than ever, and experience becomes progressively less interesting. (This is, of course, the mechanism of depression and nervous breakdown.) And this is also why explorers deliberately seek out hardship and danger – to cheat the robot and 'feel the life in them more intensely'.

* See *The Workshop of Daedalus*, ed. Robert Scholes and Richard M. Kain, 1965, p.45

Pornography is also a method of cheating the robot; it does this by producing the 'she-is-not-my-wife' effect.

The central point that has emerged from the present chapter is that real pornography began with Samuel Richardson's *Pamela* and *Clarissa* – particularly the latter – with that spirit of panting, obsessive voyeurism described by V. S. Pritchett. We might say that as well as teaching Europe how to dream, Richardson also taught it how to masturbate. The strange sexual perversions described by Krafft-Ebing and Hirschfeld are all due, indirectly, to the same imaginative revolution that produced the great romantic dreamers of the nineteenth century.

This is a strange – and rather alarming – realisation. For it clearly implies that masturbation is one of the highest faculties that human beings have yet developed. Many animals masturbate – but never without the presence of another animal, or some similar stimulus. A human being can masturbate in an empty room: a triumph of pure imagination. It is also important to observe that the human imagination is not equally strong in all departments. I can imagine burning my finger, and wince at the thought; but I do not really experience pain. I can imagine drinking iced fruit juice when I am thirsty, but it does not quench my thirst. Only when I harness the sexual imagination can I create something approximating to the real experience, *and* persuade my body to respond appropriately.

And we should note that, in doing this, I am deliberately harnessing the biological energies provided by nature for reproduction, exactly as an engineer harnesses the power of a waterfall for a hydro-electric power station. In this one respect, human beings have learned to use the natural forces of the body to gain a victory over the robot.

We should also note that, although the romantics taught Europe to dream, they were only developing a trick that man had taught himself many thousands of years earlier. It had been discovered by the first hunters who sat around a camp-fire and told stories of the past. It was brought to a high degree of perfection by the authors of the *Epic of Gilgamesh* and the Old Testament and the *Iliad*. They later learned to use music and painting and drama for the same purpose – a Greek actor named Thespis is given the credit for discovering that when the *Iliad* was read aloud with several different people interpreting the various characters, it 'came alive' far more than when it was read by one man. And for the next two thousand years, the drama was by far the most effective means of amplifying the human imagination, as well as activating human intelligence – we only have to read any of Shakespeare's plays to realise the high level attained by an ordinary Elizabethan playgoer who may well have been illiterate.

But even compared to the creation of the drama, the invention of the novel was one of the greatest steps in the evolution of human imagination. The drama needed a theatre and an audience and some kind of scenery; in the novel, the theatre was the human brain, and the scenery was the world itself. The result was the spiritual and cultural revolution that created modern man.

It was inevitable that someone should use the new invention to amplify sexual emotions, and to create the literary *genre* we call pornography – 'books that one reads with one hand'. In doing so, man increased an urge that is already one of our most powerful biological drives. From nature's point of view, that might even be regarded as an advantage, for it is undoubtedly in nature's interest to 'subsidise' the reproductory urge with a powerful flow of sexual energy; this is why the ram will continue to copulate indefinitely with new oestrous females. But where human beings are concerned, the sheer power of the urge can be a doubtful blessing. Many a rapist must spend years regretting that he ever saw his victim. A male who has gone to tremendous lengths to persuade a girl into bed may find himself wondering what he ever saw in her, once the sexual urge has subsided. A man who prides himself on his self-control may become a slave to an urge that leaves him feeling guilty and ashamed.

On the other hand, this immense force can be used to induce powerful and dangerous emotions – like canoeing down a stretch of white water. This is the trick learned by the romantics – and which produced so many of those sexual misfits whose history we must now consider in more detail.

FIVE

Rebel Angel

The Marquis de Sade was still locked in the Charenton asylum in March 1812, when a morose young poet woke up in his rooms at 8 St James's Street, London, and 'found himself famous'. His name was George Gordon, Lord Byron, and he was 24 years old. The cause of this overnight celebrity was the publication – the previous Saturday – of the first two cantos of his poem *Childe Harold*. Five hundred copies had been printed, and by Tuesday they had sold out. Byron's first intimation of fame came literally when he woke up that Monday morning, 9 March, and his valet handed him a salver full of visiting cards. It must have been a bewildering experience. On the Saturday, he was almost unknown; by Monday midday, he was being bombarded with invitations from the wealthy and influential. Women begged for introductions, and one of them – Lady Rosebery – was so overwhelmed when she talked to him that her heart began to pound violently and almost robbed her of her voice. Aware of his effect on women, Byron began to make use of what he called his 'underlook', a sudden glance upward from an averted face; it seems to have produced much the same effect as Rudolph Valentino's 'smouldering look' in the 1920s.

What was it about this lengthy – and often dull – poem that made it such a success? The poet Samuel Rogers, who had read it in proof, told his sister that it would never catch on because of its whining, discontented tone and the hero's loose mode of life. He was mistaken; the public interpreted the 'whining and discontented tone' as the melancholy brooding of a man who has drained the cup of pleasure to the dregs, and now has a hangover. As to the loose mode of life, *Childe Harold* makes it sound rather pleasant:

Whilome in Albion's isle there dwelt a youth,
Who ne in virtue's ways did take delight;
But spent his days in riot most uncouth,
And vex'd with mirth the drowsy ear of Night.
Ah me! in sooth he was a shameless wight,
Sore given to revel and ungodly glee;
Few earthly things found favour in his sight
Save concubines and carnal company,
And flaunting wassailers of high and low degree.

Unfortunately for Childe Harold (a 'childe' is the son of a noble who has not yet succeeded to the title), sex and alcohol have begun to pall, and 'he felt the fulness of satiety'. Then, with a cunning psychological twist, Byron raises him above the level of the usual drunken lecher by giving him a secret sorrow:

For he through Sin's long labyrinth had run,
Nor made atonement when he did amiss,
Had sigh'd to many though he loved but one,
And that loved one, alas! could ne'er be his.
Ah, happy she, to 'scape from him whose kiss
Had been pollution unto aught so chaste . . .

But of course, the reader is left to assume that all the debauchery is an attempt to forget this lost love; in fact, the sorrow places Childe Harold in the direct line of Saint-Preux and Young Werther. In the 1940s, Hollywood would borrow a leaf from the same book in *Casablanca*, when Humphrey Bogart renounces Ingrid Bergman, and watches her fly off into the dawn with her husband. In fact, Rick in *Casablanca* is an updated version of the Byronic hero:

And now Childe Harold was sore sick at heart,
And from his fellow bacchanals would flee;
'Tis said, at times the sullen tear would start,
But Pride congeal'd the drop within his ee:
Apart he stalk'd in joyless reverie,
And from his native land resolved to go,
And visit scorching climes beyond the sea . . .

(Byron was brought up in Aberdeen, hence the occasional Scotticism like 'ne' instead of not, and 'ee' instead of eye.) It was also to the Childe's advantage that, like his creator, he was a nobleman who lived in a disintegrating abbey; readers of Gothic novels loved crumbling castles and mildewed mansions with flapping shutters:

> The Childe departed from his father's hall:
> It was a vast and venerable pile;
> So old it seeméd only not to fall,
> Yet strength was pillar'd in each massy aisle.
> Monastic dome! condemn'd to uses vile!
> Where Superstition once had made his den.
> Now Paphian girls were known to sing and smile;
> And monks might deem their time was come agen
> If ancient tales say true, nor wrong these holy men.

The sideswipe at superstition must have caused some gasps – after all, he was talking about Christianity – while the comment about the monks, implying that they had held orgies there, amounted to adding insult to injury. With unerring instinct, Byron had drawn together the materials of a bestseller: sin, satiety, secret sorrows, and travel to distant lands to forget the girl who can ne'er be his. Moreover, England had been at war with Napoleon so long – ten years – that even the Continental travelogue that followed seemed exciting and colourful. It was unfortunate for Byron that he had sold the copyright of *Childe Harold* outright for £600 – and then given the money away to a friend – otherwise the poem would eventually have made him a rich man.

Byron was not a rich man; in fact, it was pure chance that he was a lord at all. His father, known as 'Mad Jack Byron', was a notorious rake and gambler, who had married a plain and plump Scottish heiress for her money, then deserted her after spending her money (£23,000) and getting her pregnant. He died in poverty in France three years later. His son, born 28 January 1788, had a miserable and lonely childhood; a deformed right foot caused him to limp, and his schoolfriends made fun of it. He developed a childhood passion for his cousin, Mary Chaworth, but it turned to hatred when he heard her asking her maid: 'What, do you think I could feel anything for that lame boy?' His mother, Catherine Gordon, was inclined to call him a 'lame brat'. Fortunately, when he was nine years old, a nymphomaniac servant girl, May Gray, made him aware that he was not unattractive when she slipped into his bed and taught him the techniques of love-making (although it is not clear whether they made love or merely restricted themselves to intimate caresses). He became furiously jealous when she took a lover – she even seems to have allowed him to witness their sexual encounter – and she beat him black and blue when he protested. It may have been this episode that eventually led Byron to complain about her attentions to the family lawyer, so she was dismissed. He later declared that this early initiation into sex was responsible for his later tendency to satiety and melancholy, 'having anticipated life'.

Byron's father, 'Mad Jack', had been a commoner, although his father's elder brother was the fifth Lord Byron. The latter was known as 'the Wicked Lord' because he had once killed a neighbour in a fight, for which he was tried by his peers. The heir to the title – and to the estates at Newstead Abbey, near Nottingham – was Byron's cousin, William. But William was killed, when only eighteen, at the siege of Calvi, in Corsica, in 1794. Four years later the Wicked Lord Byron died, and his great-nephew, the lame ten-year-old boy, inherited the title. But the property he inherited was run down and mortgaged – the Wicked Lord had set out to ruin his heirs after his son married against his father's wishes. And since Byron's mother had no money either, they had to live in poverty-stricken splendour. When Byron was thirteen, the government made a Civil List grant of £300 for his education, and he was sent to Harrow, where his relative poverty again made life difficult. An intelligent and affectionate mother might have made all the difference but Catherine Gordon was stupid and self-absorbed. When a fellow pupil remarked, 'Byron, your mother is a fool,' the young lord replied resignedly: 'I know it.' Byron fell in love with his cousin, Margaret Parker, but she died soon after he went to Harrow; he seemed to be haunted by death.

Byron undoubtedly had strong homosexual inclinations – directed towards those younger than himself. At Harrow, he befriended several younger boys and protected them against bullying. It was at Harrow that Byron began to write poetry, much of it addressed to young protégés, like Lord Clare and William Harness. As far as we know, these passions were all idealistic. But when a twenty-three-year-old rake named Lord Grey de Ruthyn, to whom his mother had rented Newstead, made homosexual advances, Byron fled in terror.

His real sexual initiation began when he went to Cambridge in 1805. He spent a great deal of time in London and became acquainted with the brothels of the Piccadilly area; a French procuress had to advise him to season ardour with delicacy (i.e. be less rough). He took boxing lessons from a famous pugilist, dined in good restaurants, and borrowed money at excessive interest from money-lenders. He also renewed acquaintance with his attractive, ringleted half-sister Augusta (his father, Mad Jack, had been married twice) who had recently married her cousin, Colonel George Leigh. He saved a choirboy named John Edleston from drowning, and fell passionately in love with him – although he later insisted that the friendship was 'pure'. There seems no reason to doubt that Byron's feelings about Edleston were as powerful as those he later entertained for some of his mistresses. This made him nervous, for he knew that in England homosexuality was regarded with abhorrence. Four years before Byron's birth, the author William Beckford had been driven out of England after being accused of homosexual relations with a sixteen-year-old youth. Byron's propensity to fall in love with boys undoubtedly led to feelings of guilt – about the 'love that dare not speak its name' – that contributed to Childe Harold's sense of sin.

Good living – and a taste for wine – led Byron to put on weight. To a man of his vanity, this was intolerable; he began practising in the nets – with Edleston bowling – wearing half a dozen waistcoats to induce perspiration.

He also acquired a reputation as a practical joker. When told by an indignant Cambridge Fellow that keeping a dog was against the college statutes, he brought in a bear on a chain, pointing out that the statutes said nothing about bears. He acquired himself a mistress – rumour said he bought her from a brothel for £100 – and enjoyed making her dress as a boy and passing her off as a brother. When she became pregnant, there were the usual agonies and regrets, and Byron declared himself ready to marry her; fortunately, she miscarried, and Byron wrote a poem saying farewell. This appeared in a collection of poems called *Hours of Idleness* (a title intended to provoke his Cambridge tutors), which was received so harshly by the critics that Byron contemplated suicide. The critic of the *Edinburgh Review* declared: '. . . his effusions are spread over a dead flat, and can no more get above or below the level than if they were so much stagnant water'. This caused Byron such mental agony that he declared he was going mad. Instead, he penned a lively satire in the manner of Pope called *English Bards and Scotch Reviewers*, which was received – in London at least – with rather more admiration. Then, disillusioned with Cambridge, he decided not to return; his rooms were let to an erudite young homosexual called Charles Matthews. When Byron made his acquaintance they became close friends – no doubt because they felt a certain affinity. And when Byron realised that his *Hours of Idleness* had made him something of a personality at Cambridge, he changed his mind and returned to enjoy his celebrity. This was his first taste of fame, and he found it sweet. He left the University in July 1808 with his degree, and invited his closest friends – Matthews, John Cam Hobhouse and Scrope Davies – to come and visit him at Newstead in the autumn. There they dressed in monks' habits – hired for the occasion – talked all night, and got drunk – Byron drank his wine from a skull which he had mounted as a goblet. It is fairly clear – from what transpired later – that one of the subjects of their conversation was pederasty, and that Matthews urged his companions to try it. In the following year, Byron and Hobhouse were to follow his advice.

Byron was anxious to go off on a Grand Tour of Europe, but had no money – in fact, he was £12,000 in debt. Then Scrope Davies had a wildly successful night at the gaming tables, and ended by winning enough gold to fill a chamberpot; Byron borrowed sufficient to finance his travels, and set out with Hobhouse in July 1809.

It has been demonstrated by Dr Louis Crompton* that Byron and Hobhouse set out specifically intending to practise pederasty. Byron joked in a letter to his tutor that he intended to contribute a chapter to a book by Hobhouse called *Sodomy Simplified, or Pederasty Proved to be Praiseworthy*. But a letter written to Matthews from Falmouth – from which they intended to sail – makes it clear that it was far from a joke. He says: 'I do not think Georgia itself can emulate in capabilities or incitements to the "Plen. and optabil. Coit." the port of Falmouth . . . We are surrounded by Hyacinths and other flowers . . . & I have some intention of culling a handsome Bouquet to compare with the exotics I hope to meet

* *Byron and Greek Love*, 1985

in Asia.' All this is a kind of code. Georgia is the home of the Circassian boys; Hyacinth was the beautiful boy loved by Apollo and accidentally killed by the god in a game of quoits – also spelt coits. The odd phrase 'plenum et optabilem coitum' is to be found in Petronius's homosexual novel *The Satyricon*, in which the shabby poet Eumolpus describes how he seduced a young boy under the nose of his mother and father, and ended by achieving the 'full and to-be-wished-for coitus'. This seduction occurs in the Roman province of Turkey called Asia, where Byron hoped to cull a similar 'bouquet'. Byron is telling Hobhouse that he hopes to seduce a boy in Falmouth. (He concludes: 'One specimen I shall surely carry off.')

In his reply, Matthews congratulates Byron on the success of his efforts 'in the mysterious' – that is, in his code – and says that Hobhouse has also done well. But Hobhouse must take care not to put dashes under his 'mysterious significances', because it would let the cat out of the bag if the 'tabellarians' (postmen) should read the letter. (In England at that time, an average of two homosexuals a year were executed, so they had reason to hide their secret pleasures.) He goes on to suggest that they should refer to pederasty as his 'methode', spelt with an -e. He goes on: 'Hyacinth, you may remember, was killed by a Coit, but not that "full and to-be-wished-for Coit".' Byron was apparently successful in his attempted seduction, for he mentioned two years later his encounter with a certain 'Abbé Hyacinth' at Falmouth.

So Childe Harold set off on his European tour feeling satiated with heterosexual pleasures at Newstead, where he had copulated himself into a state of languorous exhaustion with his boy/girl mistress Caroline (not to be confused with his later mistress, Caroline Lamb), as well as impregnating a servant girl named Lucy – and determined to give full rein to his bisexuality. He had half made up his mind to leave England for ever, and hints in a letter that he had some compelling reason for fleeing; it seems a reasonable assumption that he had already tried pederasty, and was afraid that his indiscretion had not gone unnoticed. (He later confessed to Lady Caroline Lamb that he had 'corrupted' his page, William Rushton, as well as three of his schoolfellows – one of whom may well have been Edleston.)

They disembarked at Lisbon, then crossed Spain to Gibraltar, where they embarked for Malta. There he sent his page Rushton back to London with an older servant, explaining to his mother that boys were not safe among the Turks. It seems more likely that he realised that his page might cramp his style with other boys in Greece and Turkey.

In Albania, they met the brigand war-lord Ali Pasha, who was highly complimentary about Byron's good looks; Byron beat a hasty retreat when Ali Pasha invited him to his bedroom. Then he and Hobhouse went on to Greece, then to Constantinople. By now they had been travelling together for a year, and Byron was relieved when Hobhouse decided to return direct to England. To begin with, Byron was intent on seducing a fifteen-year-old Greek boy named Nicolo Giraud whom he had met in Athens. He was also interested in a twelve-year-old girl, Theresa Macri, whose mother was the widow of the English vice-consul, and in whose house Byron and Hobhouse had stayed on their earlier visit to Athens; at twelve, Theresa must have looked rather boyish. But when Theresa's mother showed signs of wanting Byron to marry her daughter, he hastily moved into the monastery where Nicolo was at school, and soon succeeded in enjoying *plenum et optabilem coitum*. The two of them then went on a tour of Morea, and although Byron caught fever, he continued to be sexually insatiable – he later told Lady Melbourne that at one point he had almost expired *in coitu* – but without specifying the sex of his partner. In a letter to Hobhouse he asks him to tell Matthews that he has now obtained above two hundred 'pl & opt Cs and am almost tired of them'. But not all his adventures were homosexual. One day, returning home, he encountered a cart that contained a sack that was wriggling; it proved to contain a slave-girl who had been condemned to be thrown into the sea for indulging in sex during a Mohammedan religious festival. Byron finally induced the governor to pardon her, on condition that she left Athens. There was a persistent later story that Byron had enjoyed her favours – which is plausible, since she had been his servant's mistress, and Byron believed in share and share alike.

Byron finally left Nicolo Giraud in Malta, where he arranged for him to go to a good school, and sailed back to England, where he landed in July 1811, two years after he had set out. He was carrying the first two cantos of *Childe Burun* (an early version of 'Byron'), which he fortunately decided to re-christen *Childe Harold*.

The homecoming was not entirely auspicious. Edleston had

apparently been arrested for indecent conduct – one of Byron's biographers (Crompton) states that he had virtually become a 'tart' in London. Soon after, he died of tuberculosis. If he had been one of the schoolboys Byron had corrupted – according to Caroline Lamb – this could well explain Byron's lifelong guilt about 'destroying someone he loved'. His homosexual friend Matthews was drowned while swimming in the Cam: he was caught in the reeds, and put up a long and agonising struggle for life. And within two weeks of his return, Byron's mother had died; Byron decided, belatedly, that he *had* loved her after all, and sank into gloom and self-pity. Perhaps to dispel this, he imported some new servant girls into Newstead, and also called upon the services of his valet's wife. *Childe Harold* caused alarm amongst his friends – the cautious Hobhouse was afraid it would ruin Byron's reputation – but was warmly praised by Murray's reader.

There was no precedent for the sensation it caused when it appeared in March 1812, unless it was the fame that descended on Goethe when *Young Werther* was published. Richardson and Rousseau had achieved equal success, but no one assumed that Richardson was the naughty 'Squire B', or that Rousseau was actually Saint-Preux. Byron had become the popular hero of London society by announcing that he had run through 'Sin's long labyrinth' and was now bored and worn out. He achieved the status of a romantic idol by proclaiming himself a sated voluptuary.

What Byron had done, in fact, was to crystallise the hero that the age had been waiting for. The heroes of romantic novels were pure and noble-hearted; but people were beginning to grow a little tired of purity – it was the villains who seemed to have all the fun. Moreover, romantic novels and poems all seemed to be set in some remote never-never land. The most popular poet of the day was Sir Walter Scott (who had not yet begun to write novels), but he might have been writing about the Middle Ages. Byron's romantic travelogue was at least set in the present, and its hero was a present-day nobleman who lived in a real – if picturesquely dilapidated – abbey. Of course, his morals were rather questionable; he confessed to having wasted his youth in fornication and riotous living; but surely that was commendable frankness rather than a desire to shock? Besides, he propitiated morality by admitting that it had done him no good, but left him bored and satiated. And the fact that he was in love with someone who could ne'er be his was also a certain mitigation. So was the fact that he was a poet who loved to be alone and gaze at the stars . . .

The success of *Childe Harold* was really due to its ambiguity – or rather, to an ambiguity in the minds of its readers. Richardson's readers could feel virtuous while licking their lips at the seduction scenes; the same applied to *Julie* and *The Monk*. It was not exactly hypocrisy; just the natural human interest in wickedness. Byron had simply gauged that it was now time to take the next step, and unite the hero and villain in one man. This was the step that no one had so far dared to take. Or rather, the only man who had dared to take it was at present in the asylum at Charenton . . .

It would be fascinating to have a detailed account of Byron's first months of success; unfortunately, he was too busy to write one. We know that St James's Street was often blocked with the carriages of those who wanted to call on him, and that it was enough for a hostess to announce his intended presence at a reception to guarantee a full attendance. We know that Byron dressed in black, was exceedingly pale, and that his manner was haughty and reserved. He was only five foot eight inches tall, but exceptionally handsome, with curly chestnut hair. The Byronic limp underlined the impression of secret suffering that made him so fascinating to women, and it was soon being imitated by young men all over London. He affected to despise the success of *Childe Harold*, insisting that it was a symptom of morbid sentimentality, and that sensible people would soon go back to reading Pope, whom he esteemed above all. But his admirers had no doubt that Byron underestimated his own brilliance and originality. It now seems symbolic that Byron burst upon London in the same year as the waltz, for both marked a watershed between the eighteenth and nineteenth centuries.

One of the first to succumb to the Byronic gloom was Lady Caroline Lamb, a slim, boyish woman of twenty-seven who had read *Childe Harold* in proof – Samuel Rogers had warned her that Byron had a club foot and bit his nails, but it made no difference. When he first saw her at Lady Westmorland's, she was too shy to be introduced, and Byron took this for contempt or indifference. When they were finally introduced, he found her charming; she was capricious, moody, excitable and completely unconventional. She wrote in her diary, after this first meeting, that Byron was 'mad, bad and dangerous to know', and added: 'That beautiful pale face is my fate.' Byron was soon a regular visitor at the home of her mother-in-law, Lady Melbourne, where Caroline lived; her husband, William Lamb, who was six years her senior, was too busy with his political career to worry much about her grand passions. As to Byron, he was perfectly willing to make love to any woman who offered herself; but it was an infallible method of losing his respect. A week after she became his mistress, Byron was already writing her ambiguous love-letters studded with reservations. He convinced himself that 'like Napoleon, I have always had a great contempt for women'. As she became conscious of his contempt, she started to cause scenes and to pursue him so openly that even her husband began to be worried by the scandal. On one famous occasion she dressed herself as a page-boy and sneaked into his carriage; on another, she sent him a lock of her hair – not from her head, but her pubis. After she had caused a scene at a party and then attempted suicide, he finally broke off the affair; Caroline burnt his image in effigy and all his letters – at least, copies of them (she kept the originals).

Byron fled to the home of Lady Oxford in Herefordshire. At forty she was still beautiful, although she had a reputation for promiscuity; her husband's name was Harley, and her children were known as the Harleian Miscellany. Byron lost no time in allowing her to add his name to her list of lovers. Then he went on to the home of his half-sister, Augusta, at Six Mile Bottom, near Cambridge, and was not slow to realise that she found him as irresistible as every other woman seemed to. The idea of incest was as delicious to Byron as to de Sade. Augusta was a 'good' woman, devoted to her spendthrift husband and to her children; but since he had last seen her, Byron had overcome his shyness and developed the easy charm and compelling gaze of a seducer; it was obvious that she would not be able to resist him. So Byron seduced his half-sister, and found that the sense of sin added a new flavour to adultery. Naturally, he was unable to resist taking others into his confidence. He told Tom Moore that he was in 'a far more serious and entirely new scrape . . .' And when he confessed to Lady Melbourne that his sister had become his mistress, she was horrified and warned him: 'You are on the brink of a precipice, and if you do not retreat, you are lost for ever – it is a crime for which there is no salvation . . .' That was just what Byron wanted to hear. After an abortive affair with the wife of a friend, Lady Frances Webster – whom he decided to spare at the last moment – he took

Augusta to Newstead, and she became pregnant. Then, as if to flaunt his sin in the face of society, he wrote a long narrative poem called *The Bride of Abydos* about a brother and sister who are in love. (It is true that, in the end, Selim and Zuleika turn out to be cousins; but they think they are siblings when they fall in love.)

Having been the darling of London society, Byron was now its chief source of malicious gossip – partly through his own inability to hold his tongue. (His tendency to confide his secrets to relative strangers argues a desire to 'back into the limelight'.) He also remained a bestselling author. The sequel to *Childe Harold, The Giaour,** was based on the episode of the woman condemned to be tied up in a sack and drowned. It is heavily influenced by Scott's narrative poems, but has an Eastern flavour. There followed *The Bride of Abydos*, with its incest theme; *The Corsair*, based on the life of a real pirate; and *Lara*, in which the hero drags around the burden of some guilty secret, which he expiates in death. The modern reader will be baffled by the immense success of these works (*The Corsair* sold 14,000 copies in one day). But that is because we have become accustomed to every variety of swashbuckling hero. Byron virtually invented the swashbuckling hero, so his work had the immense advantage of originality. The impact it made was very like the impact of the early Douglas Fairbanks and Errol Flynn movies, with the bold hero who can engage in a sword-fight with a dozen enemies at once, then escape by vaulting on top of a wall and swinging on a rope above their heads. The main difference was that Byron's Giaour, Selim, Corsair and Lara were also reincarnations of Childe Harold, brooding on some terrible secret sin. This is Lara:

> There was in him a vital scorn of all:
> As if the worst had fall'n which could befall,
> He stood a stranger in this breathing world,
> An erring spirit from another hurl'd . . .

This gloomy hero lives in a ruined abbey, drinks his wine from a skull, and even has a mistress who dresses up as a page-boy . . . Byron found it impossible to resist playing with fire. As one final transparent gesture of mystification, he published the poem anonymously, although every page is signed with its authorship.

* The word is pronounced as if it rhymed with 'tower', but in one syllable

Oddly enough, Byron had decided that *Lara* should be his final work, and sent his publisher a cheque to buy back all his previous copyrights. That was typical. He was – as his journals of the period show – subject to endless changes of mood. In a young man who had just achieved overnight fame, this is understandable enough – many an older man has been destabilised by it. What made it dangerous was that Byron was inclined to be taken in by his moods; he allowed them to convince him that fame is a will-o'-the-wisp, that life is a meaningless show, that all human values are illusory. Every child experiences the same sensation when he sets out on holiday, full of eager expectation, and then, a few hours later, gazes gloomily out of the window of the train with a feeling that life has let him down. Fortunately children are not philosophers, and attempt to draw no general conclusions from these changes of mood. Byron – like the rest of his fellow romantics – lacked the insight to see that changes of mood are no more important than a stomach-ache, and may as well be ignored. Byron treated them as if they had some universal significance; in *Cain*, he even makes Lucifer accuse God of creating the universe out of boredom, and of still finding it boring.

Byron saw himself as Lucifer; but he never ceased to hope for some salvation – preferably at the hands of a woman. Not long after the publication of *Lara*, restlessness drove him to make his greatest mistake so far, and propose to a prim young lady named Annabella Milbanke, Caroline Lamb's cousin, who had piqued Byron's vanity by turning him down two years earlier. This time she accepted. No sooner were they married – in the New Year of 1815 – than he regretted it; in the carriage that was to take them on their 'treacle moon' (as Byron called it), he told her: 'Enough for me that you are my wife to make me hate you.' Annabella must have been stunned. In their room before dinner, he took the opportunity to deflower her – he had always admired Napoleon, who used to order his women to get their clothes off without even looking up from his papers. But although he told her at dinner that, now she was in his power, he would make her feel it, he seems to have found himself developing a certain affection for her. Recent biographical researches have revealed that the year-long marriage was happier than most of his biographers have given him credit for. They were soon calling one another by pet names, and Byron was admitting to Tom Moore that he was enjoying marriage. At one point she

probably saved his life, coming into a room that a blocked chimney
had filled with smoke, and reviving him with eau-de-Cologne.
Byron was soon treating her with the same affection he had shown
Nicolo Giraud – and expressing it in much the same way. In
March, they went to stay with Augusta – where Byron teased
Annabella with hints of their incest – then moved to a house in
Piccadilly, which looked impressive enough outside, but had almost
no furniture, since Byron, as usual, was deeply in debt. His admiration for the great tragic actor Kean seems to have been a bad
influence – he began ranting, firing off pistols, and generally behaving like a man possessed. He also began to drink heavily; when
Annabella announced she was pregnant, he began to feel trapped.
That December, exhausted by the birth of a daughter, Annabella
went home to recuperate. They seem to have parted on the best
of terms, with every intention of continuing their marriage. The
trouble seems to have started when she admitted to her mother
that she sometimes suspected her husband of being insane. The
reason, she revealed, was that she had looked in a drawer and found
a dirty book hidden under his papers. The book was almost certainly
a piece of homosexual pornography. What happened next is not
clear. We know that Annabella reported her suspicions about
Byron's insanity to a certain Dr Lushington, and that two doctors
were sent to London to observe him secretly and determine
whether he was really certifiable. They apparently decided he was
not. But whatever Annabella told the doctor – and her mother – so
shocked them that it was they who decided that a legal separation
was the only solution. Almost certainly, she told them that her
husband was homosexual, and that she had submitted to anal
intercourse (probably believing that it was a perfectly natural variant
of normal coitus). They assured her that her husband was a pervert
and that she had been dishonoured. From then on, Lady Byron
ignored her husband's letters and closed her ears to his attempts
at a reconciliation.

Byron's reaction was to order an elaborate travelling coach, at
the enormous cost of £500, to have a final one-night-stand with a
girl called Claire Claremont who had flung herself at his head, and
then to depart for the Continent, never to return. He had been
famous for precisely four years; for the remaining eight years of his
life he was to be infamous.

He was undoubtedly embittered by the social ostracism that

forced him to leave England and that continued to pursue him abroad. (Three months after his departure, an Englishman named Henry Brougham reported from Geneva: 'Lord Byron lives on the other side of the lake, shunned by all – both English and the Genevese.') To us, his reaction seems as naïve as de Sade's outraged astonishment at being thrown into Charenton. The truth is that Byron was being punished for exactly the same reason as de Sade: for going too far. *Childe Harold* had conveyed the impression that he had been guilty only of the normal excesses of youth – 'Paphian girls' and midnight revels. But the hints dropped in *The Giaour* and *Lara* suggested there was more to it than that. His own hints about homosexuality were removed from *Childe Harold* at the request of friends – a reference to Beckford's disgrace beginning:

> Unhappy Vathek! in an evil hour
> 'Gainst Nature's voice seduced to deeds accursed . . .

and another stanza about the oriental preference for pederasty:

> For boyish minions of unhallowed love
> The shameless torch of wild desire is lit . . .

But he made the supreme mistake of telling Lady Caroline Lamb about his own pederasty, and telling Lady Melbourne about his incestuous affair with Augusta. After the break-up of his marriage, Lady Caroline spread both stories all over London. And there were other stories – most of them founded on fact: that he had insisted on telling Annabella that he was the father of Augusta's daughter Medora, and that he was still having intercourse with her, that he got drunk and behaved like a madman, waving daggers and pistols under his wife's nose, that he had acquired himself a new mistress – an actress – soon after he was married. And there were undoubtedly rumours that he had sodomised his wife: at least, they were sufficiently well known to be set out in a poem called *Don Leon*, attributed to Byron (although probably written by the dramatist George Colman). Secret sins were all very well, provided they were confined to literature; but the suggestion that they were acted out in real life was enough to arouse the British public to one of its familiar bouts of moral indignation. An anonymous versifier in the *Morning Chronicle* celebrated his departure with a poem that began:

From native England, that endured too long
The ceaseless burden of his impious song;
His mad career of crimes and follies run,
And gray in vice, when life was scarce begun;
He goes, in foreign lands prepared to find
A life more suited to his guilty mind . . .

There was a feeling that this romantic scapegrace has proved himself to be a libertine and a pervert, and that his exile was good riddance.

The exile was to last for the remaining eight years of his life. Rumours of his conduct that drifted back to England continued to scandalise his countrymen – as did works like *Cain, Manfred* and *Don Juan* – particularly the last. *Cain* is virtually a defence of the first murderer, a romantic rebel who kills his boringly conventional brother then departs into exile with his head held high. *Manfred* is a passionate exercise in self-justification, with the doomed hero – transparently modelled on Goethe's Faust – standing on mountaintops, shaking his fist at the heavens and begging the spirits of the universe to grant him forgetfulness of his terrible secret. As to *Don Juan*, it was nothing less than a calculated affront to the British public, a series of defiantly immoral episodes, interspersed with bitter tirades on British hypocrisy, and attacks on major public figures, from the Prince Regent to William Wordsworth. Byron was paranoid about his social ostracism, but he was too good a writer to allow it to spoil his poetry. So *Manfred* remains a magnificent piece of self-justification – and self-glorification – while *Don Juan* has a lightness of touch and an impudent skill with language that make it the wittiest poem in English. If Byron had not died in Greece, England would probably have forgiven him for his sense of humour. Intelligence is the most seductive of all qualities.

After a visit to the field of Waterloo – which provided some famous stanzas for the third canto of *Childe Harold* – Byron travelled down the Rhine to Geneva. There, to his disgust, he was tracked down by Claire Claremont, who announced she was pregnant. She was with her half-sister, Mary Godwin – their father was the social philosopher, William Godwin – and Mary's lover, the poet Shelley. Driven out of the hotel by curious sightseers, they hired a villa above the lake, and there Byron began a novel about a vampire, and Mary began to write *Frankenstein*. Shelley's imagination was so excited by the ghost stories they told one another that he had a fit of hysteria, and thought that Mary's nipples had turned into eyes – an interesting example of the power of the imagination. (Such a thing would have been unthinkable in 1716.) Byron's physician Polidori had to give him a sedative.

When Shelley reproached Byron mildly for seducing Claire, he replied typically: 'No one has been more carried off than poor dear me – I've been ravished more often than anyone since the Trojan war.' There was more than an element of truth in it. (And of course, the joke of *Don Juan* is that the Don is always the seduced, never the seducer.)

In November 1816, Byron, together with Hobhouse, moved on to Venice, where he took lodgings in the house of a baker named Segati, and lost no time in allowing himself to be carried off by Segati's wife Marianna, a dark-haired beauty who soon began to tire him with her demands for sex three times a day – which may explain why her husband made no objection to her taking a lover. He also spent much time in the monastery of San Lazzaro, compiling an Armenian dictionary. The Coolidge effect ensured that he needed more than one woman, and he spent a great deal on ladies of the town, commenting that what he made with his brains he spent on his ballocks. Marianna was soon supplanted by a magnificently shapely peasant girl called Margarita Cogni, married, childless and illiterate. Margarita and Marianna soon had further reason for jealousy when Byron escorted a young married woman, Teresa Guiccioli – only recently out of a convent – to an art exhibition, and proceeded to lay siege to her virtue. This was a rash thing to do; Teresa was nineteen; her husband, Count Alessandro Guiccioli, was fifty-eight and already twice a widower, with a reputation for having poisoned his first wife and murdered the novelist Manzoni; but he eventually seems to have reconciled himself to the idea of being cuckolded by an English lord. Meanwhile, Margarita had learned to read so she could pry into Byron's love-letters; the result was an explosion of jealousy that led her to attack him with a knife and stab him in the hand. After that, Byron firmly ejected her from the *palazzo* he had rented, and she returned to her husband. The sale of Newstead brought Byron £94,500, so he was able to afford more of his favourite pleasures. His biographer Frederic Raphael remarks that 'he embarked on an orgy to challenge even the Venetian capacity to remain unshocked'.

The affair with Teresa was pleasant enough until her husband began to object. Teresa replied indignantly: 'It is hard that I should be the only woman in Romagna who is not to have her *amico*.' But when the Count and Countess parted – on her insistence – Byron became alarmed at the idea that she regarded him as a substitute husband; that would have removed every trace of spice from the affair. He was becoming increasingly dissatisfied with life – he was again growing fat, and his head was almost bald. The death of his daughter Allegra (with Claire Claremont) from fever, and the death of Shelley from drowning, in July 1822, galvanised him into leaving Italy. The cause of Greek freedom seemed as good an excuse as any for escaping from Teresa, and in July 1823 he sailed for Greece, carrying financial aid for the rebels. It all proved to be something of an anticlimax – months of monotony and boredom, without a sight of the enemy. The only consolation was that the news of his 'heroism' had spread to London and revived something of the admiration of the old *Childe Harold* days, and the latest cantos of *Don Juan* were a success. But Missolonghi, where Byron was living, was a disappointment; the troops he was supposed to lead were demoralised, incompetent and venal. Various factions were squabbling amongst themselves. He was forced to pay off some of his Albanian warriors and send them home, because they became such a threat to civil order. He was also in love with another fifteen-year-old boy, Lukas Chalandrutsanos, who seems to have declined to permit *plenum et optabilem coitum*. When he began to suffer from rheumatic fever and/or a uraemic disorder, his doctors weakened him by excessive blood-letting. On 24 April 1824, he died of fever. But anyone who reads the account of those last months in Missolonghi will agree that boredom and discouragement were really to blame.

Byron's chief problem was a simple one: *he had no idea of what to do with himself.* He knew he found social life boring and dissatisfying; but what was the alternative? A scientist might have withdrawn into his laboratory; a philosopher could have locked himself in an ivory tower. But what would Byron have *done*, even if he had locked himself in Newstead Abbey? Poetry might have occupied a few hours of each day, but he would have spent the rest of his time wondering what he could do to keep himself amused. He had expressed his most heartfelt sentiments in two famous stanzas of *Childe Harold* (Canto II):

To sit on rocks, to muse o'er flood and fell,
To slowly trace the forest's shady scene,
Where things that own not man's dominion dwell,
And mortal foot hath ne'er or rarely been;
To climb the trackless mountain all unseen,
With the wild flock that never needs a fold;
Alone o'er steeps and foaming falls to lean;
This is not solitude; 'tis but to hold
Converse with Nature's charms, and view her stores unroll'd.

But 'midst the crowd, the hum, the shock of men,
To hear, to see, to feel, and to possess,
And roam along, the world's tired denizen,
With none who bless us, none whom we can bless;
Minions of splendour shrinking from distress!
None that, with kindred consciousness endued,
If we were not, would seem to smile the less,
Of all that flatter'd, follow'd, sought, and sued;
This is to be alone; this, this is solitude!

Which is all very well; but no one can sit on rocks and muse o'er flood and fell for more than a few hours – if that. The simple truth was that, with all his dislike of 'the world's tired denizen', Byron was incapable of being alone for long. So life became an endless flight from his boredom, rolling in his carriage around Europe and making a virtue of his fatigue by complaining about it in his poems.

In Byron, we can see the essence of 'sexual perversion' with extraordinary clarity. The human sexual impulse has ceased to be a response to the smell of the female on heat, and the burden has been transferred to the imagination. So the very essence of human sexuality lies in the sense of 'forbiddenness'. When Byron became famous, he was scarcely out of his teens, and was certainly less mature than a comparable 24-year-old of the twentieth century, who has absorbed far more information about the world around him. It suddenly looked as if the whole female sex was at his disposal; but where should he begin? He plunged into an affair with Caroline Lamb; but soon she was the pursuer and he was fleeing. Disillusioned, he contemplated rushing to the opposite extreme, and getting married to the prim and virtuous Miss Milbanke. There can be no doubt that he seriously believed that this would be the solution of his difficulties; when she finally accepted him, two years later, he told her that if she had married him when he first asked her, she could have been his salvation – now it was too late. He was strongly tempted to seduce Lady Frances Webster, but realised that this would be a mere repetition of the Caroline Lamb affair. Instead, he looked around for the forbidden, and found it in his half-sister. For a while, incest was as exciting as he had hoped, and they spent idyllic weeks at Newstead. Then the Coolidge effect set in again, and he felt thoroughly let down. It was in this mood that he proposed to Annabella Milbanke a second time, although his instinct already told him that it was a mistake. He managed to introduce the element of 'forbiddenness' by sodomising her and taking a mistress. But he was like a man trying to cling to a dream as he drifts back to waking consciousness. All the wickedness and forbiddenness were an illusion; the reality that lay behind them was marriage, parenthood and ordinary human affection. But before he had time to make up his mind about this puzzling turn of events, Annabella had deserted him and he was a social outcast. So began another flight from himself. And again and again he found himself facing the same reality. 'Forbidden' affairs dissolved into a kind of domesticity. With the right woman – someone yielding and unaggressive, like Augusta – he might even have consented to settle down; but Claire was no Augusta – she was too pathetically anxious to keep him. The image of Augusta was to haunt him for the rest of his life, as the closest he had come to his feminine ideal: gentle, admiring, vulnerable, but with a mind of her own. It was ironical that she was beyond his grasp; she was even made to formally 'renounce' him after he left England. The essence of romance kept dissolving in his hands like fairy gold – Marianna, Margarita, Teresa – always leaving him face to face with the same old problem: a permanent liaison, or flight? So he ran away – to a war that proved to be another disillusionment, and a final love that seemed to prove that he had lost the power to attract. As he lay tossing with fever in Missolonghi, it must have seemed to him that there was nowhere else to go.

But to grasp what really went wrong, we have to look a little more closely at the real problem: the frustratingly ambiguous nature of the human sexual urge. Our human senses show us only a small part of the world – the present. We have to *supplement* this present-awareness with memory and imagination. The reason I feel more 'alive' when I set out on holiday is that my memory and imagination are finally pulling their weight, and supplementing the present moment with all kinds of other times and places. It is as if I am in two places at once. The same is true if I am sitting in front of a blazing fire on a cold winter night, with the snow pattering against the windows. I am in two places at once; my body is in the warm room, while my imagination is out there, in the cold. But it would be a mistake to assume that we are talking about mere imagination. We are talking about something that might be called the *sense of reality* – what the psychologist Pierre Janet called 'the reality function'. Whenever the reality function is awake, we are happy.

In short, before we can feel really alive, the mind needs to add a dimension of reality to the world of the senses. If there is such a thing as the 'great secret' of human existence, this is it.

Our greatest problem is that our reality function is so feeble; consciousness is always collapsing into mere present-awareness. It is plainly the evolutionary destiny of the human race to develop a far more powerful and efficient reality function; then life would seem to become a perpetual delight. But at present, our feeble reality function needs to be constantly stimulated by the real thing. Our senses need to be shaken awake. So Casanova seduces woman after woman in an attempt to keep his reality function permanently awake; every new conquest brings him a flash of the godlike sensation. Then the Coolidge effect comes into operation, and he has to go and look for someone else to seduce.

Yet there is obviously an element of uproarious absurdity in this feverish quest for new females-on-heat. Human beings have ceased to be dependent on the smell of oestrum to trigger sexual desire; it has been replaced by visual stimuli *and imagination*. So Casanova's restlessness is really a confession of the feebleness of his imagination – that is, of his reality function. The absurdity lies in the attempt to stimulate the reality function *from outside*, so to speak. Like the male sexual member, it is supposed to achieve erection *from inside*. The attempt to stimulate it with doses of 'forbiddenness' could be compared to an attempt to strengthen a limp penis with splints.

Yet this is precisely what all sexual perversion amounts to. Barbusse's 'outsider' is more stimulated by watching a girl undress through a hole in a wall than going to bed with a real woman (admittedly a prostitute). De Sade and Byron needed the smell of 'forbiddenness' to enjoy sex. Brothels often cater for men who have a fixation on schoolgirls or nurses or governesses. All are attempting to achieve erection – not just of the penis, but of the reality function – through a kind of play-acting. We seem to be dealing with a laughable absurdity, a kind of schoolboy howler.

Casanova revealed his lack of intelligence by pursuing the same will-o'-the-wisp for half a century. De Sade was slightly more intelligent; when the fairy gold dissolved in his fingers, he decided that the problem was that his goal was not 'forbidden' enough, and looked around for something slightly more wicked. But it made no difference what material he used for a splint; nails were no better than matchsticks, iron bars no better than nails. Yet with manic persistence, he went on looking for longer and harder splints: broom handles, lamp posts, flagpoles. As we read *Philosophy in the Bedroom* or *Juliette*, we can study this absurdity in operation. Some of his early imaginings achieve their effect of sexual stimulation. He then proceeds to demonstrate his lack of real insight into the problem by adding new touches of the 'forbidden', naïvely assuming that each one will be still more sexually exciting. In fact, he loses the average reader as soon as he embarks on fairly simple perversions and, long before he has reached murder and torture, most of us have closed the book. Nothing could demonstrate more clearly that the real trouble with human beings is the feebleness of the reality function. De Sade's perversions do not produce an effect of more and more reality; only of an increasingly surrealistic dream.

His contemporaries mistook his confusion – and his naïve persistence – for horrible wickedness, and treated him accordingly. De Sade was justifiably indignant; he regarded himself as a philosopher whose aim was a purely logical demonstration. In fact, his life reveals that he was not particularly wicked; he was merely – like some crank who believes the earth is flat or the moon is made of cheese – in the grip of a fixed idea.

Now although it sounds impossible, there is a sense in which Byron went even further than de Sade. De Sade never identified himself with his villains, like Saint-Fond or the Duc de Blangis. He remains the puppet-master, pulling the strings and expounding the ideas. But Byron decided at an early stage that the best way of achieving more or less permanent contact with 'the forbidden' was to become identified with it: to see himself as his own mixture of hero and villain. De Sade's Dolmancé gloats: 'I've got this little virgin cunt all to myself. Oh, I'm a guilty one, a villain . . .' By identifying himself with Childe Harold and Lara and Manfred, Byron was, in effect, murmuring this to himself from morning till night. As he made love to Augusta, he must have felt magnificently and supremely wicked. Yet it was not true. He was a decent, kindly, generous, affectionate person – one book about him is even entitled *Lord Byron – Christian Virtues*,* which would have horrified him. His 'wickedness' was merely a kind of play-acting, designed to strengthen his reality function.

There is supreme irony in the fact that de Sade paid for his indiscretions with a lifetime in jail and the suppression of his works, while Byron – who did his best to practise the Sadian philosophy – went on to become the most famous poet in Europe, and the greatest single inspiration of the Romantic Movement in the nineteenth century.

* by G. Wilson Knight

SIX

From Rebellion to Sex Crime

Byron would have been flattered by the sensation caused by the news of his death. Shock waves spread across Europe; thousands of young men – and women – went into mourning. Jane Welsh wrote to her fiancé, Thomas Carlyle: 'My God, if they had said that the sun or moon was gone out of the heavens, it could not have struck me with the idea of a more awful and dreary blank in creation than the words "Byron is dead!"' In Greece, all shops closed for three days and the government announced the suspension of Easter festivities. Hobhouse heard the news in 'an agony of grief'; Augusta was thrown into 'a pitiable state'. Matthew Arnold wrote:

> When Byron's eyes were shut in death,
> We bow'd our head and held our breath.
> He taught us little: but our soul
> Had *felt* him like the thunders roll.

The real Byron was forgotten; he had become a heroic ideal, a natural force. The only thing he might have done to increase the impact of his death was to have died in battle, like his own Lara. But it made no difference; as far as his contemporaries were concerned, he *had* died in battle. *The Times* published a glowing obituary that included the words: 'That noblest of enterprises, the deliverance of Greece , employed the whole of Lord Byron's latter days.' Those who disliked him ironically quoted *Macbeth*:

> nothing in his life
> Became him like the leaving it . . .

Nevertheless, his death rounded off the legend and completed the identification of Byron with his own heroes.

In retrospect, we can see that the Byronic hero had almost as great an impact on the European imagination as Richardson's *Pamela*. He became the favourite hero in fiction; Charlotte Brontë's Heathcliff, Pushkin's Eugene Onegin, Lermontov's Grigory Pechorin, are all variants on Childe Harold and Lara. And – perhaps oddest of all – Byron himself appears in the second part of Goethe's *Faust* as Euphorion, the child of Faust and Helen of Troy, who makes himself wings to fly and crashes to his death at their feet.

Goethe's admiration for Byron offers us the vital key to Byron's grip on the European imagination. At first it seems baffling. Goethe was a middle-aged writer whose romantic period lay fifty years behind him, and who had long since turned his back on it. He now felt contemptuous of the hysteria that had been aroused by his *Young Werther*, which had made him famous at twenty-four. Now, aged seventy-five, he preached self-discipline and classicism. Yet, from his first reading of *Lara* and *The Corsair* (in 1816), he had been almost a Byron disciple, questioning every Englishman who crossed his path about the English lord, and even ploughing through a vast and unskilful novel called *Glenarvon* by Lady Caroline Lamb because he had heard that the hero was based on Byron. Why was he not contemptuous of Byron's histrionic self-pity? The answer can be seen if we compare *Manfred* and *Faust*. Faust is an ageing scholar who feels that all knowledge is an illusion and that we can know nothing; he sells his soul to the devil in exchange for a love-affair with a peasant girl; only the intervention of angels saves his soul from Hell. In the last analysis, Faust is rather a negative character, a victim of his own pessimism. By comparison, Manfred is superbly heroic, shaking his fist at the heavens and defying the spirits of the universe. Compared to the Byronic hero, young Werther is distinctly 'wet', while Goethe's later hero, Wilhelm Meister, is a typical phlegmatic German. Byron made Goethe realise that his own attitude might have been more challenging and heroic. Moreover, Byron's death plunged Goethe back into something like his own early romanticism. 'Byron's death . . . had destroyed for ever Goethe's waning belief in the essential harmony and stability underlying the chaotic and stormy waste of waters which we call the world.'* In short, it seems that contact with

* *Byron and Goethe* by E. M. Butler, p. 208

Byron's genius made Goethe realise that he had allowed himself to become a little too complacent.

So it made no difference that Byron lacked self-discipline, that he was the victim of boredom and self-pity. What mattered was that he was capable of challenging God, of demanding to know why human life seems so chaotic and meaningless; he wanted to know why we are in the world, and what we are supposed to do now we are here. In that sense, he deserves to be called the father of existentialism, for he antedates Kierkegaard by several decades. No one before Byron had ever thought of putting that question with quite the same angry persistence – except, perhaps, Satan in the Bible. And this is why the Byronic hero made such an impact. He was not merely a sinner; he was a Questioner.

What was really at issue was a feeling that a man *ought to be the master of his own life*, that he ought not to be a helpless puppet in the hands of his fate. Byron spent most of his life as a victim of boredom and *ennui*; yet he had a deep intuition that these are somehow absurd – that, in certain moments, man has a superb feeling of *control* over his life. The same 'absurd' vision lay at the heart of de Sade's philosophy; but he spoilt it by going too far. In the final scene of *Juliette*, Noirceuil shouts: 'Oh infamy on high' (he means God) 'remove these curbs that make me little, when I would imitate thee and commit evil.' Then he seizes Juliette's little daughter and rapes her, at the same time crying: 'Sell me the slut, Juliette . . . Let's both soil ourselves . . . Yes, Juliette, let's assassinate your daughter . . . Stay, Juliette, have yourself fucked before you decide, don't answer me until you have a couple of pricks in your body.' And as penises penetrate her in front and behind, and she looses 'discharge upon discharge', she shouts: 'Do what you please with Marianne, whoreson knave, she is yours.' And Noirceuil hurls Marianne into the fire. De Sade's philosophy rests upon the 'godlike' sensation of the orgasm, upon the feeling that Yeats described as 'fire blazing into the head'. This seems to be the closest man ever gets to feeling himself a god. In which case, it seems to follow that a good orgasm justifies anything. Byron never went as far as de Sade, but his *Don Juan* was also conceived as a slap in the face for English morality – the morality that had driven him to become a wanderer. As far as he was concerned, he had every right to sodomise Nicolo Giraud, and to commit adultery with Caroline Lamb and Lady Oxford, and incest with his own sister; committing 'forbidden' acts gave him a glimpse of the 'god-like' sensation. And, like Noirceuil, his deepest desire was to 'remove these curbs that keep me little'. This is why the Byronic hero dominated literature in the first half of the nineteenth century; he expressed the very essence of romanticism: the feeling that man is, in some paradoxical sense, a god. *This* was the aspect of Byron that exercised such a powerful influence over his followers.

The greatest of these was the Russian poet, Alexander Pushkin, eleven years Byron's junior, whose life bears many interesting resemblances to Byron's. Pushkin was also an aristocrat who liked to boast about his '600-year-old nobility'. His mother was the granddaughter of Peter the Great's Chief Engineer, General Hannibal, who was an Abyssinian. (Pushkin's features were distinctly negroid.) But his parents were Moscow socialites who ignored their children. A voracious reader, he was writing precociously brilliant poetry by the age of fifteen. He was educated in a private school that occupied a wing of the royal palace at Tsarskoe Selo – a training ground for future ministers and royal advisers. So recognition came easily; when he was only fifteen, his talent was recognised by the leading Russian poet, Derzhavin. And at twenty, he became famous with the publication of his long poem *Ruslan and Liudmilla*, a Russian fairy-tale featuring a gigantic severed head. Unfortunately, Pushkin was also what would now be called a 'leftist', and when some of his revolutionary epigrams came to the attention of the Tsar, he was exiled from St Petersburg. He caught fever, and was sent to the Caucasus to recuperate.

There he discovered Byron. He was staying with the family of General Nicolai Rayevsky, whose four daughters adored Byron's work and whose son Alexander did his best to look and behave like the English poet. The impact of Byron's poetry, and the magnificent mountain scenery of the Caucasus – not to mention attractive girls – was tremendous. Pushkin badly needed fresh air and exercise – at twenty-one he was nearly as enfeebled by alcoholic and sexual excesses as Byron had been at twenty-four. So while he listened to the cynical 'Byronic' commonplaces of Alexander Rayevsky, he planned a long narrative poem, in which the weary, disillusioned hero is himself. *The Prisoner of the Caucasus* is about a beautiful Circassian girl who falls in love with the Byronic hero and helps him to escape. But he is too sexually experienced and emotionally drained to be able to return her love. After filing his chains, she

drowns herself in the river; he makes no attempt to rescue her . . .
When *The Prisoner of the Caucasus* appeared in 1822, it was an
even greater success than *Ruslan and Liudmilla*. It established
Pushkin as the Russian Byron; every educated young man in Russia
knew his lyrics by heart. (These included *The Dagger*, a poem
celebrating the assassination of tyrants, which aroused the dis-
pleasure of the authorities.) And, inevitably, most young women
found him irresistible.

After this, Pushkin demonstrated his affinity with de Sade in a
ribald poem called *The Gavriliad*. Thoroughly bored by being
forced to attend church – as a government functionary – he produced a 500-line poem in which the Virgin Mary – who is portrayed
as a sweet and irresistible young girl, rather like Terry Southern's
Candy – is ravished by Satan, then by the Archangel Gabriel
(Gavril), then by God in the form of a dove (producing, we assume,
the Immaculate Conception). It remained unpublished during the
course of Pushkin's life, but was widely circulated in manuscript.

Meanwhile, Pushkin remained in his exile, mostly in dreary
provincial towns where he was inclined to quarrel with his su-
periors. In Kishinev, he fought a duel with a colonel in a raging
snowstorm – both missed. When he fought an officer – whom he
had accused of cheating – Pushkin stood munching cherries while
the other fired – and missed – then declined to take his own shot.
His opponent rushed over to try and embrace him, but Pushkin
raised his hand coldly: 'No, that would be *too* much' – and walked
off, still eating cherries. News of Byron's death led him to write a
moving poem that began:

> Another genius has left us,
> Another master of our thoughts . . .

Meanwhile, in Odessa, he pursued a dozen or so ladies, including
the Governor's wife, thus earning the official's undying enmity.
And when one of Pushkin's letters announcing his conversion to
atheism was intercepted, he was expelled from the Civil Service and
ordered to go and live on his mother's estate in the country. There
he quarrelled bitterly with his father, and continued to work on his
masterpiece, *Eugene Onegin*. But the exile proved to be a blessing
in disguise, for the Decembrist Revolt against the new tsar, Nicholas
I, took place in 1825 and Pushkin, as a friend of many of the

conspirators, would certainly have ended on the gallows or in Siberia. Instead, Pushkin was recalled from exile by the new tsar, who had decided that the simplest way of drawing the teeth of this revolutionary would be to keep a close eye on him. And for the remaining decade of his life, Pushkin was like a caged animal, stifled by the boring social life of St Petersburg – but at least writing masterpieces to relieve his boredom and frustration.

Although it was only a decade since he had been Russia's most famous poet, younger poets already regarded him as a kind of literary dinosaur. His great play, *Boris Godunov*, was a critical failure. He turned to prose, and produced some of the finest short stories that have come out of Russia, and one masterly novel, *The Captain's Daughter*. In 1831, he made the same devastating mistake as his hero, Byron, and married – a beautiful but empty-headed girl who was many years his junior. The tsar made Pushkin a 'gentleman of the bedchamber' merely to have his lovely wife at court. And it was when he thought that his wife had taken a lover that Pushkin challenged his rival – whose name was D'Anthès – to a duel, and was fatally wounded. He died at precisely the same age as Byron, thirty-seven.

Unlike Byron, Pushkin seems to have had no guilty secrets that weighed him down; his sex life was cheerfully heterosexual, and he ceased to pose as a Byronic hero at a fairly early stage in his career. But his most enduring work – and his masterpiece – *Eugene Onegin*, was typically Byronic. And since it also happened to be a novel in verse, at a time when there were no Russian novels, it also exercised an immense influence on the great Russian fiction of the nineteenth century. Dostoevsky once remarked about Russian novelists: 'We all came out of Gogol's *Overcoat*.' But it would be equally true to say that they all came out of *Eugene Onegin* – and thus out of *Childe Harold* and *Don Juan*.

Onegin opens with a Byronic flourish:

> My Uncle's shown his good intentions
> By falling desperately ill . . .*

And the bored and love-weary hero inherits his uncle's estate in a remote part of Russia, where he lives the life of a gloomy recluse, until an old friend invites him to dinner with a neighbouring family,

* Translation by Babette Deutsch

the Larins. The friend is interested in the beautiful older sister, Olga; neither of them pay much attention to the younger girl, Tatiana. But Tatiana falls violently in love with Onegin, and finally summons up the courage to write and tell him so. He calls, and finds her alone in the garden. There he explains that it is a waste of time to love him: 'I was not born for happiness.' His heart is already worn out with past love-affairs. He advises her to try and think of him as a brother, then leaves her.

Two years later, the tables are turned when Onegin returns from his travels and attends a *soirée*. There he sees a dazzling apparition, a woman whose beauty stops him in his tracks. It is his hostess, Tatiana, now married to a fat general. Onegin writes her passionate letters, but she ignores them. Finally, he manages to see her alone. She admits that she is still in love with him but firmly rejects his devotion. Now she is married, and will remain faithful to her husband until death . . .

Whether Pushkin gave the poem this un-Byronic ending to convince the tsar that he was a reformed character is a matter for speculation. What is clear is that it was the Byronism of the rest of the poem that made it the Russian equivalent of *Childe Harold*; Byronic heroes proliferated in Russian fiction, from Lermontov's Pechorin to Dostoevsky's Stavrogin in *The Possessed*.

Pechorin is the creation of Pushkin's greatest heir. Mikhail Lermontov's mother died when he was three, and he was appropriated by his grandmother, a wealthy landowner, and brought up in the Caucasus, where he was thoroughly spoiled. Byron's death occurred when Lermontov was ten years old, and by the time he was thirteen he saw himself as another Childe Harold. At eighteen he became a cavalry cadet, and devoted himself to riotous living. Promoted to ensign in the Hussars – stationed at Tsarskoe Selo – he wrote pornographic verses, got drunk regularly, and complained that he was unable to copulate with peasant girls because they stank. His natural tendency to aloofness was increased by a sense of social inferiority; his father had only been a member of the minor gentry, so – unlike Pushkin – Lermontov was unable to penetrate the higher echelons of Petersburg society.

When Pushkin was killed in January 1837, Lermontov poured out his indignation in a poem called *Death of a Poet*. It was impossible to publish it, since Pushkin was a forbidden subject (even his final portrait was suppressed), but manuscript copies circulated among the Petersburg intelligentsia and brought the poet instant notoriety. The result was that Lermontov was arrested, tried, and transferred to a regiment of the line in the Caucasus. But his exile was brief and, back in St Petersburg, he was welcomed as a successor to Pushkin. But as soon as he found himself successful in society, he experienced a Byronic change of heart, and began to despise it; his arrogance soon made him highly unpopular. But his work became more pure and classical in style – the earlier poetry is often romantic and obscure, like a storm-cloud full of lightning - and works like *The Novice*, *The Demon* and *The Tambov Treasurer's Wife* compare with the best of Pushkin or Byron. The latter is a delightful squib, written in the same metres as *Eugene Onegin*, about a dishonest old treasurer who loses his pretty wife in a game of cards to a dashing young officer; the casual, conversational style owes as much to *Don Juan* as to *Onegin*:

> And that's the end of my sad story –
> Which, strictly speaking, isn't true.
> Now tell me: did you find it boring?
> Did you want passion – actions, too? . . .
> Too bad. My story's at an end.
> That's all you're going to get, my friends.*

This was written when Lermontov was twenty-three. Two years later, his prose masterpiece, *A Hero of Our Time* – regarded by many Russians as the greatest Russian novel – was published without success. A year later, Lermontov was dead, at the age of twenty-six, killed in a duel by an old schoolfellow whom he had constantly provoked.

A Hero of Our Time is more than a belated study in romantic Byronism; it is an attempt to analyse the psychology of an 'outsider', a man who is too intelligent for his own good. The form of the novel is also unusual; it consists of five stories, in each of which a little more of Pechorin's character is revealed. In the opening story, *Bela*, he appears as a cold sensualist and a ruthless egoist; in the second, he seems to be an unpleasant snob. By the end of the book, the reader realises that, although he has certain faults, his real problem is that 'he sees too deep and too much', and that as a result

* Translated by Guy Daniels

he is profoundly self-divided. T. E. Lawrence expressed the feeling
in *Seven Pillars of Wisdom*:

> The lower creation I avoided, as a reflection upon our failure to
> attain real intellectuality. If they forced themselves on me, I
> hated them. To put my hand on a living thing was defilement,
> and it made me tremble if they touched me or took too great an
> interest in me . . . The opposite would have been my choice if
> my head had not been tyrannous. I . . . lamented myself most
> when I saw a soldier with a girl, or a man fondling a dog, because
> my wish was to be as superficial and as perfected, and my jailer
> held me back.

Here we see the problem of Byron and Pushkin as well as of
Lermontov. A certain cold clarity of intellect makes him contemptuous of 'the lower creation', and of the trivialities that most people
accept as the essence of life. Yet he has not yet discovered anything
to *put in the place* of these trivialities. He is angry with himself for
being trapped in the boredom of the present moment; he feels that
his imagination should be capable of carrying him away to other
times and other places. Of course, poetry is a method of concentrat-
ing the imagination; but it never lasts for long enough. Getting
drunk is almost as effective . . . Romanticism is a frantic attempt
to escape the limitations of the body and the emotions. This explains
why Byron treated his mistresses so badly. He needed them as he
needed alcohol; but he was contemptuous of himself for needing
them.

These men were 'Outsiders' in the most precise sense of the word:
that is, they were 'in-betweeners', men whose unhappiness arose
from finding themselves stranded between two states of being, as
if they had fallen between two stools.

Looked at in this light, we can see that romanticism might be
regarded as an evolutionary attempt to escape these limitations of
the body and the emotions. When we look back on the previous
century – the century of Dryden and Pope, Swift and Congreve –
we feel that its writers were trapped in a narrow and stifling social
reality, endlessly gossiping and stabbing one another in the back.
This narrowness drove Swift half insane, yet he never discovered
how to break out of it. When we turn to Blake and Wordsworth,
Byron and Shelley, it is like stepping out of an overheated drawing-

room into the open air. They had discovered the secret of achieving glimpses of a wider type of consciousness – a sense of what Wordsworth called 'unknown modes of being'. Yet they achieved this at enormous cost – *a strengthening of the imagination that reduced their power to cope with reality.* Blake's orphan boy asks:

> Father, O Father! what do we here
> In this land of unbelief and fear?
> The Land of Dreams is better far
> Above the light of the Morning Star.

But emerging from the Land of Dreams into the real world is like walking out of a hot bath into a freezing gale. Moreover the power of imagination can be dangerous – Wordsworth once admitted that he was afraid of it, because it could carry him away into a world of negative fantasies. This is what happened to Shelley when he thought Mary's nipples had turned into eyes. It was a healthy instinct that drove Byron to feats of athleticism, like swimming the Hellespont; yet as we read *Childe Harold* and *Manfred*, we can see that he remained trapped inside his own head.

This was the problem of the Romantics. Imagination was like a new wonder-drug with dangerous side-effects. Byron and the Byronic hero died of the side-effects. As Manfred shakes his fist at the sky, he is not really defying God; he is only threatening to sue the manufacturer.

We can see the essence of the romantic problem in Pushkin's friend and contemporary, Nikolai Gogol. Born in the little market-town of Sorochintsy in 1809, Gogol was the son of a member of the minor gentry. Unlike Pushkin and Lermontov, he was not an attractive child. Vladimir Nabokov puts it with his usual vigour in his little book on Gogol:

> He was a weakling, a trembling mouse of a boy, with dirty hands and greasy locks, and pus trickling out of his ear. He gorged himself with sticky sweets. His schoolmates avoided touching the books he had been using. Upon completing his schooling at Nejin in the Ukraine he left for St Petersburg to look for some job. His arrival in the capital was marred by a bad cold which was all the more unpleasant through not being able to feel his frost-bitten nose . . .

The bad cold and the frost-bitten nose are somehow typical of Gogol, and things were made worse by the fact that he had an exceptionally long nose that looked as if it had been designed for eating ants or plucking bananas off a tree. (One of his party tricks was to cover his nose with his lower lip.)

The story goes that he immediately went to call on Pushkin, but was told that the poet was still in bed.

'Dear me, has he been writing all night?'

'Writing?' said the servant. 'No, he's been playing cards.'

Hoping for overnight fame, he published a long poem called *Hans Kuchelgarten*; this was received by the critics with such derision that he bought up all the copies and destroyed them. Next he entered the Civil Service and began to write prose stories; he was taken up by the literary set, finally met Pushkin, and became overbearingly conceited. An appointment as a professor of history proved a disaster – he was too lazy to apply himself to study – but a first volume of Ukrainian stories called *Evenings on a Farm near Dikanka* (1831) was an instant and tremendous success, and made Gogol famous at the age of twenty-two. No one had ever read anything like it before. All the scenes are painted in clear primary colours, like one of those Russian dolls; fantasy and actuality blend as if in a dream. The tone is casual and conversational; the narrator is supposed to be a bee-keeper, but he sounds rather more like Tristram Shandy. The charm of the stories lies in the fact that, in spite of the touches of realism, Gogol was actually writing a kind of poetry. The first story, 'Sorochintsky Fair', begins: 'How intoxicating, how magnificent is a summer day in the Ukraine! How luxuriously warm it is when midday glitters in stillness and sultry heat, and the blue expanse of sky, arching like a cupola, seems to be slumbering . . .' This is not the real Ukraine – it is a Ukraine in Gogol's head. And when, a page later, he describes a peasant girl, she is not a real peasant girl either, but a kind of Walt Disney princess. 'On a wagon sat his pretty daughter, a girl with a round face, black eyebrows arching evenly above her clear brown eyes, and merrily smiling rosy lips. Red and blue ribbons were twisted in the long plaits which, with a bunch of wild flowers, crowned her charming head.' All Gogol's girls are like this – the kind of girls confectionery manufacturers used to put on chocolate boxes. And this is perhaps inevitable, for Gogol was tongue-tied in the presence of real young ladies. There seems to be a general agreement among his biographers that the only sexual pleasures he ever knew were solitary – which may also explain the guilt that darkened his last years.

Gogol was a strange, paradoxical character who seemed to be oddly out of touch with reality. At times he was morbidly shy and withdrawn; at others, manically egoistic and conceited. He may have inherited a touch of insanity from his mother, who bore Gogol at the age of eighteen (two earlier children had died) and who spent much of her time in a state of 'sickly dreaminess'. She not only adored her son, but was firmly convinced that he was responsible for all recent technological advances, including the telegraph and the railroads. Gogol was also subject to long moods of boredom, 'spleen', 'melancholy', and states of 'stupefaction' and 'senseless somnolence', when he became incapable of action. He was also a lifelong hypochondriac who was never 'indisposed', but always 'dangerously ill'. His literary fame brought him many friends and admirers, but even his closest friend, the novelist Aksakov, confessed that he did not particularly like Gogol. He admitted to his son that he knew no one who loved Gogol as a friend, irrespective of his talent, and said that he himself venerated Gogol as 'the vessel in which the great gift of creative art was enclosed', but that he disliked the vessel. It seems hardly surprising that Gogol failed to attract a woman.

Sexual frustration may account for the element of horror and morbidity that runs through stories like 'The Terrible Revenge' and 'Viy'. The former is about a wicked magician who has murdered his wife and is now determined to seduce his daughter. It is full of startling and dramatic effects:

> A cross on one of the graves tottered, and a withered corpse rose up out of the earth. Its beard reached to its waist; the claws on the fingers were longer than the fingers themselves. It slowly raised its hand upwards. Its face was all twisted and distorted. One could see that it was suffering terrible torments. 'I am stifling, I am stifling,' it moaned.

At this stage of his career, there seemed to be nothing that Gogol could not do. In *Taras Bulba* he even attempted a kind of Homeric epic about the Cossacks, and succeeded magnificently. Yet it was his sense of his own absurdity and weakness of character that made him the father of Russian realism. In *The Nose*, a civil servant wakes up to find that his nose is missing, and tries to track it down all over St Petersburg; the nose ends up posing as a state councillor and driving a coach and four all over town. His most famous story, *The Overcoat*, begins as a fantasy about an insignificant little clerk who stretches his resources to the limit to buy himself a new coat; after this is stolen, the story ends in supernatural fantasy, with the clerk's ghost snatching coats from the backs of late-night wanderers through the streets of St Petersburg.

In 1835, at Pushkin's suggestion, Gogol wrote a play called *The Government Inspector*, about a penniless rogue who is mistaken by the inhabitants of a small town for an inspector from the Civil Service – something of the sort had actually happened to Pushkin himself. Incredibly, the play was passed by the censor and, in spite of some bad reviews, was a considerable success. The Tsar Nicholas I laughed heartily, saying: 'Everybody's caught it, me most of all . . .' Conservative critics attacked Gogol as a rebel, and he reacted with his usual paranoia: 'This prophet is without honour in his own country. Everyone is against him . . .' But he became the darling of the liberals, and was soon convinced that he had a vocation to save his own countrymen.

In 1836, a romantic wanderlust drove him abroad – Gogol was the sort of person who always imagined that magical experiences lay around the next corner – and he stayed away for the next twelve years. He was shattered by the death of his friend Pushkin in 1837 – to such an extent that one commentator wrote that D'Anthès's bullet had killed not one writer but two – but pressed on with his novel *Dead Souls*, which he was convinced would have the effect of morally regenerating Russia.

Dead Souls is the story of a confidence man, Chichikov, who has learnt that a certain Trustees Committee will advance money on serfs. But serfs (or 'souls') who have died since the last census are still officially regarded as alive. So Chichikov makes a tour of landowners, offering to buy their 'dead souls' for a trifling sum – the novel is simply the story of his various encounters with a gallery of Russian 'types'. Whether the landowners in *Dead Souls* – the genial Manilov, the drunken Nozdrev, the miser Plyushkin, the glutton Pyetukh – are real characters or drawn straight from Gogol's imagination, it is now impossible to say; but it is probably safe to assume that they never really existed. At the end of the first part, Chichikov is arrested for forging a will; but a rascally lawyer succeeds in confusing the issue by dragging in every scandal in the province, and the officials are glad to let Chichikov go, on condition he leaves town.

Like *The Government Inspector*, *Dead Souls* was badly received by most critics. One described it as being like 'a dirty inn – a slander on Russia', and another as 'filth upon filth'. But Gogol was undismayed; more convinced than ever of his mission, he returned to Rome to write the second and third parts of *Dead Souls* – for he was convinced that the first part was merely the front steps to a magnificent dream palace – and began to study the Gospels. What followed has been described by the critic Mirsky as 'one of the strangest and most disconcerting passages in the history of the Russian mind'. Perhaps under the burden of his strange illness with its long periods of depression and debilitation, his fragile contact with reality snapped altogether, and he plunged into religious mania. He broke off the second part of *Dead Souls* and then, after an attack of illness, threw it on the fire. Then he decided to preach his moral message directly to his fellow countrymen, and prepared a volume called *Selected Passages from Correspondence with Friends*, consisting of religious and moral exhortations mingled with justifications of such institutions as serfdom and corporal punishment. The Russian liberals – his chief supporters – were horrified, and even Aksakov wrote him a letter accusing him of Satanic pride. Belinsky, one of the warmest defenders of *Dead Souls*, declared that Gogol adored reaction and barbarity. The attacks only increased Gogol's misery and self-division, and plunged him still further into religious mysticism. He made a pilgrimage to the Holy Land, then returned to Russia and moved from place to place like a tormented soul. In a state of deep melancholy, he almost stopped eating; in February 1852 he died of an undiagnosed illness based on starvation.

Throughout his life, Gogol made obscure references to what he called 'the riddle of my existence'. His biographer, David Magarshack, has suggested that Gogol provided the key in his essay *Woman*, in which he asked: 'What is woman? The language of the gods! She is poetry, she is thought, and we are only her embodiment in reality . . . While his idea is still in the head of the artist, while it is being created and has not yet assumed its corporeal form – it is woman; when it materialises and becomes tangible – it is man.' Magarshack suggests that 'this transcendental idea of woman made man lies at the core of Gogol's conception of sex and his disgust with its ordinary manifestations . . .'

In fact, we can see that Gogol's image merely means that he identifies 'woman' with intuition or inspiration – those formless impulses which, we would now say, originate in the 'right brain', while the left brain has to capture them and turn them into logic and language, both 'masculine' functions.

Gogol's real problem was his sense of being only half formed – what Musil called a 'man without qualities'. His 'riddle' lay in the strange contradiction between his rather weak and unlovable character, and the almost demonic force of his imaginative creation, which reminded his contemporaries of Dickens, but which more often reminds us of Tolkien, or even of H. P. Lovecraft. So he was in the strange position of feeling himself a personal non-entity – one of Dostoevsky's 'insignificant men' – while creating work of tremendous imaginative vitality like *Taras Bulba* and *Dead Souls*. And the sense of insignificance condemned him to admire woman from a distance . . . Why do men wish for fame? One of the major reasons is that it makes them more attractive to the opposite sex. Gogol was an admirer of Byron, and he had the example of Pushkin before him. Yet his own nation-wide fame left him as sexually isolated as ever; his only outlet was a practice that was regarded in the nineteenth century as one of the seven deadly sins. In the same position, other men of genius might have taken a working-class mistress, or frequented prostitutes; Gogol was too nervous and sensitive for that. If he ever made any tentative sexual experiments, it seems likely that he would have suffered from what Stendhal called 'le fiasco'. (This may be what one critic was hinting at when he spoke of a 'defect in Gogol's nature, a lack of something that everyone has, that no one is deprived of'.) In his story *Shponka and his Aunt*, Gogol describes a long, Freudian nightmare of a young man who is told he has to marry a neighbour's daughter, and who wakes up sweating with terror. In his comedy *The Marriage*, a man decides to employ the services of a marriage broker to find him a wife, but at the last minute loses his nerve and jumps out of the window. Gogol's own solution, in his final years, was to propose a 'wholly spiritual marriage' to a young countess with whom he had fallen in love – in effect, warning her in advance not to expect any sex. Understandably, she turned him down, and he was shattered.

Gogol's problem was the sheer strength of his imagination. His contemporaries failed to see this because of his superficial realism, and his own assurances that he was incapable of inventing anything. *Dead Souls* opens with a description of Chichikov's arrival at the inn, which sounds almost fussily precise: 'A small, rather smart, well-sprung four-wheel carriage with a folding top drove through the gates of an inn of the provincial town of N—; it was the sort of carriage bachelors usually drive in . . .' We overhear the remarks of two peasants standing opposite.

> 'Lord!' said one of them to the other, 'what a wheel! What do you think? Would a wheel like that, if put to it, ever get to Moscow, or wouldn't it?'
> 'It would all right,' replied the other.
> 'But it wouldn't get to Kazan, would it?'
> 'No, it wouldn't get to Kazan,' replied the other.

Gogol also describes a young man who happens to be passing,

> wearing very narrow and very short white canvas trousers, swallow-tail coat with some pretensions to fashion, disclosing a shirt-front fastened with a pin of Tula manufacture in the shape of a bronze pistol. This young man turned round, took a look at the carriage, held on to his cap which a gust of wind nearly blew off his head, and went on his way.

We might feel justified in expecting this young man, so carefully described, to play some part in the story; in fact, he promptly vanishes. And it is in the next paragraph that the attentive reader begins to understand Gogol's technique.

> When the carriage had driven into the courtyard, the gentleman was met by a servant of the inn, or a floorman as waiters are called in Russian inns, who was so lively and restless that it was quite impossible to make out what kind of a face he had . . .

No one could be *that* restless. The inn servant is faceless because he is a character in a dream, just like the two peasants and the young man with the tie-pin in the shape of a bronze pistol – a detail typical of the absurd precision of a dream. A century before Kafka, Gogol had stumbled upon the technique of turning dreams into literature.

Hoffmann remarks in his novel *Kater Murr*: 'Every man really has an innate inclination to fly, and I have known serious, respectable people who in the late evening merely fill themselves with champagne as a gas for ascending to the heights . . .' The problem with this balloon known as imagination is that it can carry us to dangerous heights. Byron, Pushkin and Lermontov did their best to keep their feet on the ground – but, then, they had the advantage of an aristocratic training. Gogol, the scrofulous, sickly mother's boy, lacked that kind of self-discipline. So he was carried aloft, his feet kicking frantically, clinging for dear life to the balloon that condemned him to 'Outsiderism' and frustration. The burning of the second part of *Dead Souls* was a kind of symbolic suicide. After that, he lay down on his bed, refused to speak to anyone or to see a doctor, and starved himself to death. Like Dostoevsky's Ivan Karamazov, he was 'handing God back his entrance ticket'. Imagination had left him drained and exhausted.

In England, there had also been many changes since the age of Fielding and Smollett. First of all, there had been a powerful reaction against the 'coarseness' of the Age of Reason. There was a new tone of high-mindedness – undoubtedly due to the influence of the Romantics. The reading public wanted Gothic castles and gloomy pinewoods and mountains with their foothills wreathed in mist. The Scots must have been delighted at the influx of tourists that followed publication of Sir Walter Scott's *Lady of the Lake* and *Marmion*, and MacPherson's pseudo-Celtic concoction, *Ossian*. When Scott found that his poetry was being outsold by Byron, he turned to the novel and produced a series of masterpieces in an incredibly short space of time. (*Guy Mannering* was written in six weeks, and *The Bride of Lammermoor* in only a fortnight.) Scott had invented a time-machine that could transport his readers to the Holy Land with Richard the Lionheart or to the battlefields of France with Quentin Durward. In Italy, Scott's greatest follower, Manzoni, succeeded in producing only one masterpiece, *The Betrothed*. But in France, Scott was soon being overtaken by a host of young novelists, including Balzac, Hugo, Dumas and Stendhal. Honoré de Balzac was so gripped by imaginative fever that he created whole cities, with their cobbled streets and dark houses, and whole generations of inhabitants. Yet in Balzac we can again see the paradox of the great romantic artist. The sheer scale of his work demonstrates his belief in the god-like powers of the human mind, yet his commitment to 'realism' meant that he spoilt the grand design with a shallow pessimism, a conviction that life is meaningless and that human beings are hopelessly corrupt. Finally, like Gogol, Balzac died of creative exhaustion and a sense of futility.

The 'puritan revolution' of the Romantics explains why John Cleland found so few imitators. In the age of Goethe and Rousseau, pornography seemed old-fashioned. And in the age of Jane Austen, Maria Edgeworth, Sir Walter Scott and Charles Lamb, only the depraved wanted to read books with titles like *The Loves of Cleopatra* and *The Voluptuarian Cabinet*. But all this romantic high-mindedness was bound to produce its reaction. And the very fact that the European reading public was learning to use its imagination meant that, sooner or later, the imagination would be harnessed for sexual purposes. This seems to have happened round about the year 1820. As far as we can judge from Spencer Ashbee's monumental *Bibliography of Prohibited Books* (1877), there was surprisingly little pornography produced in the sixty years that followed *Fanny Hill*. Works like *The Pleasures of Love* (1755) and *The Pupil of Pleasure* are obvious imitations of Cleland, with young rakes seducing various ladies; but they sound as if they might have been written a century earlier.

But by the 1820s, a new generation of pornographers was learning from de Sade as well as Cleland. In *The Bedfellows, or Young Misses Manual* (1820), two teenage girls who share a bed tell their amorous experiences each night, gradually becoming increasingly candid until they recount the story of the loss of their virginity 'in minute and voluptuous detail' (as Ashbee says). They also engage in lesbian activities. But comparison with *Fanny Hill* reveals an obvious difference. Cleland is a typical man of the eighteenth century: humorous, pragmatic, down-to-earth; the physical aspects of love seem to amuse him as much as they had amused Rabelais two centuries earlier. We feel he enjoyed practising sex as much as writing about it – probably more. The author of *The Bedfellows* is much more involved in his subject; the idea of two teenage girls losing their virginity obviously makes his mouth water. So the book has that feverish, obsessive quality that V. S. Pritchett observed in Samuel Richardson advancing on tiptoe towards the keyhole. The same applies to *The Lustful Turk* (1828), *The Seducing Cardinal* (1830), *The Ladies' Telltale* (1830) and other pornographic works of the period. The latter, subtitled *The Decameron of Pleasure*, describes a club in which all the members have to tell stories of their sexual experiences. The opening tale, 'Little Miss Curious', is typical. A ten-year-old girl spies on the butler between the chinks of his bedroom door, and watches him masturbating. One day, chasing a butterfly, she falls on a rake and loses her virginity; the butler extracts the stake and applies remedies to the wounded part, thus 'breaking the ice'. One day, he finds her asleep in the summerhouse in a position that exposes her genitals, and after some preliminary masturbation, he makes an attempt on her virtue. She wakes up, and he hastily hides his member away. But Little Miss Curious has no intention of being baulked; she unbuttons his flies, takes out his member, and brings him to orgasm. That night, at her request, he slips into her 'little bed' and makes a woman of her.

In another story, 'The Schoolmaster and Schoolmistress's Tale', the schoolmaster seduces the schoolmistress, then the two agree to co-operate in seducing their pupils. He hides behind the door while she administers a whipping to a young girl, then enters and begs her to stop. The schoolmistress allows herself to be persuaded to let him take the girl to his own room to give her a 'task'. In fact, he seduces her. Meanwhile, the schoolmistress seduces a shy schoolboy who is secretly in love with her. Finally, the schoolboy bumps into the newly deflowered schoolgirl as she leaves the schoolmaster's room, and they confide in one another. Then, in spite of feeling sore, she allows the schoolboy to repeat the lesson . . .

The whole point of these stories is to make the reader feel that sex is wickedly exciting, something to be associated with peeping through cracks in doors and masturbating in lavatories. Fielding or Smollett – or even Cleland – would have regarded such an attitude as sick. For them, sex was a down-to-earth activity which involved certain preliminaries and certain consequences – occasionally getting pregnant or catching pox. For the post-Sadian pornographer, it was a dreamlike activity with no more connection with reality than 'Monk' Lewis's world of demons or Hoffmann's fairy tales.

But from the vantage of the twentieth century, we can also see that it is simply a development of romanticism. As young Werther watches Lotte slicing bread and butter, he sees her as a kind of goddess; it would be only one step from this attitude to day-dreaming about removing her clothes. The same applies to the virtuous heroines of Jane Austen. The very fact that they wouldn't dream of speaking to a man without being introduced somehow makes them a far more suitable object for sexual fantasy than Moll Flanders or Fanny Hill. The more high-minded the Romantics became on the subject of 'the eternal feminine', the more they created a low-minded counter-reaction.

By the time the eighteen-year-old Queen Victoria came to the throne in 1837, pornography had become one of England's major imports. In 1853, an Obscenity Act enabled the Customs to seize indecent books and pictures; the result was a sudden growth in the home-produced pornography industry. Victorian prudery only intensified the pleasures of 'the forbidden'. There were even erotic magazines with titles like *The Pearl*, *The Boudoir* and *The Cremorne*. *The Pearl*, which ran for eighteen months from July 1879, reveals the increasing Victorian obsession with flogging and the deflowering of virgins. Its heroes and heroines are all – of course – sexually insatiable.

> Five times that night did I put her through the manual exercise of love, and five times did she die away in the most ecstatic enjoyments . . . It was with sincere regret that Madame le Maire parted from me at dawn of day to join her sleeping husband, to whose brows had just been added a pair of horns. They were short, to be sure, but there appeared every prospect of their branching to large antlers.

And when Walter takes his virginal cousin Annie for a country walk, she shows herself oddly complaisant for a well-brought-up Victorian miss. '"Annie! Oh! Annie!" I gasped. "Give me the tip of your tongue, love." She tipped me the velvet without the slightest hesitation, drawing at the same time what seemed a deep sigh of delightful anticipation as she yielded to my slightest wish.' A few minutes later they are engaged in mutual oral sex. Then, 'King Priapus having burst through all obstacles to our enjoyment', and 'the sheath being now well lubricated', 'we spent three or four times in a delirium of voluptuousness'. After her sixth orgasm, Annie sighs: 'Oh, can it be possible to hurt one's self by such a delightful pleasure?'

A story called 'Lady Pokingham or They All Do It' is lifted straight from 'Little Miss Curious's Tale'. But there is one significant difference. When the child Alice peeps through the crack in the pantry door, the butler, whose trousers are unbuttoned, is reading a volume of pornography. In the forty years since *The Ladies' Telltale*, pornography has become part of the Victorian way of life. This is the result of covering ladies with crinolines that trail on the ground, so that even the glimpse of an ankle is exciting, and of covering up table-legs with frills in case the very thought of legs should give rise to impure thoughts.

It is significant that *The Pearl* ran for only eighteen months; it was obviously impossible to go on inventing new sexual situations. After all, the basic act of love-making is crudely simple, and the number of 'forbidden' situations is strictly limited, as even de Sade discovered. *The Pearl* runs through every variation: schoolgirl lesbians, deflowering of virgins, many kinds of flagellation, child sex, group sex, voyeurism, incest, homosexuality; there is even a scene in which Dick Turpin and his men rape a coachload of schoolgirls. But long before the end, the sex has become almost arbitrary; the authors have run out of epithets and out of invention.

A decade later, the anonymous author of *The Power of Mesmerism* succeeded in devising a new situation. A young student learns the secrets of hypnosis in Germany and, when he returns home, uses it to seduce his sister. Then brother and sister acknowledge a sexual attraction towards their parents; he hypnotises them and then possesses his mother, while his sister is possessed by her father. At the crucial moment he wakes them up, and they are horrified to find themselves engaged in incest; then they decide that it is rather pleasant after all, and join their children in an orgy. In the remainder of the book, various other people are hypnotised – including the vicar and his two nieces – to 'the joint delight of his father, mother and sister'.

What this book makes clear is that the basic erotic fantasy is of some magical power to choose sexual partners at will. In de Sade's fantasies, this power is achieved by brute force; but the result is that his situations are nauseating rather than erotic. But the author of *The Power of Mesmerism* has penetrated to the true nature of sexual fantasy. Most human beings are not sadistic, so de Sade's novels would leave them cold. But all human beings are conscious of being surrounded by 'the forbidden'. The result is that most human beings, even the most respectable, are susceptible to 'magical' day-dreams of the forbidden. Many years ago, a Viennese publisher told the present writer how he had bought a copy of a famous pornographic novel, *Josephine Mutzenbacher* (attributed to Felix Salten, the author of *Bambi*), and how every member of his family – including mother and grandmother – had clamoured to borrow it. Similarly, Gurdjieff's follower, Fritz Peters, tells a story of how Gurdjieff invited a group of wealthy New Yorkers to dinner and, before they arrived, asked Peters to teach him every obscene Anglo-Saxon word he knew. Over dinner, Gurdjieff began to explain to his guests that most people are really motivated by their sex drives. He told a well-dressed woman that the care she took of her appearance was really a 'desire to fuck'. He began to speak of his own sexual prowess, using the words Peters had taught him. After the meal, the guests began to flirt with one another, and many were soon in a state of partial undress. Suddenly, Gurdjieff called them all to attention, then began to mock them, telling them that they now knew what kind of people they really were. He ended by asking for contributions to his Institute, and received cheques amounting to thousands of dollars. Gurdjieff was simply taking advantage of the universal human appetite that pornography is designed to satisfy.

It is doubtful whether Gurdjieff would have been able to achieve a similar effect with an audience of contemporaries of Fielding and Smollett; they would merely have chuckled appreciatively. But contemporaries of Dickens would certainly have been susceptible to the 'lure of the forbidden' (although Gurdjieff would have had to use a subtler technique to avoid shocking Victorian prudery). The century between *Tom Jones* and *David Copperfield* had produced a powerful sexual obsession, a morbid fascination with 'sin'. This is why, towards the end of the century, Freud was able to to obtain such a stunning effect with his crudely exaggerated theories about sex and neurosis; Victorian guilt made them horrifyingly plausible.

The history of pornography sheds a new light on the problem of human sexuality. It should now be clear, for example, that pornography is simply a special case of romanticism. Novalis and Hoffmann and Jean Paul created dream landscapes like nothing ever seen on earth; the Victorian pornographers created sexual fantasies that bear no resemblance to the reality of human relations. Ten-year-old girls do not really seduce the butler; shy virgins do not really fling themselves into sexual orgies; young students do not really use mesmerism to seduce their sisters and parents. Pornographers are simply low-minded romantics as opposed to high-minded romantics. While the high-minded romantics dreamed of 'the light that never was on sea or land', the low-minded romantics fantasised about the sex that never was on sea or land.

And when we compare Victorian pornography with the indecent books of the previous century, we can see clearly that something odd has taken place. As we read Fielding or Cleland, we are aware that sex is simply nature's device for propagating the race, and that sexual preference is also a purely biological affair. What a woman really wants from a male is not – as de Sade says – 'to be fucked from morning till night', but to be offered a secure and fruitful life. She sees him as a potential husband and a father for her children. And what a male wants from a female is not endless sexual ecstasy, but an interesting and stable relationship. Fielding and Smollett and Sterne – and even Cleland – never lose sight of this fact. The authors of *The Ladies' Telltale* and *The Pearl* lose sight of it on the first page, and we are invited to believe that all teenage girls are nymphomaniacs and that all grandfathers dream of incest with their granddaughters. Yet the result of these absurd premises is a certain feverish intensity which is as different from Cleland's down-to-earth bawdiness as the poetry of Keats or Shelley is from that of Dryden or Pope. We might say that Victorian pornographers learned the trick of producing 'superheated sex' as Victorian engineers learned the trick of producing superheated steam. They do this by a deliberate technique involving the use of the 'forbidden'.

Now we have already noted that, in human beings, the 'forbidden' plays the same role as the smell of oestrum in animals – the 'she-is-not-my-wife' effect. But there is obviously a basic difference. We have seen that a ram or bull will go on copulating indefinitely, provided it is offered a choice of new females on heat. But zoologists have not noted any increased *intensity* in the copulation with different females. As far as the ram is concerned, one sheep on heat is very much like another. On the other hand, all human beings seem to have the ability to vary the intensity of their sexual response by an act of imagination. In 1793, William Blake was writing:

The moment of desire! the moment of desire! The virgin
That pines for man shall awaken her womb to enormous joys
In the secret shadows of her chamber; the youth shut up from

The lustful joy shall forget to generate & create an amorous
   image
In the shadows of his curtains and in the folds of his silent
   pillow . . .

Blake obviously knew all about the use of imagination in sexual
fantasy.

In other words, human beings understand the use of imagination
to raise the pressure of sexual desire, to create 'superheated sex'.
And this offers an obvious explanation for what we have called 'the
Barbusse phenomenon' – the fact that Barbusse's hero is far less
excited by a prostitute than by a glimpse up a girl's skirt. The
distant glimpse of 'the forbidden' produces instant 'superheated
sex'. On the other hand, the actuality of intercourse with a prostitute
simply *fails to focus* his sexual imagination.

This notion of 'focusing' is obviously of central importance. It is
as if the human mind is a rather inefficient microscope. If we wish
to examine some tiny object, it will focus momentarily, then almost
immediately slip out of focus, so we see only a blur. The first time
a man makes love to a woman, his whole being seems to be
concentrated on her; the fiftieth time, she is little more than a blur.
But a touch of the 'forbidden' will instantly sharpen the focus. *The
Pearl* contains a chapter describing a girl's wedding night with a
worn-out lecher; after flogging her and sodomising her, he has her
penetrated by his servant while he sodomises the servant. We can
see immediately that it is not the man's body that has been worn
out by debauchery, but his imagination. The result: his sexual
desires need to be stimulated 'into focus' with heavy doses of 'the
forbidden'.

We can also see that this 'blurring' phenomenon will, sooner or
later, lead to sex crime. If a man is excited by a glimpse up a strange
woman's skirt and disappointed by the actuality of sex with a woman
he knows, then he may decide that the answer lies in sex with the
stranger; and since, by definition, she ceases to be a stranger the
moment she is willing to yield, then the logical solution would
seem to be sex without her consent.

Now, oddly enough, sex crime was rare in the eighteenth century. We have already seen that, in fifteenth-century Venice, 'sex
crime' meant adultery, fornication and homosexuality; there was
apparently no sex crime in the sense that the Marquis de Sade

would have understood the term. The same was, in general, true of eighteenth-century Europe. The first comprehensive account of crime in England, *The Newgate Calendar* (1774), contains almost no sex crime; the rare exception is a rape committed by a drunken man. *The Pearl* reprints an account of a trial of 1775 in which a certain Captain Powell lured Margaret Edson, a child 'under twelve', to his room and sodomised and raped her. Captain Powell was charged merely with common assault; evidently his crime was regarded as a misdemeanour.

One of the earliest known examples of true sex crime (if we except 'freak' cases like Ivan the Terrible and Gilles de Rais) is the case of Andrew Bichel, a professional fortune-teller who lived in Regensdorf, Bavaria. Very little is known of his motives for killing girls – since the court accepted his unlikely story that he did it for the sake of their clothes – yet it seems quite clear that he was driven by some perverse sexual urge.

Bichel, born about 1770, was apparently regarded as a model citizen, 'esteemed for his piety', although he had once been accused by an innkeeper of stealing hay from his loft. In 1807, a girl named Barbara Reisinger came looking for a job as a servant; according to Bichel, she was his first victim. Bichel promised to show her her fortune in a 'magic glass', but told her she must first be blindfolded and have her hands tied behind her. Then he stabbed her in the neck, cut the body in half, and buried it in the corner of the woodshed. The ease with which he had committed the murder made him decide to try it again. But his next three intended victims all failed to walk into the trap. It was not until the following year that he succeeded in persuading a girl name Catherine Seidel to have her fortune told, and to bring three changes of clothes. She was killed in the same way, dismembered, and then buried nearby. Major Arthur Griffiths, who recounts the case in *Mysteries of Police and Crime* (1898), states that there were other victims, but offers no details.

Fate took a hand when Catherine Seidel's sister happened to see a tailor making up a waistcoat from a piece of dimity that she recognised as being part of her sister's best dress. Bichel was questioned, and a chest full of women's clothes was found in his room, including some belonging to Catherine Seidel. Finally, a dog sniffing persistently in the corner of the woodshed led them to dig there. They found the remains of a body that had been cut in half. A head was found buried under a pile of logs, and another dissected body nearby. Bichel at first proclaimed his innocence, but in prison, 'his imagination overcame his obstinacy', and he confessed. He claimed that his motive was to steal the girl's clothes. The judge accepted this story, and Bichel was sentenced to be broken on the wheel; this was commuted, and he was beheaded.

Krafft-Ebing, who studied the case, had no doubt that Bichel was sexually abnormal. He quotes him as saying: 'I opened her breast and with a knife cut through the fleshy parts of the body. Then I arranged the whole body as a butcher does beef, and hacked it with an axe into pieces of a size to fit the hole which I had dug . . . I may say that while opening the body I was so excited that I trembled, and could have cut out a piece and eaten it.' Krafft-Ebing suggests that Bichel may have been guilty of acts of 'bestiality' with the corpse, such as wallowing in the intestines. But the fact that he kept the clothes of the women, rather than selling them, suggests that he may also have dressed up in them.

England's first sex murder occurred fifty years later, in 1867. On a Saturday morning in the July of that year, a young clerk named Frederick Baker, of Alton, Hampshire, persuaded an eight-year-old girl named Fanny Adams to leave her friends and go for a walk. He took her to a nearby hop-garden, then killed her, hacked her to pieces, and strewed the parts of the body over a wide area. When the girl's mother met Baker a few hours later and asked him what he had done with her daughter, he seemed perfectly calm, and assured her that Fanny had gone off to buy sweets. The lack of blood on his clothing suggests that he had stripped himself naked before killing the child. The dismembered body was soon found; the head lay on the ground, and the genitals proved to be missing. Baker's diary contained the entry: 'Killed a young girl today. It was fine and hot.' He was sentenced to death and hanged. The *Illustrated Police News*, which described the case in some detail, omitted the missing genitalia, and stated simply that Baker was suffering from 'mania'. It seems possible that the Victorians simply failed to recognise it as a sexual crime.

There were many similar sex crimes in the remaining decades of the nineteenth century. In 1871, a French youth named Eusebius Pieydagnelle went on a killing rampage after being forced by his father to leave his job in a butcher's shop to become apprenticed to a lawyer. Pieydagnelle admitted to becoming sexually excited at the smell of blood, which had led him to become a butcher's assistant. After leaving this job, he entered the bedroom of a sleeping girl, intent on rape, then noticed a knife and instead stabbed her to death. He experienced orgasm as he killed her. Pieydagnelle then committed six more murders – including the butcher who had employed him – before he gave himself up to the police.

In the same year, a twenty-two-year-old Italian youth named Vincent Verzeni was charged with two sex murders; he was mentally subnormal. In his confession, it emerged that he obtained sexual satisfaction from the act of throttling women, 'experiencing during the act erections and real sexual pleasure'. In August 1871 he attacked a 28-year-old woman in the fields and, after strangling her, cut open her abdomen and pulled out her intestines. The following day he made an attempt on the life of his nineteen-year-old cousin Maria, but she succeeded in persuading him to let her go. When he strangled a fourteen-year-old girl named Johanna Motta, he tore out the intestines and (as he later admitted) drank some of her blood. At the trial, it emerged that he had made several other attempts to strangle women, the first when he was eighteen; the victim on that occasion had been his nurse, who was ill in bed. He told the judge that he had first realised that he enjoyed strangling when he was twelve, when he found that it gave him sexual pleasure to throttle chickens. Verzeni was sentenced to life imprisonment.

In Boston, Massachusetts, in 1874, a fourteen-year-old youth named Jesse Pomeroy admitted to two murders of children – one of a four-year-old boy, one of a ten-year-old girl. He had already been arrested at the age of twelve for stripping two boys and flogging them with a knotted rope. Pomeroy – an exceptionally ugly boy with a harelip and a 'white eye' – was sentenced to life imprisonment.

It would, of course, be totally inaccurate to suggest that there was some connection between the rise of pornography and the rise of sex crime; there is no evidence whatever that Bichel or Verzeni or Baker had been influenced by pornography. All the same, we can feel clearly that sex crime was the end-product of a process that had begun with Richardson and Cleland. A *state of mind* had gradually spread until, to some extent, it affected every level of society. By the second half of the nineteenth century, imagination – which had seemed so harmless in *Pamela* – was suddenly revealing its darker and more disquieting aspects.

SEVEN

Victorian Misfits

On the afternoon of 4 August 1866, two men paused at a newspaper seller in Piccadilly to buy a copy of the *Saturday Review*. The taller of the two was a publisher's representative, James Bertrand Payne. The smaller man was a striking figure, with a huge aureole of red-gold hair, a receding chin, and shoulders that sloped so steeply that he looked like a walking wine-bottle. This was the twenty-nine-year-old poet, Algernon Charles Swinburne.

As Swinburne started to read, he suddenly burst into shrill shrieks of rage; an interested crowd began to gather. His companion tried to calm him, and ushered him into a nearby café. It was useless; as Swinburne went on reading, his face became as red as his hair, and his language became so foul that the waiters scurried for cover. Payne had to beg him to swear in French to avoid a scandal.

What Swinburne was reading was a review of his first volume of poems, *Poems and Ballads*, and it was brilliant and damning. The author was himself a rising young man of letters named John Morley. Swinburne, said Morley, 'deserves credit for the audacious courage with which he has revealed to the world a mind all aflame with the feverish carnality of the schoolboy over the dirtiest passages in Lemprière['s Classical Dictionary]. It is not everyone who would ask us all to go and hear him tuning his lyre in a stye.' What made Morley's review so damning was that he was obviously not some boring old conservative who was shocked by an audacious young poet. 'We should be sorry to be guilty of anything so offensive to Mr Swinburne as we are quite sure an appeal to the morality of all the wisest and the best men would be . . . But it may be presumed that common sense is not too insulting a standard by which to measure the worth and place of this new volume.'

Morley makes it clear that what shocks him about Swinburne is the distinct note of sadism and masochism:

> By the ravenous teeth that have smitten
> Through the kisses that blossom and bud,
> By lips intertwisted and bitten
> Till the foam has a savour of blood . . .

This was from a poem addressed to Dolores, 'Our Lady of Pain'. 'Faustine' was almost as bad:

> Stray breaths of Sapphic song that blew
>   Through Mitylene
> Shook the fierce quivering blood in you
>   By night, Faustine.
>
> The shameless nameless love that makes
>   Hell's iron gin
> Shut on you like a trap that breaks
>   The soul, Faustine . . .
>
> Red lips long since half-kissed away
>   Still sweet and keen,
> You'd give him – poison shall we say?
>   Or what, Faustine?

You did not even have to know that Mitylene was the birthplace of the lesbian poetess Sappho to guess that something wickedly indecent was being hinted at. Even the most innocent-looking poems might be booby-trapped. The beautiful 'Itylus', that began:

> Swallow, my sister, O sister swallow,
> How can thine heart be full of the spring?

was actually about a king who raped his wife's sister, then cut out her tongue so that she could not tell anyone; his queen avenged herself by killing their child Itylus and serving the father with his flesh for dinner.

In fact, Morley's murderous review had the effect of destroying the sale of *Poems and Ballads*, and temporarily destroying the poet's reputation. Swinburne – who was inclined to hysteria – thought it was the end of the world. It was not quite as bad as that. Although – as his friend Edmund Gosse remarked – *Poems and Ballads* roused a scandal unparalleled since Byron left England exactly half a century before, the younger generation read him avidly and, within two or three years, he was worshipped as if he was a god. He was certainly the Byron of this new generation, the fearless young rebel, advising the young to abandon

> The lilies and languor of virtue
> For the raptures and roses of vice.

Students at Oxford and Cambridge went around chanting aloud his magnificent rhythms:

> I will go back to the great sweet mother,
> Mother and lover of men, the sea.
> I will go down to her, I and none other,
> Close with her, kiss her and mix her with me;
> Cling to her, strive with her, hold her fast;
> O fair white mother in days long past
> Born without sister, born without brother,
> Set free my soul as thy soul is free.

In the long run, Morley's attack was the best publicity Swinburne could have wished for.

Morley was right, of course; Swinburne *was* a sexual pervert, although of a fairly harmless variety. Ever since he was a child, he had had an obsession with flogging – or rather, being flogged. Most of his biographers assume that this began at Eton, which was notorious for its 'swishings' – one headmaster was said to be more familiar with his pupil's behinds than with their faces – but it was almost certainly an inborn tendency. Long before he went to Eton, Swinburne and his cousin, Mary Gordon – three years his junior – used to play flogging games in which they pretended they were pupils at a school with savage disciplinary standards.

Swinburne was the child of aristocratic parents, his father an admiral, his mother, Lady Jane, the daughter of an earl. He was a strange child, physically frail yet wildly courageous – he once climbed Culver Cliff, eastern headland of the Isle of Wight, simply

to test his nerve. In 1849, at the age of twelve, Swinburne was sent
to Eton, where he lived with his tutor, James Joynes, and his young
wife. Joynes – who was twenty-five – had also been a pupil at Eton,
so it is just conceivable that he realised how much pleasure he was
giving Swinburne with his frequent birchings. He would prepare
the flogging room with burnt scent, or make Swinburne put eau-de-
Cologne on his face before being beaten – apparently with the aim
of increasing his sensitivity to the rod, although Swinburne found
that the scent greatly increased his pleasure. In later life, he
expressed nostalgia for the 'glorious Eton beatings', and was grateful
to his friend George Powell for a photograph of the flogging block
– although he complained that he would 'give anything for a good
photograph taken at the right minute – say the tenth cut or so'.

Sir Osbert Sitwell records meeting an octogenarian Etonian who
told him how the head boy had pointed out a little fellow with red
hair and said: 'Kick him if you are near enough, and if not, throw
a stone at him.' The old man added: 'I have often wondered what
became of him – his name was Swinburne.' Swinburne seems to
have been the kind of little boy that other boys disliked – withdrawn,
nervous, continually wrapped up in a dream world – he devoured
Dickens and Victor Hugo, and was enthralled by the world of
ancient Greece and Rome. He also read the Elizabethan dramatists,
lent to him by Joynes, who forbade him to read Ford's *'Tis Pity
She's a Whore* about a brother who makes his sister pregnant; we
can be sure that the prohibition led Swinburne to give the play his
special attention. He had four younger sisters, and later liked to
tell his friends that he had incestuous designs on all of them. (He
was also fascinated by Byron's affair with Augusta, and talked about
it *ad nauseam*, until his friend Rossetti remarked wearily: 'If Byron
fucked his sister, he fucked her, and there's an end of it.') He wrote
a play modelled on Tourneur's *Revenger's Tragedy, The Unhappy
Revenge*, in which (as he later explained) he tried to pack twice as
many rapes and three times as many murders. By the time he was
seventeen he was known as 'Mad Swinburne', and was apparently
removed from Eton by the mutual consent of his parents and tutor.

Inspired by the charge of the Light Brigade, he dreamed of
becoming a cavalry officer, but was dissuaded by his father, the
admiral. Instead, he went up to Oxford, where he learned to drink,
but also to work hard; his tutor was the great Benjamin Jowett,
who once told a young girl: 'My dear, you must believe in God in

spite of what the clergy tell you.' There Swinburne also met the 'pre-Raphaelite' painter and poet, Dante Gabriel Rossetti, who had volunteered to paint murals in the Union building, together with William Morris, Burne-Jones and other members of the 'Pre-Raphaelite Brotherhood'. They immediately welcomed Swinburne as a fellow spirit. But Swinburne's drunkenness and high spirits finally exhausted the patience of the authorities, and he left – much as he had left Eton – by mutual consent of his parents and his tutor.

In London in 1861, he met Richard Monckton Milnes, who later became Lord Houghton, author of a classic life of Keats. Milnes was a celebrated wit and an avid collector of pornography. It was Milnes who introduced Swinburne to the works of the Marquis de Sade, which became a lifelong influence. He also introduced Swinburne to the ferocious, scarred adventurer Sir Richard Burton, who seems to have regarded it as his life's mission to make the Victorians aware of the narrowness of their sexual morality by trying to draw their attention to the extraordinary sexual practices of savage tribes. (His wife burned most of his more bizarre manuscripts after his death.) He and Swinburne were fellow spirits; intellectually speaking, both were arrested at that adolescent stage at which anything to do with sex seems unutterably wicked and alluring. They used to withdraw into a corner at parties and talk in low voices, punctuated by shrieks of wild amusement.

Swinburne had never ceased writing. By this time he had already written many of the poems and ballads that were to outrage John Morley when they appeared five years later. He was also the author of an uproarious novel written in French, *La Fille du Policeman*, about how Prince Albert tried to stage a *coup d'état* against Queen Victoria, and a play called *La Sœur de la Reine*, in which Queen Victoria is revealed as a nymphomaniac who first lost her virginity to the poet Wordsworth. He also made an attempt to become a novelist, with a novel in letters called *Love's Cross Currents*, about two unsuccessful seductions, and an unfinished work called *Lesbia Brandon*, about a schoolboy who is endlessly 'swished' by his tutor who is passionately in love with the schoolboy's sister and dreams of flogging her as he beats his pupil's behind. He read chapters aloud to his cousin, Mary Gordon, and we may speculate that it inspired them to mutual swishings. *Lesbia Brandon* also contains a strongly incestuous element, as well as – as the title suggests – a lesbian theme. Swinburne remained fascinated by lesbians all his life.

But he was also writing a 'Greek' play, *Atalanta in Calydon*, and when it appeared in 1865 – when Swinburne was 28 – it received high praise from the critics. They were overwhelmed by the superb sense of rhythm, and by the obvious verbal mastery:

> When the hounds of spring are on winter's traces,
> The mother of months in meadow or plain
> Fills the shadows and windy places
> With lisp of leaves and ripple of rain . . .

And if it seemed to be full of a rather heavy sensuality, no doubt this was merely a reflection of the spirit of ancient Greece:

> For winter's rains and ruins are over,
> And all the season of snows and sins;
> The days dividing lover and lover,
> The light that loses, the night that wins;
> And time remembered is grief forgotten,
> And frosts are slain and flowers begotten,
> And in green underwood and cover
> Blossom by blossom the spring begins.

With rhythms so intoxicating, it would have been churlish to ask why winter should be a 'season of snows and sins', or precisely what he meant by 'time remembered is grief forgotten'.

The triumph of *Atalanta* made Swinburne more unmanageable than ever; he drank more heavily – usually brandy – and tried harder than ever to *épater* any *bourgeoisie* within hearing. Asked to meet Tennyson, Swinburne turned up half drunk; he strode between the respectfully standing guests, said a few brief words to Tennyson, then turned his back on him and retired to the next room, from which he proceeded to announce in his shrill, piercing tones the genius of William Blake.

Then, in August 1866, came the publication of *Poems and Ballads*. With horror, the Victorians realised that their neo-classical poet was an advocate of vice and profligacy, and disciple of the unspeakable Frenchman, Baudelaire. Morley's devastating review was a signal for the British press to turn on Swinburne; *Punch* announced that the true form of his name was obviously Swine-born. In America, Morley's review was reprinted, with the result that the American edition of *Poems and Ballads* sold out. But Swinburne's response to these attacks was to become more defiant than ever and to increase his intake of brandy. He was frequently brought home by cabmen or policemen at four in the morning, too drunk to stand upright. At the Arts Club in Hanover Square, he drank himself unconscious with dreary frequency, usually passing through a stage in which he talked in a loud voice about lesbianism, sodomy and sadism, or shrieked obscenities while he performed an impromptu dance like a demented puppet; in 1870, he resigned, in order to avoid expulsion. Admiral Swinburne was frequently summoned by telegram, and dragged the ailing prodigal back to the country for convalescence. In 1871 he was sent to recuperate to Etretat, on the Normandy coast, and found it so delightful that he bought himself a cottage, which he christened *Dolmancé's Cottage* after the chief libertine in de Sade's *Philosophy in the Bedroom.*

His career almost came to a premature close after a few days in Normandy; he went swimming when the tide was on its way out, and was swept out to sea. A coastguard heard his cries and was able to send a fishing smack to save him. Swinburne showed his appreciation of his rescue by telling the sailors how much he approved of the French Revolution, and reciting the poems of Victor Hugo until he was taken ashore.

The rescue was witnessed by an eighteen-year-old youth who wanted to become a writer, and he succeeded in angling an invitation to lunch; his name was Guy de Maupassant. Swinburne was sharing the Chaumière de Dolmancé with a friend named George Powell, a fellow devotee of the rod, and Maupassant speculated whether they were homosexuals. After lunch, a large portfolio of pornographic photographs was produced, one showing an English soldier masturbating. Maupassant concluded that if Swinburne and Powell indulged in sex, it was not with one another, but with a pet monkey named Nip, and with a handsome young house-boy. The next time he visited, Maupassant was served roast monkey for lunch – not Nip, but one obtained locally. He said the smell and taste was appalling, but he may also have been deterred by the flayed hand of a parricide, with dried blood stuck to the muscles, which also lay on the table. There is, in fact, no evidence whatever that Swinburne was homosexual, or even bisexual; the evidence of his poetry argues strongly against it. But with his adulation of de Sade, he no doubt liked to keep an open mind.

In London, one night in 1867, Swinburne answered a knock on his door and found an attractive American woman smiling at him; she said she admired his poems and had come to offer her body to the poet. Her name was Adah Mencken, and she was an American actress, at present appearing in London; her real name, oddly enough, was Dolores. In fact, she had been asked by Swinburne's friends to seduce the poet, one rumour asserting that Rossetti had paid her £10. She spent that night, and many subsequent nights, in Swinburne's rooms in Dorset Street, but is said to have returned the fee to Rossetti, admitting that she could not get the poet 'up to scratch', or convince him that biting was no real substitute for intercourse. Swinburne admitted to becoming excited at the view of her shapely behind, but this was undoubtedly connected with his flogging fixation. A photograph shows her seated in a chair while Swinburne stands beside her – she was a great deal taller than he was – with his eyes averted like a schoolboy receiving a dressing-down from the headmaster.

During the course of this affair, Swinburne was introduced to a brothel in Circus Road, St John's Wood, where statuesque and golden-haired young ladies were willing to pretend they were governesses and administered floggings, and where other young ladies were well paid to allow themselves to be beaten and generally humiliated. (One angry husband who had caught his wife with a lover agreed to forgive her on condition she went to Circus Road to be flogged.) Generally speaking, it seems to have been rather tame, although the sight of the diminutive naked poet, bounding around the room with mingled cries of agony and delight, pursued by a buxom wench wielding a cat-o'-nine-tails, must have been hilarious. But in 1868, when the demands of the procuress grew exorbitant, Swinburne abruptly broke with her establishment. The child in him wanted to indulge in fantasies of 'correction'; the adult objected to being taken for a fool.

During the 1870s, Swinburne's friends became deeply concerned about his drinking, as well as about the caricatures of him that were appearing in the popular press. Among these friends were his former Master, Jowett, the great Italian patriot, Mazzini – whom Swinburne worshipped – and his younger friend, Edmund Gosse. By inviting Swinburne to reading parties and other such functions,

Jowett gradually managed to impose some degree of moral restraint. He also made use of Swinburne's mastery of Greek, persuading the poet to revise Jowett's own translation of Plato. (There is an amusing story of Jowett administering a dressing-down to one of his pupils when there was a shriek of laughter from the next room, and Swinburne's voice shouted: 'Another howler, Master!' 'Thank you, Algernon,' said Jowett meekly, and closed the door.)

However, it was not Jowett, but a solicitor named Theodore Watts, who had the dubious distinction of 'taming' the poet. Their first meeting had been inauspicious; Swinburne had been dancing naked and chased Watts from the house. But Watts gave invaluable advice when Swinburne wanted to change publishers, and since they lived within a few doors of one another, they gradually became close friends. Watts was undoubtedly respectable; he had no taste for alcohol, flogging or the works of de Sade. But he had boundless admiration for Swinburne's genius. And when Admiral Swinburne died in 1877, Watts took over the role of the poet's rescuer after bouts of alcoholism, escorting him to Putney to stay with his sister and taking him for walks on Wimbledon Common. Swinburne had spent a great deal of money on brothels and brandy and, after the death of the admiral, suddenly realised that he might well end his days in poverty. That and a healthy instinct of self-preservation seem to have made Swinburne decide to give up the attempt to drink himself to death, and to accept Watts's offer of a home in Putney. In 1879, the two men moved their furniture from their London rooms and became tenants of The Pines.

And that, in effect, was the end of Swinburne's career as a major poet. Not that he ceased to publish; during the remaining thirty years of his life, he produced a dozen volumes of poetry and some excellent critical studies, many on great Elizabethan poets. But for the most part, the poetry was as flat and disappointing as that of Wordsworth's later years. In fact, there had already been a falling off in quality in *Songs Before Sunrise* (1871) with their political inspiration, and the *Poems and Ballads* second series (1878). Swinburne was the kind of poet whose senses needed stirring with unrequited love (perhaps his greatest poem, 'The Triumph of Time', was written after an eleven-year-old girl had rejected his offer of marriage) or with lurid day-dreams of Sadeian orgies. The peaceful, healthy life at Putney, with one bottle of beer a day, was good for his health but fatal for his genius. Watts (who changed his name to

Watts-Dunton, prompting Whistler's telegram: 'Theodore – what's Dunton?') went on to write a fine novel, *Aylwin*, but Swinburne, whose talents may have lain in the direction of the novel, preferred to work on turgid verse dramas. At seventy-three, Watts-Dunton married a girl of twenty-one, but Swinburne remained celibate. When he died in 1909 – the era of Shaw, Wells and Chesterton – most newspaper readers were probably surprised to discover that he had not died a quarter of a century earlier.

But Swinburne's problem was not merely that of a poet who goes into decline. More than any other poet, he symbolises the problem of romanticism itself. He had caught the 'spirit of the age' like a case of influenza – the spirit of outrageous pornography, of defiance of all authority, of endless sexual day-dreams. (He even contributed flagellation poems to *The Pearl* under a pseudonym.) But, unlike his mentor de Sade, he never made the slightest attempt to justify his case intellectually. The American poet Bayard Taylor described him as 'a wilful, perverse, unreasonable, spoiled child', and, like a spoiled child, he cared only for his own emotions. In *Poems and Ballads*, he expressed these emotions – the fascination with pain, wickedness and vice – with the naturalness of a child having a tantrum. The outrage he provoked led him to draw in his horns; in *Songs Before Sunrise* he tried to convince his critics that his rebelliousness was basically a concern for political freedom. But in private he continued to preach the total rebellion of de Sade. As late as 1876 he was writing gleefully to Milnes about accounts of massacre, rape and torture in Bulgaria by the Turks. One Turkish leader, Sadick Bey, was reported to have raped more than a hundred girls, and for the next year Swinburne's letters are full of delighted references to his new hero. Even the name (Sadique) seemed to indicate that he was a reincarnation of de Sade.

We can see that Swinburne was doing his best to avoid the fundamental question that was at least discussed obsessively by de Sade: that of 'the rights of others'. It is true that every individual seeks his own satisfaction. At the same time, we all recognise that this satisfaction should not be at the expense of others. De Sade's 'originality' lay in flatly denying this. He pointed out that animals eat one another, as we eat animals; we do this without moral misgivings because they are our 'inferiors', our 'subjects'. Then why can we not accept the logic of this atittude, and recognise that there is no moral reason why all 'rulers' should not use their human subjects for their own satisfaction, raping them, flogging them – even eating them? It is only hypocrisy to pretend that there is some absolute gap between human beings and cows . . .

The answer is obvious. A society run on 'Sadeian' lines would self-destruct within days. De Sade insists that the basic law of society should be 'Every man for himself'. In fact, he insists that this *is* the basic law of society, and that we are simply too cowardly to recognise it. This happens to be untrue; the very existence of language disproves it: it is an attempt to communicate, and presupposes a certain sympathy between human beings. The burglars, child molesters, rapists and murderers are basically nuisances, like members of a club who refuse to pay their dues; the sensible reaction is to expel them, or suspend them until they *are* willing to pay.

Swinburne's reaction to the attacks on *Poems and Ballads* reveals that he recognised this; he promptly 'paid his dues' with *Songs Before Sunrise*. But in private he continued to be the unrepentant devil's disciple, advocating revolt, tyrannicide, rape, flagellation and cannibalism – in short, his right to absolute selfishness. So, intellectually speaking, he remained in a state of suspended animation for the rest of his life, the spoilt child in him refusing to step aside for the adult.

At the time Swinburne was writing the *Songs Before Sunrise* a young Frenchman was confronting the same moral dilemma. A tall, round-shouldered young man named Isidore Ducasse was engaged in writing a long sadistic prose-poem called *Les Chants de Maldoror*.

There are those who write to gain the applause of men by inventing noble sentiments . . . As for me, I use my genius to depict the delights of cruelty . . . One should let one's fingernails grow for fifteen days. O, how sweet it is to snatch some child brutally from his bed . . . Then suddenly, when he is least expecting it, to plunge your long nails deep into his soft breast, in such a manner as not to destroy life; for should he die you could not later enjoy his sufferings. Then you drink the blood, passing your tongue over the wounds . . .

In 1869, Ducasse paid a Belgian printer to produce the book privately – he used the pseudonym Le Comte de Lautréamont – but the printer lost his nerve and refused to issue it. In the following year, the poet died of some unknown illness, at the age of twenty-four. Nine years later, the printer went bankrupt, and his successor found the unbound sheets and issued them. Lautréamont was much admired by Maeterlinck, Huysmans and Remy de Gourmont, and *Maldoror* became a minor classic. And at this point, someone discovered the only other work by Lautréamont, the preface to an unwritten book of poems. It displayed a complete change of heart, a return to traditional values. A letter written just before his death confirms this: 'I have now completely changed my method . . . from now on I will sing only of HOPE, FAITH, CALM HAPPINESS and DUTY.' Unfortunately, no one knows how the change of heart came about; it was not, as in the case of Swinburne, because of public outrage. We can only assume that, having poured his sadism, vampirism and urge to blasphemy out of his system, he recognised the impossibility and illogicality of maintaining 'the right to absolute selfishness' as a lifelong attitude.

The truth is that neither Swinburne nor Byron nor de Sade nor Lautréamont really believed in the 'right to absolute selfishness', as their lives reveal. When Swinburne fell in love with an underage girl, his response was not to kidnap and rape her, but to propose marriage. He may well have fantasised about kidnapping and raping her – de Sade most certainly would – but he knew that it was out of the question. And here we can see the essence of the problem. A man who is powerfully attracted by a pretty girl may day-dream of tearing off her clothes but, in practice, he knows that he has to persuade her to co-operate. It is, in effect, as if he has to establish a kind of telepathic link between them. And if the girl happens to be too young to respond, then he has to accept that she is beyond his reach.

As a curious – and rather gruesome – postscript to this discussion, we may consider the case of another Victorian 'misfit', Sergeant Bertrand of the 74th Regiment. In 1848, various cemeteries in Paris were raided by a man of peculiar sexual tastes. Newly buried corpses of young women – in one case a seven-year-old girl – were dug up and violated. When surveillance was increased, the necrophile simply moved to another cemetery. In later cases, he usually cut open the body and tore out the entrails.

One night, watchers who were keeping an all-night vigil in Père la Chaise cemetery saw a shadowy figure climbing the wall; they fired, but the man escaped. A torn scrap of uniform revealed that he was a soldier. A few days later, a gravedigger heard a sapper remark that one of their comrades, a certain Sergeant Bertrand, had been accidentally wounded, and was now in the Val de Grace military hospital. When confronted by detectives, Bertrand confessed to being the unknown violator of corpses, and was tried by a military court on 10 July 1849.

Bertrand was twenty-seven years old. He came from a peasant background and had spent some time in a seminary. He was known as a good soldier, highly popular with his comrades, although disinclined to engage in obscene talk – he was a regular churchgoer. But ever since childhood he had been the victim of intense sexual desires; in his teens he masturbated seven or eight times a day, and the sight of an article of female clothing was enough to induce an erection. He began to imagine being in a room full of women, and torturing and violating them. At the age of twenty-four, he began to ill-treat animals while masturbating. Then, in 1847, came the experience that led to his career of graverobbing. He was walking in a graveyard near Béré with a friend when he saw a half-filled grave; the gravediggers had left it during a shower. Bertrand made an excuse to get rid of his comrade, then returned to the grave and uncovered the corpse of a woman. He was in such a state of excitement that he began to beat the body with the shovel. A workman came to see what was happening, and Bertrand escaped over the wall. He sat in a nearby wood for hours in a dazed state. Two days later, he returned to the cemetery, dug up the corpse with his hands, and tore out the entrails.

During the next few months he dug up more corpses and masturbated over them. In November 1847 he performed the sexual act on the corpse of a sixteen-year-old girl, kissing and caressing it for a quarter of an hour. 'I cannot describe what I felt during that time. But all my enjoyment with living women is nothing compared to it.' (In fact, Bertrand had had many mistresses, and had always been found a satisfactory lover.) During the course of the next year, his destructive urges became more intense, and he hacked off heads and limbs. ('I wanted to annihilate them completely.') But if the corpses proved to be male, he turned away in disgust.

When he was possessed by the necrophiliac urge, no obstacles could discourage him. He once swam a freezing river in midwinter to get into a graveyard. On another occasion, he was shot by a booby-trap while climbing a cemetery wall, but still dug up and violated the corpse, afterwards mutilating it.

Bertrand was sentenced to a year in prison. After his release, he left Paris and disappeared.

Perhaps the most interesting feature of the case is that Bertrand was described as being of a gentle and sensitive disposition, and his statements about the case reveal an intelligence and lucidity above the ordinary. Here was a case of a man suffering from 'hypersexuality', who might well have become a rapist, but who resolved the conflict between his inborn sadism and his natural sensitivity by becoming a necrophile. It is clear that Bertrand would have rejected de Sade's doctrine of the right to absolute selfishness.

In 1862, when Swinburne regarded himself as a disciple of Rossetti, one of Rossetti's friends described him as 'the intolerable little prig'. The critical acquaintance was Arthur Joseph Munby, a minor poet and civil servant who was nine years Swinburne's senior. To his friends, Munby was known as one of those warm-hearted Victorian philanthropists who was also a good companion. In his diary, Munby records meeting in Oxford Street an eight-year-old boy who was trying to make his way back to Brompton Road with no money; the kindly Munby put him on an omnibus and paid his fare.

What few of his friends knew was that he had a positive obsession with working-class girls. His diary gives no hint as to how this originated, although it has been suggested that it was through seeing the legs of maidservants as they scrubbed the floor. The Victorians had little opportunity for casual sexual stimulation, which is why anything that involved nakedness – such as flogging – was likely to develop into a fixation. (The publication of Gladstone's diaries in 1974 revealed that even he read pornography and flagellated himself.) At all events, Munby spent a great deal of time engaging working-class girls in conversation and questioning them about their lives. But unlike Swinburne – whom he never came to like – Munby was not capable of regarding women purely as sexual objects. So instead of paying them for sex, he derived some kind of satisfaction from learning the details of their lives, which were often tragic. One girl had lost her nose in an accident, and was looking forward to having an artificial one that would fit on with a hook; she believed this would enable her to obtain work as a servant. Another had such appalling scrofula that she wore a kerchief over the lower part of her face, and was hoping to buy a mask to cover it entirely. In 1859, the thirty-one-year-old Munby went off to Boulogne for the weekend, merely to satisfy his passion for observing working-class girls. He was not disappointed. One twelve-year-old girl followed him along the cliffs asking for ha'pennies, and finally lifted her skirt to her waist. Munby's 'reproof' made no difference, and he had to drive her away. Another woman tried to pick him up and persuade him to go to a quiet corner of the beach; when Munby asked if she was married, she admitted she was, but said that her husband was away. (Munby refused, of course.)

What fascinated him, obviously, was that these delicious feminine creatures should be so 'available'. He describes walking along the beach with four shrimp-girls. 'On either side of [me] are two of the "softer sex"; yet these young ladies have no veils or parasols to keep the sun off, no gloves to nurse their hands, no dainty boots to protect their feet from the rocks . . .' And – the part that obviously delights him – 'below the waist, save a short kilt, she wears – nothing!'

Munby's sex urge does not seem to have been strong, but he was not entirely celibate. In 1854 – when he was crossing Grosvenor Street, he saw a tall, erect girl with rosy cheeks and a black bonnet, and spoke to her. She replied civilly, and they walked along in conversation. Her name was Hannah Culwick, and she was a servant girl from Shropshire; she was just twenty-one, five years Munby's junior. He began meeting her on her afternoons off, and made her describe in detail her day's work – he even persuaded her to keep a diary recording everything she had done. Hannah seems to have enjoyed playing this game. She used to sit at Munby's feet, black his boots – which always seems to have given him a fetishistic thrill – and call him 'Massa', as if she were a negro slave. She would sit on his knee and they would kiss; but for many years the relationship remained totally innocent. For Munby, the situation could not have been more delightful: a slim, attractive, 'ladylike' girl sitting adoringly at his feet, looking up to him as a kind of god, willing to endure any humiliation for his sake (such as hiding under beds and staying there for hours when visitors arrived unexpectedly, or following him patiently through the streets until they could find a quiet spot where they could talk). It is not clear when they finally became lovers, but in January 1873, almost twenty years after their first meeting, he married her, and she moved into his chambers in the Temple (Munby had been an unsuccessful barrister before he became a civil servant who worked for the Church Commissioners). But she continued to dress as a servant, and Munby liked her to look as dirty as possible. And in the evenings, when Munby went out to teach at the Working Men's (or Women's) College, which he had helped to found, or to mix with friends like Rossetti, Ruskin and R. D. Blackmore, Hannah helped him to dress, then sat quietly at home until he came back.

But Munby had been a bachelor too long to settle down as a married man. Strains in the relationship increased; in 1877 he went off for a continental holiday with one of his old male friends, and Hannah went back to Shropshire. They spent three weeks of October together in London, then she went back to Shropshire, while he acquired the tenancy of a farm near Pyrford, in Surrey. In 1888, his habit of accosting women of the streets nearly led to his being arrested on suspicion of being Jack the Ripper. In 1890, he retired from the Civil Service and moved down to his pleasant farm near Pyrford, where no one knew he was married; meanwhile Hannah lived on alone in a working-man's cottage at Hadley in Shropshire; in 1903, at the age of seventy, she moved into a semi-detached cottage in her home village of Shifnal, and Munby often came to stay with her – they made no secret of their marriage before Hannah's friends and family. And so, sadly, they ended their lives living apart. Hannah died at the age of seventy-six, in 1909. A few weeks before his own death at the age of eighty-one, Munby finally let his brother George into the secret of his marriage. Then, in January 1910, he died. It was more than half a century later that his diaries were examined by the author Derek Hudson, whose book *Munby, Man of Two Worlds* finally revealed the strange love-story of Hannah Culwick and her 'Massa'. Of the real significance of that love story we shall speak in a moment.

In 1971, a young experimental psychologist named Nicholas Humphrey went to Rwanda, in central Africa, to dissect some mountain gorillas which had been killed by poachers. And as he studied the gorillas in their natural habitat, on the slopes of a volcano, he became increasingly intrigued by one simple mystery. Apart from the chimpanzee, the gorilla has the largest brain – in proportion to its body mass – of any land animal. Yet the lives of the gorillas seemed incredibly simple: they did nothing but eat, sleep, and move on to new feeding grounds. Why did the gorilla *need* such a large brain? A bird evolved wings because of the need to fly; an elephant evolved its trunk in order to hold food. What was there in the simple life of the gorilla that required a highly evolved intelligence? Gradually, Humphrey began to see the solution. The most important thing in a gorilla's life is *its relation to other gorillas*. The family life of a gorilla is its equivalent of a university education; it learns everything it needs to survive from other gorillas. And if a university is to perform its task efficiently, it needs to run smoothly, without conflict. The gorilla's family life looks simple because the gorilla's social responses make it simple. Its sensitivity to the moods, feelings and reactions of other gorillas ensures a smooth and conflict-free existence.

In fact, Humphrey has probably stumbled on the answer to one of the greatest mysteries in the story of humanity: why man evolved his unusually large brain in the past half-million years or so. Zoologists have made all kinds of interesting suggestions, including the alarming notion that it was due to the use of weapons, and the need to co-ordinate the hand and eye when using a spear or a club. But Humphrey has almost certainly got it right: man's intelligence evolved because, as he began to live with his own kind in larger and larger groups, he had to become a skilled psychologist. It was necessary, in effect, to develop a kind of *telepathy* with other members of the group – a delicate and instant sensitivity to their feelings. The more a human being can place himself 'behind the eyes' of other people, the better his chances of survival and of success. This is why the nations we tend to regard as the most 'civilised' – for example, the Chinese and Japanese – display such a high level of social sensitivity.

Evolution favours social sensitivity. This is the ultimate objection to de Sade. A species that adopted de Sade's philosophy would be extinct within a few generations.

The same comment can enable us to understand why so many of the great Romantics, from Rousseau to Swinburne, lived unhappy lives. Their 'rebellion' led them to claim the right to absolute selfishness, and this led to personal complications which often had

the effect of poisoning their lives. Rousseau was weighed down by
a sense of guilt, of which he tried to unburden himself in his
Confessions. De Sade denied the guilt, but tacitly admitted it by
trying to disown his own work. The Byronic hero is weighed down
by a sense of sin and – worse still – of boredom and futility.
Swinburne's dazzling display of rebellion ended in forty years of
mediocrity. In each case, we can trace the unhappiness to the
philosophy of the 'right to selfishness' – even though, as we can
now see, the right to selfishness was really no more than a demand
for what Ibsen would later call the right to individual self-
development.

Yet Munby, who was as obsessed by working-class girls as Swinburne was with flagellation, led a relatively happy and fulfilled
existence. And, as the diary makes clear, this is because he never,
for a moment, entertained the notion that his sexual obsession
granted him some kind of 'right to selfishness'. His interest in
working-class women was satisfied by literally 'taking an interest'
in them, by getting to know them, by going to their homes and
drinking tea and dispensing half-crowns. It is true that his sense of
guilt led him to make the mistake of marrying Hannah Culwick
when it would have been far more sensible to leave things as
they were; yet, even so, the relationship remained satisfying and
affectionate. If intelligence is social sensitivity, then Munby was a
more intelligent man than Rousseau, Byron or Swinburne.

And this, oddly enough, also applies to Sergeant Bertrand. He
was born with powerful sadistic impulses, the desire to tear and
destroy. (He admitted at his trial that he could not even own a pipe
for more than a day or two without smashing it.) Yet it never
occurred to him to satisfy these impulses on other people – either
on the men under his command or on his mistresses, none of whom
suspected the violence beneath the surface. It was not until he
passed an open grave that he saw the means of satisfying his
obsession without harm to other people. The court recognised the
fundamental harmlessness of his horrible obsession by sentencing
him to only one year in prison in an age when a man who stole a
loaf might be deported to Devil's Island.

There was one nameless contemporary of Munby and Sergeant
Bertrand who chose to pursue his sexual obsession with a single-
mindedness that was unique, even among the Romantics. He is

nameless because his autobiography – *My Secret Life* – was published anonymously, and no one has ever cleared up the mystery of who wrote it. The problem is not particularly important – the author who calls himself 'Walter' has no intellectual distinction, and was almost certainly unknown to distinguished contemporaries like Swinburne and Munby. *My Secret Life* is nevertheless unique in being the only full-length autobiography ever written by a satyr – the male version of a nymphomaniac.

From internal evidence, we can deduce that Walter was born around 1825; his father seems to have been a wealthy businessman (he goes out of his way to suppress any details that might identify him) and, until he was twelve, Walter was taught at home by a governess. When he was in his early teens, his father came close to bankruptcy, then died after a long illness; for the next few years the family lived in reduced circumstances. But Walter's godfather left him a fortune, and Walter spent the first half of his twenties sowing his wild oats. He wasted his fortune and was forced to marry for money. This was a miserable period, and when he came into another inheritance, he deserted his wife and went off to the Continent looking for sexual adventures. She died while he was away, and he inherited her money. A few years later, he fell in love and married again; but although he professed to adore his wife, his mania for sex remained irresistible, and he continued his single-minded pursuit of casual experiences. Over the years, he had kept a kind of diary of his sex life, describing his encounters in detail. Sometime in the mid-1880s, he paid a printer in Amsterdam – or possibly Paris – to bring it out. Eleven volumes were printed over the course of ten years, by which time the author would have been in his seventies. It has been suggested that 'Walter' was Spencer Ashbee, the author of the *Bibliography of Prohibited Books*, but this seems unlikely; Walter's style is utterly without literary finesse, and suggests a man who had never bothered to acquire more than a minimal education.

The main interest of *My Secret Life* is that it was written by a man for whom sex was the most delightful and fascinating subject in the world; if he ever thought of anything else for five minutes, there is certainly no evidence for it. Sex is his holy grail, his equivalent of Novalis's blue flower. It would not be entirely inappropriate to call him 'the Saint of Sex', for it is obvious that sex possessed for him the fascination of a mystical vision. He admits that he himself finds it puzzling. 'Why . . . I have sought the . . . strumpets which I have done, I cannot explain, nor the frame of mind which led me into lascivious vagaries and admirations, fancies and caprices . . .' He was driven by the same irresistible urge that made Sergeant Bertrand uncover a corpse and beat it with a spade, and there were occasions when, afterwards, Walter experienced that same feeling of exhausted bewilderment that Bertrand describes after his first experience of necrophilia.

His sexual education began at the age of twelve; his instructor was his cousin, Fred, who seems to have been a coarse and nasty child. Inspired by Fred's 'bawdy talk', Walter lifted his baby sister's nightdress when she was asleep and examined her genitals; later, he and Fred crept into the bedroom occupied by Fred's sisters early in the morning, when the girls had kicked off their bedclothes, and succeeded in examining them at leisure; afterwards, back in their bedroom, they 'danced with joy'. On another occasion, he succeeded in catching a glimpse of his aunt in the nude. He makes the interesting observation 'These [sexual] feelings got intensified when I thought of my aunt's backside, and the cunts of my cousins, but when I thought of the heroines [in novels], it seemed strange that such beautiful creatures should have any.' Walter has, of course, put his finger on the very essence of the male sexual urge: the notion that women are somehow pure and untouchable, and that to be allowed the familiarity of love-making is therefore at once wicked and delicious. In his coarse way, Walter is as romantic as Byron and Pushkin. One day when he was ill, he lay with his head in the lap of a servant girl, and persuaded her to kiss him while he slipped his hand up her skirt. 'Then came over me a voluptuous sensation, as if I was fainting with pleasure, I seem to have a dream of her lips meeting mine, of her saying oh! for shame! of the tips of my fingers entangling in hair, of the warmth of the flesh of her thighs upon my hand, of a sense of moisture on it, but I recollect nothing more distinctly.' The same girl was persuaded to give him long kisses before he went to sleep, feeling his genitals while he groped under her skirt. This led Walter to discover the joys of masturbation. Soon after this, he pursued a seventeen-year-old servant girl called Charlotte, who would allow him to kiss her but resisted further liberties. Finally, when his mother was out, he succeeded in throwing her on the bed and, by luck rather than judgement, managed to take her virginity. 'The next instant something seemed to tighten round its knob, another furious thrust, – another – a sharp cry of pain (resistance was gone), and my prick was buried up in her . . .' A love-affair developed, which ended only when her parents began to suspect what was happening, and ordered her back home.

He lost no time in trying to seduce the cook, Mary, and after a long and hard pursuit, with many repulses, finally succeeded in possessing her on the sofa. 'What a heavenly sense of satisfaction at being up a cunt again.' (Walter is never less than brutally specific.) And eventually he was able to persuade Mary to accompany him to a 'house', where he discovered that she was a more skilled and accomplished lover than Charlotte. He was already developing some personal tastes. 'I loved to see a woman piddle, used to make Charlotte do it as often as I could, to place my hand under the stream, and feel it splash on my fingers.' And he remains extraordinarily frank and analytical about his feelings. 'Charlotte I loved, and used to feel as if she were part and parcel of me for life when I was up her; with Mary I thought of thighs, backside, cunt, and her other parts, without much liking her beyond the desire of spending in her.' Soon after this, Mary also left to return home.

Staying with his cousin, Walter learned that Fred had succeeded in seducing a farm girl. At the first opportunity, Walter hastened to the girl's cottage and offered her five shillings. He was so excited that he reached orgasm quickly, at which the girl said: 'Ye may ha' me agin an yer loike,' and aroused him to further effort with skilful manipulations. On a later occasion, she co-operated with him in the seduction of her sixteen-year-old sister. He took her virginity while she was drunk, and she fell asleep immediately afterwards, clutching in her hands the two sovereigns he had given her.

Back in London, he discovered a friend whose father owned a gun shop; from the basement, they could peer up through the grating at the women who stopped to stare in at the window. 'There were two states of the weather which favoured us; if muddy, women lifted their clothes up high. Having no modern squeamishness [1890 talking about 1840!], all they cared about was to prevent them getting muddy; and then, with the common classes, we got many a glimpse of the split. But a brilliant day was the best. Then the reflected light being strong, we could see higher up if the lady was in a favourable position . . .' During these sessions they would masturbate themselves, or one another. But Walter found this so frustrating that he occasionally flung his sperm violently upwards, hoping to make it reach 'its intended destination'.

Walter had by now discovered that in Victorian London most working girls were sexually available to a 'gentleman' with a few guineas in his pocket. (Standard cost for intercourse was five shillings.) Much of the contents of Volume One – and the subsequent ten – can be suggested by selective quoting of chapter headings: 'My second adultery – a poke in the open – clapped – a big cunted one – Charlotte reappears – Consequences – My first child – Cook Brown and housemaid Harriet – Charwoman and daughter – At a keyhole – A fat rumped Devonian – a bum-hole offered – Erotic madness – Remorse'. (Walter failed to acquire de Sade's taste for sodomy; after this experience he was physically sick 'and scarce slept that night for horror of myself'.)

The sub-headings of a subsequent chapter are almost a mini-novel in themselves: 'Sarah and Susan – At the keyhole – A village fair – Up against a wall – An unknown woman – Clapped again – My deaf relative – Some weeks' felicity – Sarah's secret – Susan's history – Sarah with child – Amidst black beetles – Susan's virginity – Susan with child – Sisters' disclosures – A row – A child born – Emigration'. The chapter describes his seduction of two sisters, the cook and housemaid, and we are struck by his incredible persistence – hours and hours of bending down at a keyhole to catch the briefest glimpse of pubic hair or urine splashing into a pot, days of careful planning to get the housemaid alone while the family are at church – for a few stolen kisses – endless lewd innuendo and 'baudy talk'. Both sisters were duly seduced, impregnated, and packed off to Canada. Soon after this, Walter came into his godfather's legacy, and decided that he had finished with 'harlots of small degrees', and would investigate more expensive whores.

One of his more successful experiments in this direction was with a French girl named Camille. 'Never had I seen a girl take off such fine linen before, never such legs in handsome silk stockings and beautiful boots . . . Then she sat on the pot, pissed, and looked at me, whilst I sat in fear, saying nothing, doing nothing, my cock shrivelled to the size of a gooseberry.' But the touch of a professional hand soon restores his potency, and 'I was on to her without uttering a word and had plugged her almost before I had said "no," which I had meant to say. What a cunt! What movement! What manner! I had till then never known what a high-class, well practised professional fucker could do. How well they understand the nature and wants of the man who is up them . . .'

He asks Camille to help him secure a virgin; she goes back to France, and returns with a handsome young girl called Louise. As Louise leans out of the window, staring at the sights of London, Camille softly lifts her skirt to give Walter a glimpse of the delights he is to be offered. 'The thighs finished me; I shoved my hands up Camille's petticoats on to her arse, got her into the bedroom, and with her clothes in a lump on her belly, drove up my prick, spending directly I got up her cunt.' A few days later, with Camille away, he gets Louise into the bedroom.

My prick moved forward, something which had tightened round and clipped it gave way; suddenly it glided up her cunt, still tighter I clasped her, as she moved with pain beneath me, my balls were dangling on her bum, my sperm shooting against the neck of her womb, and I had finished the toughest virginity I ever had yet. The job was done, months of anticipation, hopes, fears and desire were over; my prick was in the cunt of a French virgin, at a cost of two hundred pounds.

It is only at this point that he learns that Louise is Camille's sister.

Even for a volume of 'confessions', the coarseness of the languge seems unnecessary. It gradually dawns on the reader that this is an essential part of Walter's retrospective pleasure; he is trying to re-create his sensual enjoyment by conjuring it up in words; but words are clumsy and inadequate, so he is forced to exaggerate. 'A few minutes afterwards, that lucky lad's prick was in her virgin niche, her hymen was but a bleeding split, his sperm was sticking his balls on to her buttocks . . .' If, in fact, he was having an orgasm inside her, then his sperm would *not* be 'sticking his balls on to her buttocks', but, for Walter, this extra touch is necessary to bring the scene to life. For the same reason, he needs to hear women using Anglo-Saxon obscenities.

A desire came to make her youthful mouth utter baudiness.
'Say cunt, dear.'
'Cunt.'
'Say fuck.'
'Fuck.'

'You know what fucking is?'
'Putting that into this,' said she with a chuckle.

The girl, who is fifteen, is sent out to buy a French letter – in those days, a piece of sheep's intestine, obtained from the nearest slaughterhouse, and still warm.

'It don't feel nice,' said the girl.
A few shoves more, and I lost all prudence, pulled it off, and drove my naked prick with such a thrust up her little quim, that she cried out. Her cry of pain gave me pleasure, and fetched me.

It is soon apparent that it is Walter's *imagination* that is possessed by sex. 'After that I occasionally frigged myself at the privy, and used to picture to myself the girls sitting there, their clothes up round their rumps, and slightly up in front showing their limbs, and their piddle squirting . . .' It is difficult to imagine James Boswell or John Cleland working themselves into a state of excitement with such day-dreams, for the eighteenth century had not yet arrived at the notion that what happens in lavatories is 'forbidden'. Even de Sade would have felt that it was a little *infra dig*. But Walter, in the mid-1840s, has been affected by the 'spirit of the age', by *The Lustful Turk* and 'Little Miss Curious' and *The Amatory Experiences of a Surgeon*, and the very sight of a keyhole induces a Pavlovian stirring in the genitals. He is a lifelong victim of the Coolidge effect. 'When I came to London, Camille received my attentions but I was not constant to her, for a change of women was necessary for me.' The absurdity is that this obsessive desire for change brings no satisfaction. 'I longed for one woman whom I could like better than the others, and go to when tired of strangers . . .' But even when he found her – his second wife – he remained a slave to the old craving for strangers.

In Walter we can see a highly developed example of the imaginative sexual obsession that would bring the era of sex crime. Locked in an asylum, like de Sade, the result would probably have been full-fledged sexual perversion. But since he was at liberty, he was able to indulge an almost pathological craving for sexual variety. As early as Volume Three he is explaining: 'I don't know why my erotic fancies took the desire for a young lass, but they did. My taste had for the most part run upon the big, fleshy, fat-cunted, and large-arsed; now, perhaps for contrast, perhaps from sheer curiosity, the letch took possession of me. A small cunt, tight and hairless perhaps – I wondered how it looked and felt, and if pleasure would be increased by it . . .' He passes two girls in the street, the elder fifteen, and invites them into the nearest bawdy-house; there he possesses the elder of the two. Then, although he finds the other one ugly, he finds himself attracted by the thought that she is probably a virgin. He persuades her to undress. 'My eyesight failed me, the demon of desire said, "It's fresh, it's virgin – bore it, – bung it, – plug it, – stretch it, – split it, – spunk in it."' Finally,

in my blind battering I at last lodged the tip well between the lips. The next instant with a cunt-splitting thrust I was up the howling little bitch who wriggled like an eel; but I held her skinny arse up to me like a vice, kept my leg fixed and unmovably up her in spite of her. Her wriggles alone would have kept it stiff enough, and fetched me. 'Be quiet, – I am up you, – I can't h-hurt – you, – ah!' – and my spunk was up the virgin quim of the ugly little devil.

And when it is over, he and the other girl look up 'the little quim bunged up with sperm mixed with blood'. For Walter, this is obviously a supreme moment; he has not only achieved his satisfaction; *he has succeeded in becoming conscious of having achieved it*. And this is the mainspring, not only of Walter's sex drive, but of the whole 'superheated' sex drive that produced nineteenth-century pornography and the rise of sex crime. Walter's most powerful craving is not for sexual experience, but for *consciousness* of sexual experience. There is a scene in Volume Two in which he describes picking up a forty-year-old woman and a ten-year-old child, and going home with them. He then has intercourse with the child standing in front of a mirror, 'holding her like a baby on me, her hands round my neck, she whining that I was hurting her . . .' The scene is symbolic; he needs to *see* what is happening, to convince himself that it is really happening. And suddenly we become aware of the inner meaning of this 'superheated' Victorian sexuality. Animal sex is unreflective, a mechanical response to the smell of oestrum; but in de Sade and Swinburne and 'Walter', sex is striving to become *self-reflective*. Animal sex is a simple physical pleasure, like eating or sunbathing; the Victorians had learned to turn it into a *mental* experience, like appreciating poetry or listening to music. Animal sex is a passive experience; the Victorians were trying to use it as a device for the control of consciousness.

This explains the sheer repetitiveness of Walter's pursuit of sex. Because he achieves the 'self-reflective' experience, the sense of total control, only at long intervals, he keeps pushing at the same lever, so to speak, like a laboratory rat trying to release a food pellet.

His experimentalism has its origin in the same source. He may experience a 'sudden letch' for a young girl, for a pregnant woman, for two women at the same time, even for an old woman, and almost without exception he finds it disappointing. (After his session with the ten-year-old girl, he admits that it 'could not give the pleasure that a fully developed woman could'.) Worse still, it often leaves him in a state of violent self-disgust. In Volume Eight he describes his experiments with a man, ending with sodomy. 'A fierce, bloody minded baudiness possessed me, a determination to do it – *to ascertain if it was a pleasure*' [my italics]. In the act of orgasm, 'I shouted out loudly and baudily (Sarah told me), but I was unconscious of that.' And as soon as it is over: 'I had an ineffable disgust at him and myself – a terrible fear – a loathing – I could scarcely be in the room with him . . .' Walter recognises that he is subject to 'erotic madness' when, like the votaries of Dionysus, he is possessed.

Here again Walter makes us aware of the essence of human sexuality, and of sexual 'perversion'. There is a sense in which physical intimacy is not natural to human beings. Scott Fitzgerald captures its intensity in a passage in *This Side of Paradise*, in which two children are 'spooning'.

She slipped her hand into his, her head drooped against his shoulder. Sudden revulsion seized Amory, disgust, loathing for the whole incident. He desired frantically to be away, never to see Myra again, never to kiss anyone; he became conscious of his face and hers, of their clinging hands, and he wanted to creep out of his body and hide somewhere safe out of sight, up in the corner of his mind.

'Kiss me again.' Her voice came out of a great void.

'I don't want to,' he heard himself saying. There was another pause.

'I don't want to!' he repeated passionately.

Most children find the idea of 'French kissing' disgusting – the mingling of saliva. Most of us can recall experiencing disgust on first reading Joyce's *Ulysses*, with its description of Marion Bloom forcing chewed seed-cake out of her mouth into her lover's, and of Mr Bloom kissing her behind with its 'yellow smellow furrow'. Yet adults may perform these or similar sexual acts without revulsion; the reproductory instinct has caused the 'distaste for the alien' to evaporate. The sexual impulse has the power of producing 'erotic madness', of overwhelming the usual bounds of personal consciousness, and creating something akin to the mystical experience – a sense of total affirmation.

And this, we can now see, is the key to the Marquis de Sade. The sheer violence of his work is otherwise baffling – surely he cannot *really* expect us to become sexually excited at the idea of torturing someone or burning them alive? The answer is no, he doesn't *really*; de Sade is not writing about the real. He is trying to conjure up reality *through the medium of language*, and the language has undergone a certain inflation. De Sade's language is an attempt to flog his imagination into a certain response. Like the hero of Barbusse's *L'Enfer*, he feels that 'These words are all dead – they leave untouched, powerless to affect it, the intensity of what was.' And his quest for 'the intensity of what was' leads him to exaggerate, just as Walter is forced to exaggerate. ('It's virgin – bore it – bung it – plug it – stretch it – split it.') De Sade's violence reminds us of a singer trying to reach a high note that is beyond the range of his voice.

Now, in fact, both de Sade and Walter behaved rather better than they admit. De Sade made no attempt to revenge himself on his mother-in-law; Walter often behaved with decency and generosity. They saved their brutality for the realm of language. But then, both were 'gentlemen', who had been taught to express themselves. It was inevitable that those who were less fortunate should be tempted to cross the gap that divides sexual fantasy from sex crime.

*

Early in the morning of 31 August 1888, a carter named George Cross was walking along Bucks Row, Whitechapel – in London's East End – when he saw what he thought was a bundle of tarpaulin lying on the pavement. It proved to be a woman with her skirt above her waist. In the local mortuary, it was discovered that she had been disembowelled. Mary Ann Nicholls was almost certainly the first victim of the sadistic killer who became known as Jack the Ripper. (He provided himself with the nickname in a series of letters that he wrote to the Central News Agency.) Just over a week later, he killed and disembowelled a prostitute named Annie Chapman in a Whitechapel backyard. On the morning of 30 September, he was interrupted soon after he had cut the throat of a third victim – a woman called Elizabeth Stride – and immediately went and killed and then disembowelled another woman, Catherine Eddowes. On the morning of 9 November, he committed his last murder indoors, and spent hours dissecting the body of Mary Kelly by the light of a pile of rags burning in the grate. By this time Londoners were in a state of hysteria, and the Chief of Police was forced to resign. But the Whitechapel murders were at an end.

Jack the Ripper certainly qualifies as an archetypal sexual misfit – he was driven by Walter's 'erotic madness', a 'fierce, bloody minded baudiness' – and it is regrettable that we have no clues to his identity. But from what has been said already, we can make certain statements with a fair degree of certainty. All theories suggesting that the Ripper was a 'gentleman' – an insane doctor, a cricket-playing lawyer, a member of the royal family – are almost certainly wide of the mark.* The kind of frustration that produced the Ripper murders is characteristic of someone who lacks other means of self-expression, someone who is illiterate or only semi-literate. Such a suspect came to the attention of Daniel Farson after he had directed a television programme about Jack the Ripper.† He received a letter (signed G.W.B.) from a seventy-seven-year-old man in Melbourne, Australia, who claimed that his father had confessed to being the Ripper.

> My father was a terrible drunkard and night after night he would come home and kick my mother and us kids about something

* See *Jack the Ripper: Summing Up and Verdict* by Colin Wilson and Robin Odell, 1987

† *Jack the Ripper* by Daniel Farson, London, 1972, p. 108

cruelly. About the year 1902 I was taught boxing and after feeling proficient to hold my own I threatened my father that if he laid a hand on my mother or brothers I would thrash him. He never did after that, but we lived in the same house and never spoke to each other. Later, I emigrated to Australia . . . and my mother asked me to say goodbye to my father. It was then he told me his foul history and why he did these terrible murders, and advised me to change my name because he would confess before he died.

He goes on to explain: 'He did not know what he was doing but his ambition was to get drunk and an urge to kill every prostitute that accosted him.' Whether or not G.W.B.'s father – whose job was collecting horse-manure – was Jack the Ripper, he is certainly a far more likely suspect than a member of 'Walter's' social class.

To us, it seems obvious that Jack the Ripper's murders were sex crimes (for example, the impulse that drove him to seek out another victim when he was interrupted while killing Elizabeth Stride). But it was by no means obvious to the Victorians, who preferred to think in terms of religious mania and 'moral insanity'. Sexual murders were a new phenomenon in the 1880s, and the average Victorian still found it puzzling that anyone should want to kill for the sake of sexual satisfaction.

The Whitechapel murders changed all this: they produced a deep disquiet, a morbid thrill of horror that made the name of Jack the Ripper a byword all over the world. It was an instinctive recognition that some strange and frightening change had taken place. In retrospect, we can see that the Ripper murders were a kind of watershed between the century of Victorian values and the age of violence that was to come.

EIGHT

Guilt and Defiance

In 1886, the year when *Psychopathia Sexualis* made such a sensational impact in Germany, a young Viennese doctor named Sigmund Freud was studying under the great Charcot at the Salpêtrière in Paris. Freud, an intensely ambitious man, had already achieved a certain dubious notoriety by publishing a paper in which he recommended cocaine – 'the magic substance' – as a general cure for all kinds of illness, without recognising that it was a dangerous drug. So when he went to Paris he was already under something of a cloud.

Jean-Martin Charcot was at that time perhaps the most famous 'mind doctor' in the world – he was even known as the 'Napoleon of Neuroses'. Four years earlier, he had delivered a remarkable lecture which had converted the Academy of Sciences to the controversial practice of hypnosis – a subject that had been regarded with disfavour since the days of the 'charlatan' Mesmer. Charcot had tried hypnosis on hysterical patients and found that it worked – that, for example, a man suffering from 'hysterical paralysis' of the arm could be cured by hypnotic suggestion. Now Charcot gave spectacular lectures in which hypnotised patients would bark like dogs, flap their arms like birds, or eat a piece of charcoal when told that it was chocolate. Freud was overwhelmed. He wrote home: 'I sometimes come out of his lectures as from out of Notre Dame, with an entirely new idea of perfection . . .' And when Freud translated one of Charcot's books, the two men became close personal associates.

When Freud returned to Vienna in April 1886, he was brooding on a profoundly important problem. How *could* hysteria – or hypnosis for that matter – cause such remarkable physical effects? How, for example, could it make a woman's stomach swell up into

GUILT AND DEFIANCE · 173

a 'hysterical pregnancy' that looked indistinguishable from the real thing? And how could a hypnotised patient, who had been told that a piece of ice was a red-hot poker, develop a real blister? Surely there must be some part of the mind that was far more powerful than everyday consciousness? Freud created a revolution in psychiatry by labelling this part of the mind 'the unconscious'. The unconscious mind could be compared to the ballast in a ship; no one can see it, and it has no obvious effect; yet without it, the ship would overturn in the first high wind. But – more important – if something causes the ship's ballast to move, it can cause the ship to heel over, or even overturn. This, Freud recognised, is what had happened to Charcot's hysterical patients.

It was when he came to think about the exact nature of this ballast that Freud reached his most controversial conclusion. Before leaving for Paris, he had been greatly intrigued by a case that was treated by his colleague, Josef Breuer. A young girl called Bertha Pappenheim had developed strange hysterical symptoms after the death of her father. She had turned into two personalities, one of whom spoke only English; this *alter ego* would suddenly take over, and perform thoroughly irrational acts. One night when Breuer was called to her bedside, her hips were gyrating up and down in wild convulsions, as if in the throes of sexual intercourse. This convinced Breuer that she had sexual designs on him, and he hurriedly left Vienna the following day.

Freud had also been deeply struck by a remark made by a colleague about a hysterical female patient: that what she really needed was 'repeated doses of a normal penis'. He began to develop a frightening conviction that sex lay at the root of all neuroses. And it *was* frightening, for it could easily mean his professional ruin. Emperor Franz Joseph's Vienna was as prudish as Queen Victoria's London; sex was not a subject that was ever mentioned in decent family circles. When he first began to develop the 'sexual theory', Freud must have felt as if he was holding an unexploded bomb, an idea whose implications could undermine civilisation. He had come to believe, for example, that most neurotic women have been seduced by their fathers when they were children. He had come to believe that children are interested in sex at a far earlier age than we suppose, and that sons and daughters are likely to fall in love with the parent of the opposite sex. As Bertha Pappenheim had sat by the bedside of her dying father, she had dreamt that a black snake was writhing towards him; Freud suspected that the snake was a symbol of the father's penis and that Bertha unconsciously wanted her father to become her lover; later, she transferred this feeling to Breuer . . .

In fact, most of Freud's patients seemed to enjoy answering questions about their intimate sex lives, and many women assured him that they *had* been seduced by their own fathers – it was only later that Freud realised they were fantasising. Finally convinced of the truth of the 'sexual theory', Freud began to publish it in works like *Studies in Hysteria* (with Breuer) and *The Interpretation of Dreams*. The scandal was as great as he had anticipated, and he soon became one of the most controversial – and hated – men in Vienna. Even Breuer felt that Freud was going too far in stating that sex was the basis of *all* neurosis, and the two men ceased to be friends. Other colleagues simply accused Freud of being incurably dirty-minded. But because sex had been regarded as unmentionable for so many years, its sudden eruption into a scientific respectability made an impact that sent tremors across the civilised world. More than any other single event, it signalled the end of the Victorian era.

Krafft-Ebing regarded Freud as a natural ally and supported his promotion to a professorship at the University of Vienna. Freud in turn had no doubt that Krafft-Ebing's cases were 'new valuable evidence of the soundness of my material'. Oddly enough, the two men shared the same rather puritanical attitude towards sex; Krafft-Ebing was inclined to explain perversion in terms of 'hereditary taints': alcoholism, syphilis, epilepsy, insanity and so on. We feel that his attitude is tolerant but mildly disapproving, like a defence lawyer with an incorrigible client. Freud also held a rigidly moral attitude towards sex. His own sex life with his wife Martha came to an end at a fairly early stage, according to his biographer, Ernest Jones: and he would certainly have been shocked, if not surprised, to learn that his follower, Jung, made a habit of having affairs with his patients.

Freud's problem was that, like some religious prophet, he insisted on imposing his own interpretations on his patients. He became convinced, for example, that a seventeen-year-old girl called Dora was in a repressed state of love for Herr K., a friend of her father's – whose wife was committing adultery with Dora's father. He told Dora that a recent attack of appendicitis was a hysterical symptom representing her defloration by Herr K. Dora expressed disbelief, but Freud insisted, pounding away with his own interpretations until she was subdued and acquiescent. But she became sick of this bullying and terminated her analysis. Freud had become so hypnotised by his own sexual theories that he became incapable of objectivity – and, very often, of common sense. In the case of a four-year-old child named Little Hans, Freud decided that the boy's phobia about being bitten by a horse was not – as seemed plain enough – because someone had warned him that a horse might bite off his fingers, but because he wanted to sleep with his mother and was jealous of his father's penis. Little Hans recovered without Freud's help.

Another school of 'sexologists' took a more objective and flexible approach. Alfred Binet's starting point was fetishism (a word he coined), and he pointed out that it was a simple matter of association of ideas, like Pavlov's conditioned reflexes. If a man comes to associate sexual excitement with a girl's underwear, or her shoes, or her hair – or, for that matter, his mother's nightcap – then these things will produce the same desire as the naked girl. The key lies in the concept of sexual starvation; the overflowing impulse will brim over and carve its own channels. Binet pointed out that the same thing applies to sadism and masochism. A younger colleague of Freud's, Albert Moll – who criticised Freud's sexual theories and was consequently detested by him – seized on the concept of romantic imagination, giving as examples the feelings of the nine-year-old Dante for Beatrice, or the eight-year-old Byron for Mary Duff. His starting point was what he called the 'detumescent drive'. He recognised that sexual desire begins with a pleasant tingling of energy in the genitals, and a desire to discharge this energy – and produce detumescence – by bringing the genitals into intimate contact with the desired object. Nature obviously intended this object to be the genitals of a member of the opposite sex. But sexual desire may begin long before this is possible – Moll cited a seven-year-old girl who indulged in mutual sex play with her three-year-old brother. So the sexual object may be *anything* that is associated with a desired person, or even with the very idea of sex and the 'forbidden'.

In fact, a moment's thought will show us that this 'fetishistic' mechanism will, by its very nature, soon produce all kinds of new varieties of sex. 'Normal' sex depends upon the mutual attraction of two consenting parties, but neither of them may regard the other as an ideal partner. But the fetishist can achieve full satisfaction with some item belonging to a girl he regards as otherwise unattainable, which means that his 'conquests' are limited only by his imagination. 'Walter' was rich – and attractive – enough to spend his life in sexual experimentation; the fetishist can perform all these experiments in his own mental laboratory. If Byron had been a fetishist (as Hirschfeld suggests Goethe was), he could have 'possessed' Mary Duff without her even suspecting it.

It seems strange that none of the 'sexologists' recognised the obvious and simple fact that most of the perversions they were writing about dated from their own century. Indeed, Krafft-Ebing was inclined to obscure this fact by talking about the sadism of the Roman emperors, or the widespread immorality of the seventeenth and eighteenth centuries. But we have only to glance through a dozen pages of *Psychopathia Sexualis* to see that most of the cases are unique, and that they are the result of Moll's 'fetishistic mechanism' – of *imagination* producing new and strange varieties of perversity. We read of a man who masturbates while caressing a furry dog, of a man who wants to be masturbated by a prostitute with mud on her fingers, of a girl who wants to perform anilingus on old men, of a man who wants to watch a prostitute torturing rabbits, and so on. The variety is due to the fact that the imagination is *free to choose* what will produce sexual satisfaction. And before the nineteenth century, men had simply not learned to use their imaginations in this way.

Moll's recognition of the role of sexual energy was an enormous step forward in the understanding of sexual perversion. Krafft-Ebing, as we have seen, was inclined to regard it as hereditary – which begged the question of how it came about in the first place. Hirschfeld, when he first came to write about it in 1896, was inclined to look for the cause in the brain and the endocrine glands. But Moll recognised that the basic sexual urge is a matter of a certain energy that expresses itself through the genitals. It is only one step from this to recognising that the agency that directs the flow of this energy is the imagination.

Most children who have attended a chemistry class will recall a device known as a Kipp's Apparatus, which produces carbon dioxide. When a tap is turned, gas pressure is released, allowing acid to flow into a vessel containing marble chips. The mixture turns into a seething mass, which produces carbon dioxide. When the tap is closed, the carbon dioxide builds up, driving the acid out of the vessel containing the marble chips. A similar process occurs in sexual excitement. In animals, the smell of oestrum acts as the acid. But in human beings, the imagination alone can release the acid into the marble chips. When Cleland produced *Fanny Hill* he had, in effect, invented a Kipp's Apparatus for producing instant sexual excitement. ('Walter' liked to put an illustrated edition of the book into the hands of servant girls he wanted to seduce.)

But *Fanny Hill* only emphasises the strange freedom of the human imagination. With his vast library of pornography, Monckton Milnes could *choose* his sexual stimulant. Did he wish to be excited by fantasies of flogging? Or of rape? Or of seduction of schoolgirls? Or of incest? Or sodomy? Or de Sade's hundred forms of sexual violence? He was like a drinker faced with a wide variety of wines and liqueurs. Yet all this only emphasises that the human mind is, in *itself*, a kind of Kipp's Apparatus. Animals need to have the 'acid' introduced by an external source – the smell of the female on heat. The human Kipp's Apparatus is complete in itself. *We* add the acid by an act of choice.

This insight affords us a glimpse into the basic mechanism of 'perversion'. We might say that, for a god, the sexual response is entirely physical, while for the fetishist it is entirely psychological. But the normal human being lies somewhere between these two extremes. A man in bed with a woman is responding to her femaleness, but he reinforces this with a certain psychological element. Like Walter, he tries to grasp his situation *imaginatively*. And we have already seen that even Walter, with his hyperactive sex drive, has to reinforce his desire by *telling* himself what is happening – or, better still, getting his partner to tell him. ('Where is my prick?' 'In my cunt.')

An unintelligent man with a strong animal sex drive needs very little of this reinforcement. A more sensitive or imaginative man may need a great deal. And in certain cases, the 'fetishistic' response may outweigh the purely physical response. This is clearly what happened in the case of Carl Hajdu. Although sexually 'normal', he had a powerful fetishistic response to 'intimate' female clothing. So when he sat in bed, covered with his girlfriend's silk dressing gown, he experienced sexual excitement even though the girl herself was on the other side of the room making coffee. But this was still 'normal' – the girl was present. But when his girlfriend failed to keep an appointment, and he put on the stockings he had bought for her, the fetishistic element had outweighed the 'normal' element. And it is easy to see how the same mechanism led de Sade to become a sadist, Swinburne to become a masochist, Bertrand to become a necrophile, and so on.

The same process can clearly be seen in the case of the most influential 'sexologist' of the early twentieth century, Havelock Ellis. Ellis, who was born in 1859, was troubled during his adolescence by seminal emissions during sleep, and he decided at the age of sixteen to devote his life to the scientific study of sexuality. But what really troubled Ellis was his own 'little perversion', urolagnia, or a desire to watch women urinate. This originated when he was a child and he and his mother were walking in the gardens of the Regent's Park Zoo; she stopped, and he heard the splash of water and saw his mother squatting over a puddle. She murmured shyly: 'I did not mean you to see that,' but Ellis comments in later life that it would have been perfectly easy for her to have gone to the nearest 'Ladies'. And some time later, she made him stand guard while she urinated in the bushes. From this time onward, young Harry (as he was known to his family) was obsessed by what he later called 'golden streams'. (When Ellis later told his sister about these events, she commented perceptively: 'She was flirting with you.')

Ellis grew up to be an intensely romantic young man, inclined to worship every pretty girl as an embodiment of the Eternal Feminine. But he was doubtful about his own attractions, being tall and thin, with a high squeaky voice; he recognised in himself a strong feminine streak. After a period in Australia, Ellis returned to a London seething with intellectual ferment – feminism, socialism, Ibsenism – and promptly developed a passionate sexual interest in his younger sister, Louie. This never developed into incest, but the two always remained close.

Ellis's romanticism made him nervous about strange women, and this is what happened in the case of the South African novelist, Olive Schreiner. She was a determined advocate of women's rights, but her feminism had received a severe shock when she fell in love with a sadist and discovered that she enjoyed being humiliated and beaten. When her lover deserted her, she turned to Ellis, hoping he would combine intellectual mastery with physical domination.

In fact, his knees turned to water at the thought of trying to sound masterful – let alone flogging her. So Olive returned to South Africa.

Ellis had obtained his medical degree, but decided he preferred literature. His suggestion that the Elizabethan playwrights should be published unexpurgated led to his editorship of the Mermaid Series, and his book *The New Spirit* brought him a certain celebrity among idealistic members of the younger generation, particularly the so-called 'new women'. One of these admirers was a tiny, blue-eyed woman named Edith Lees, who had hated her father and now had a deep distrust of all males. She and Ellis spent a great deal of time together on a walking tour in Cornwall and decided that they were soul mates. They must have made an odd pair – the tall Ellis with his squeaky voice, and the tiny Edith with her unexpectedly deep voice. It is not clear whether Ellis realised at the time of their marriage that Edith was a lesbian; if so, he may have been relieved that she would make no sexual demands on him. But a few months after their marriage, he was badly shaken to receive a letter from her – she was staying in a country cottage – explaining that she had developed a deep passion for a woman friend; after a painful interior struggle, he wrote to give his approval to the affair. It was the first of many. Edith, for her part, failed to show the same tolerance, and when Ellis confessed that he had kissed a female guest on a walk, she threw her out of the house.

It was in 1892 that Ellis formed a partnership with the poet and critic, John Addington Symonds, to write a book on sexual 'inversion' (i.e. homosexuality) for a Contemporary Science Series edited by Ellis. Symonds had been aware that he was a homosexual since his schooldays, although his friendships with younger boys had always been 'pure'. It was not until he went to Italy that he made the delighted discovery that many young gondoliers and fishermen found his desires perfectly natural and were willing to participate. In fact, Symonds died while he and Ellis were still collaborating, and Ellis finished *Sexual Inversion* alone. It was first published in German in 1896, and made an immediate impact on the world of 'sexology', being read with deep interest by Freud, Krafft-Ebing and Hirschfeld. It appeared in England in the following year. But it was in 1898 that Ellis suddenly achieved unwelcome notoriety when a bookseller named George Bedborough was prosecuted for selling 'this obscene publication' (as the judge called it) and fined £100 on condition that he pleaded guilty. Ellis wanted to fight the case, but the bookseller was afraid of prison. So *Sexual Inversion* was officially banned in England, and Ellis published the remaining volumes of his *Studies in the Psychology of Sex* in America. At least the case had the effect of turning Ellis into a celebrity. In the second volume of the series – on auto-eroticism – Ellis quoted Freud and Breuer with approval, and added a great deal of material of his own on infantile sexuality – recording, for example, a case of an eight-month-old girl who could achieve complete orgasm by closing her eyes, clenching her fists and tightly crossing her thighs. These views caused widespread controversy – and scandal – several years before the ideas of Freud achieved notoriety outside Austria and Germany.

Edith Ellis was incensed by the banning of *Sexual Inversion*; she hurled herself into authorship and lecturing, and became a celebrity in her own right. But a lecture tour in America exhausted her, and she died in 1916.

In the following year, Ellis met the Frenchwoman who had been translating one of Edith's books, Françoise Cyon. She was in severe financial straits and depressed about the failure of her marriage to a Russian. Ellis became, in effect, her psychiatrist, and Françoise was soon – like most women he met – in love with him. She admitted as much in a letter and, when they met again, they spent some time lying in each other's arms, fully clothed. After this, Ellis followed her into the bedroom – not to seduce her, but to 'minister to her needs'. What he meant by this phrase is not quite clear from her subsequent description in her autobiography, but she admits that she was reduced to 'delicious bashfulness' as Ellis sat with his head between her thighs and she caressed his leonine locks. Presumably Ellis persuaded her to urinate for him, and probably rhapsodised about the mysterious beauty of 'golden streams'. From then on, Françoise showed herself completely willing to participate in his fantasies. He called her Naiad – water nymph – and liked to persuade her to urinate as they walked in the rain; on one particularly satisfying occasion, he made her do it standing among the crowds at Oxford Circus – her long dress preventing anyone else from noticing the golden stream that flowed down into the gutter in the rain. Françoise's eager co-operation apparently restored Ellis's potency, and their sexual relationship remained satisfactory to the end of his life. But it was not until the publication of Phyllis

Grosskurth's biography of Ellis in 1980 that it was finally revealed that Ellis made a habit of rhapsodising to his many female admirers about 'golden streams', and that most of them were willing to oblige someone they admired so deeply. One girl, Winifred de Kok, wrote after spending some time with him: 'It seems lonely and strange to be making golden streams alone, and not in a lovely garden with the great god Pan in loving attendance.' But the poetess Hilda Doolittle was upset when, in an essay in the third series of *Impressions and Comments*, Ellis described how, one day at twilight, she had stood before him, with 'those straight adolescent legs still more ravishing in their unyielding pride', and 'a large stream gushed afar in the glistering liquid arch', while on her face she wore – understandably – 'a shy and diffident smile'. But she eventually gave her permission for it to be published.

What seems most extraordinary was not that Ellis persuaded so many respectable young ladies to urinate in front of him, but that he himself was convinced that this was an exquisite aesthetic experience that deserved to be classified with Greek sculpture or the Greek experience of love between males. It never seems to have struck him that he was merely a case of arrested development. His rationalisation of his urolagnia brings to mind Carl Hajdu's similar – if more elaborate – rationalisation of transvestism.

One great emotional upheaval was still to come. In 1915 Ellis had met a strikingly handsome young novelist named Hugh de Selincourt, who professed to be one of Ellis's most devoted admirers, writing in one letter: 'O King, O King! my love to you, Havelock, ears back, you know, tail lowered and wagging . . .' But he was also a tireless seducer, and his admiration took the form of wanting to sleep with Ellis's female disciples. In 1920, Ellis was unwise enough to take Selincourt to lunch with the birth-control advocate, Margaret Sanger, who had been in love with Ellis since the days of his marriage. When de Selincourt invited her to his Sussex home and introduced her to his wife and his wife's lover, she was impressed by such 'civilised' behaviour, and soon became his mistress. De Selincourt then persuaded Ellis to take him to meet Françoise; she was at first shy and awkward, but also succumbed to his charm. One day, as Ellis and Françoise were lying in one another's arms, she confessesd that she was having an affair with de Selincourt. Again, he was shattered, although he assured himself – and Françoise – that he was incapable of jealousy; he was convinced that the fault lay in his own wicked possessiveness. But it was beginning to dawn on him that he regarded sexual fidelity as 'one of the fundamental facts of life'.

When Ellis died, at the age of eighty, in 1939, his early fame had long evaporated, his theories on sexuality having been superseded by the more 'scientific' ideas of Freud. Yet in many ways, his insights on perversion are more profound than Freud's (who had, for example, to evoke a 'death impulse' to explain sadism). Ellis recognised that fetishism is unique to human beings, and that it is the result of an object 'parasitically absorbing' the normal sexual energy. Yet, like Krafft-Ebing and other pioneer sexologists, he also failed to recognise that this development had taken place mainly in the nineteenth century, and was due to the energising of the sexual impulse by the imagination. But at least Ellis saw through the error that vitiates the work of Krafft-Ebing: the notion that sexual perversions are simply the result of hereditary taints.

In *Sexual Inversion*, Ellis also took an important step beyond Krafft-Ebing in recognising that homosexuality should not be classified among the sexual perversions. Krafft-Ebing believed that it was an acquired habit; Ellis recognised that it is inborn and basically biological in origin (thereby anticipating the modern view that will be discussed in a moment).

The importance of Ellis's insight in the 1890s can hardly be overestimated. A large proportion of the British public had never heard of homosexuality before the trial of Oscar Wilde in 1895, and this had given the impression that homosexuality was an unspeakable depravity. It was revealed that Wilde had spent a great deal of time with telegraph boys and others of 'low' origin. His appetite seems to have been enormous; he admitted having as many as five youths in one evening. He preferred them dirty, and liked to kiss them all over their bodies. So the general impression left by the trial was that homosexuals were men of perverted tastes who preferred a male's anus to a woman's vagina because it was somehow more dirty and disgusting. This was why homosexuality was 'the love that dare not speak its name'.

The same view, of course, had prevailed since the time of Beckford and Byron. The consequence was that, although the death penalty for sodomy was reduced to life imprisonment in 1861 (which explains, no doubt, why Wilde insisted so passionately that he had

not committed sodomy), most homosexuals spent their lives in a
frenzy of shame and concealment, and were prone to nervous
breakdowns. Ellis's collaborator, John Addington Symonds, had
several. So did the composer, Tchaikovsky. The underlying sadness
of his music betrays the misery of concealment. He made a heroic
effort to 'cure' himself by marrying a female pupil who fell in love
with him, and he was driven to attempt suicide when he found
she was a nymphomaniac. (She later died in a lunatic asylum.)
Tchaikovsky's death in 1893 (at the age of fifty-three) is usually
attributed to cholera contracted by drinking a glass of unboiled
water. But in 1978 a Soviet scholar, Alexandra Orlova, published
a narrative that had been dictated to her twelve years earlier by
Alexander Voitov, of the Russian museum in Leningrad. According
to this, Tchaikovsky had been accused of a liaison with Voitov's
nephew, and a member of the aristocracy wrote a letter to the tsar.
A hastily convened 'court', including six of Tchaikovsky's former
schoolfellows, met to consider how the disgrace might be averted,
and Tchaikovsky was ordered to commit suicide, which he did
by taking arsenic. The story has been branded 'an outrageous
fabrication' by the music scholar, Nicholas Slonimsky;* yet what is
important is that the story *could* easily be true. In St Petersburg
in the 1890s, homosexuality was regarded with as much disgust as
in Victorian London.

Wilde's condemnation aroused widespread sympathy on the
Continent. In France, Italy and Holland – where there were no
laws against homosexuality – it was regarded as a typical piece of
British hypocrisy; and even in Germany – where a law known as
Paragraph 175 punished homosexuals with heavy prison sentences
and loss of social status – Magnus Hirschfeld and the critic Leo
Berg drew widespread support for a public protest in which they
labelled Wilde's imprisonment 'a judicial crime against the greatest
poet of the generation'. And although their petition for Wilde's
release was not successful, it helped to create a sympathetic climate
of opinion for Hirschfeld's lifelong endeavour to persuade the public
to regard homosexuality as completely natural. He liked to refer to
homosexuals as the Third Sex.

Magnus Hirschfeld, the son of a Jewish doctor, was born in 1868.

* *Baker's Biographical Dictionary of Musicians and Composers*, 7th edition,
1984

He recognised his own homosexual inclinations from an early age, and was deeply shocked when one of his patients, a young officer, committed suicide on the eve of his marriage because he felt guilty about his 'unnatural desire' for men. This resulted in Hirschfeld's first medical publication, a pamphlet called 'Sappho and Socrates – How can one explain the love of men and women for their own sex?'. In 1896, the year Ellis's *Sexual Inversion* was published in Germany, Hirschfeld also argued that homosexuality is biological in origin. In her biography of Hirschfeld (1986), Dr Charlotte Wolff dismisses Hirschfeld's theories as 'confused and contradictory', and argues that hormones have little, if anything, to do with homosexuality. Yet modern scientific research is on Hirschfeld's side. We now know that the natural form of the human being is the female. The ovary that contains the unborn child has both male and female components. It carries an X chromosome. If it is fertilised by a sperm carrying an X chromosome, the result is a girl. If it is fertilised by a sperm carrying a Y chromosome, the result is a boy. In that case, the gonads become testes, and a chemical absorbs the female parts that would turn into a womb. Then the testes produce the major male hormone, testosterone, which prevents the male parts from degenerating. From the very beginning, the male foetus has to fight to become male.

An East German scientist, Dr Gunter Dorner, became convinced that the basic difference between male and female lies in a definite part of the brain and that, in homosexuals, this part of the brain is still female. He proved this, to his own satisfaction, by injecting a homosexual with the female hormone oestrogen, then measuring the signals that came back from this part of the brain. The oestrogen 'told' the homosexual's brain that he had just finished ovulating, and his brain sent back signals to the phantom womb that would normally be sent by a woman's brain. The experiment was repeated with twenty homosexuals; each one sent back female signals. Dorner concluded that the homosexual is a male with a female brain, and that this is due to a shortage of testosterone when the foetus was in the womb. Dorner believed that this can be the result of stress, and he supported his argument by pointing out that a far higher number of homosexuals were born in Germany during the war years than in the years immediately preceding or immediately following the war. (Lesbianism, he believes, is caused by the effect of too much testosterone.)

So it would seem that Hirschfeld was basically correct; the root of homosexuality lies in the brain, and is due to hormones. He even guessed the vital role of the gonads, and hypothesised the existence of a male and female hormone (which he called andrin and gynecin) more than three decades before testosterone and oestrogen were isolated in the laboratory.

Hirschfeld was also the first to make a close study of transvestites – he invented the word – and to write a book on them – he was so fascinated by them that he came under suspicion of being one himself. Krafft-Ebing had announced arbitrarily that all transvestites are homosexuals, and Freud's leading disciple, Stekel, agreed with him. Hirschfeld pointed out that this is not necessarily true; his own investigations showed that only about 35 per cent were homosexual. Hirschfeld also made the important observation that about 15 per cent of transvestites were what he called 'auto-monosexual' – that is, experienced orgasm while wearing the dress of the opposite sex, as Charlotte Bach did – this is an important observation to which we must return later.

Hirschfeld's most important contribution was in recognising that, in the modern world, an increasing number of people are 'sexually sick', and that these people should not be condemned as degenerates – still less as criminals – but should be treated like anyone else with an illness. In 1919, Hirschfeld acquired the mansion of a former ambassador in Berlin, and set up his *Institut für Sexualwissenschaft* – Institute for Sexual Science – with a notice outside which read AMORI ET DOLORI SACRI – 'sacred to love and sorrow'. All kinds of sexual 'misfits' came to him for treatment, and he recorded many of the cases in his book *Sexual Disasters* (*Sexualkatastrophen*, 1926). Hirschfeld was particularly moved by the case of a doctor who was accused of exposing himself to a thirteen-year-old girl. The doctor had been subject to epilepsy and sleepwalking since childhood. At the time of the offence, he was severely depressed. He was treating a child, Ilse K., for an eczema that covered her entire body. The child had come to his surgery alone, and the doctor asked her to strip completely. As he was drawing her head down towards him to examine behind her ears, he experienced an erection. He turned her round, opened her legs, and rubbed his penis against her back; then he turned her round and rubbed against her body until he experienced orgasm. According to the doctor, he had no memory of what happened from the moment he drew her head towards him until he 'woke up' to find the child, crying, between his knees, and his penis hanging out of his trousers. Hirschfeld believed his story about the 'blackout', and testified in court on behalf of the doctor, describing him as a case of 'psycho-sexual infantilism'. As a result, the man was acquitted.

The classification is important, for it makes clear that Hirschfeld regarded sexual perversions as a form of emotional immaturity. Havelock Ellis, we may recall, refused to admit that his desire to watch girls urinate was an infantile regression, and insisted that his appreciation of 'golden streams' was on the same level as an appreciation of painting or sculpture. Hirschfeld was more honest – or perhaps merely more detached; while he showed boundless sympathy for sexual deviates, he recognised that their problem was usually an inability to reach emotional maturity. The implication – which would have been rejected by Ellis – was clearly that, although sexual satisfaction is important, there are far more important things in life, and that a person who remains obsessed with achieving sexual satisfaction is failing to achieve his full potential as a human being.

As early as 1920, Hirschfeld was already under attack from right-wing political elements, who declared that he was a corrupter of German youth. Thugs interrupted his lectures, and after one of them he was knocked unconscious. He was seriously injured, and foreign newspapers even reported his death. A Dresden newspaper regretted that 'this shameless and horrible poisoner of our people has not found his well-deserved end'. In spite of this, Hirschfeld refused to be diverted from his purpose, and went on to complete his classic three-volume *Sexual Pathology*. With the rise of the Nazis, life became increasingly dangerous, and Hirschfeld's praise of the Soviet Russian experiment offered his enemies a new stick to beat him with. In 1928, he became a founder member and president (together with Havelock Ellis and August Forel) of the Second International Congress for Sexual Reform, which developed into the World League for Sexual Reform. But in the autumn of 1930, he left Germany on a world lecture tour which took him from America to Japan, China, Bali, Ceylon, India, Egypt and Palestine, returning to Europe on a ship called (symbolically) the *Byron*. But his collaborator and lover, Karl Giese (Hirschfeld was sexually attracted to effeminate men) warned him that it would be too dangerous to return to Berlin. He was in Switzerland when Hitler came to power in January 1933. The Institute was closed down almost immediately; all its books and papers were burned on a bonfire, and a bronze bust of Hirschfeld was thrown into the flames. Depressed and in failing health, Hirschfeld went to live in Paris, then in Nice. But in his final days, he at least had the satisfaction of knowing that he had become an international celebrity. He died of a stroke on his sixty-seventh birthday, 14 May 1934.

By the time Hirschfeld died, the 'sexual revolution' had been virtually accomplished. Hirschfeld and his fellow 'sexologists' had been largely responsible; but dramatists and novelists had also played a central role. Creative artists tend to have a higher level of 'dominance' than the rest of the community and therefore to be less prudish; they have always objected to having puritanism thrust upon them. The first shots were fired in 1881 by Henrik Ibsen, who wrote a play about hereditary syphilis. One of Ibsen's most ardent champions called *Ghosts* 'one of the filthiest things ever written in Scandinavia'. It was banned in England until 1913, but a private performance drew such descriptions as 'an open drain', 'a loathsome sore unbandaged' and 'candid foulness'. In 1882, Zola's novel *Pot-Bouille* (*Piping Hot*) described adultery, fornication and rape in a respectable block of middle-class Paris apartments and led *Le Figaro* to exclaim: 'It is about time Paris avenged herself on M. Zola's outrages.' (The earlier *Nana*, about a courtesan, had upset the moralists, but Zola had propitiated them by making her die of a particularly nasty smallpox.) But in 1887, Zola's *Earth* was universally condemned; it portrays the lives of French peasants almost entirely in terms of avarice, brutality and lust, and a scene in which a farmer rapes his pregnant sister-in-law while his wife holds her down was regarded as unalloyed pornography. In London the following year, the publisher Henry Vizetelly was fined £100 for publishing *Earth*, then sent to prison for three months for defiantly continuing to publish 'obscene' French writers like Flaubert and Maupassant.

In 1894, Bernard Shaw's play *Mrs Warren's Profession* was also banned from the English stage; it was about the white slave traffic, and was designed to drive home the truth that prostitution was not the outcome of licentiousness, but of paying women starvation wages. A private performance in London provoked even more violent reviews than Ibsen's *Ghosts*, and when it was performed in

New York in 1905 half the cast was arrested. But by the turn of the century the battle was more than half won. It was patently absurd to prosecute serious writers who were trying to draw attention to social evils, particularly since these works contained nothing that was remotely sexually stimulating. But the new century saw the emergence of a new trend: writers who felt that sexual freedom deserved defending for its own sake. The *succès de scandale* of 1907 was Elinor Glyn's novel *Three Weeks*, about a young Englishman who meets a beautiful Russian princess in Switzerland, just as she is about to go and marry a wicked and debauched eastern potentate, and they spend a three-week 'honeymoon' together. That it is a non-stop sexual orgy is only hinted at ('He clasped her in his arms with a frenzy of mad, passionate joy . . . And this night was the most divine of any they had spent on the Bürgenstock. But there was in it an essence of which only angels could write.') Morality is propitiated when she dies at the hands of her jealous husband ('And so, as ever, the woman paid the price'), and the book went on to sell five million copies.

In 1909, H. G. Wells caused deep offence by bringing adultery nearer home; *Ann Veronica* is about a 'nice' middle-class girl who offers her virginity to her college teacher – arguing that it is hers to dispose of – and induces him to leave his wife. The outrage was increased by the awareness of most critics that Wells had deserted his first wife under identical circumstances, and that Ann Veronica Stanley was based on Wells's latest young mistress. The book was labelled 'literary filth', and caused a storm of outrage that helped to make Wells – and his publisher – a great deal of money.

In the following year, Scotland Yard stepped in when the publisher John Lane brought out a translation of Hermann Sudermann's *Das Hohe Lied (The Song of Songs)*, about a girl who has a dozen or so lovers, and still manages to live happily ever after, and the book was withdrawn from circulation.

One of the most puzzling episodes in the history of censorship occurred in 1915 with the suppression of D. H. Lawrence's *The Rainbow*. One newspaper described it as 'a monotonous wilderness of phallicism', while another declared that it was 'worse than Zola'. In fact, there are no explicitly sexual scenes in it, although the heroine gets herself pregnant by a man to whom she is not married – one, moreover, whom she later refuses to marry. What really upset the critics was that Lawrence was determined to treat sex as one of the most serious and important things in life, and most of them felt – perhaps justifiably – that this was an absurd exaggeration. At all events, the publisher apologised abjectly, and the remaining copies of the book were destroyed. It later emerged that no one in court, including the judge, had actually read it.

Meanwhile, the French were displaying their usual common sense in declining to be outraged by the publication – volume by volume – of Proust's *À la recherche du temps perdu* (*Remembrance of Things Past*) between 1913 and 1927. The abstract quality of the prose (Proust has been described as the Einstein of the novel) and the sheer length of the sentences prevented anyone from accusing Proust of writing pornography; yet, in his quiet and demure way, Proust had certainly gone a step further than Zola. On the second page he describes a wet dream:

> Sometimes, too, as Eve was created from a rib of Adam, a woman would be born during my sleep from some strain in the position of my thighs. Conceived from the pleasure I was on the point of consummating, she it was, I imagined, who offered me the pleasure. My body, conscious that its own warmth was permeating hers, would strive to become one with her, and I would awake.

And in the second volume he describes, in the same, almost prim tone of voice, how the young Marcel has an orgasm as he wrestles with a little girl.

> I tried to pull her towards me, and she resisted; her cheeks, inflamed by the effort, were as red and round as two cherries; she laughed as though I were tickling her; I held her gripped between my legs like a young tree which I was trying to climb; and, in the middle of my gymnastics, when I was already out of breath with the muscular exercise and the heat of the game, I felt, like a few drops of sweat wrung from me by the effort, my pleasure express itself in a form which I could not even pause for a moment to analyse . . .

In the same precise, almost pedantic manner, he describes peeping in through a window and witnessing a lesbian scene between two young girls, and eavesdropping when his friend, the Baron de

Charlus, makes love with a young man he has just picked up. Meanwhile, Proust preserves the fiction that his autobiographical hero is interested only in the opposite sex – so skilfully that even André Gide (himself a homosexual) was completely taken in, and was startled when he later learned of Proust's true proclivities. For, after all, the main plot of the novel is about the hero's involvement with a girl called Albertine, who deserts him and then is killed in a riding accident. Until long after his death, it was generally assumed that Proust's preoccupation with 'inverts' was a kind of botanising, undertaken in a spirit of scientific enquiry.

In fact, Proust had a sadistic streak that would have qualified him for inclusion in *Psychopathia Sexualis*. He was fascinated by butchers, and his manservant Albert (on whom Albertine was based) had to procure him a young man who claimed to be a butcher's boy, and whom Proust would question in detail about his work. ('Did it bleed much? Did you touch the blood?') In a butcher's shop, Proust asked the apprentice: 'Let me see how you kill a calf.' In the male brothel he frequented, he had a peculiar ritual involving photographs of those he loved, including his mother. The youth who had been hired for the evening was instructed to look through these and ask insulting questions like, 'Who the hell's this little tart?' But his most unpleasant habit was certainly hiring a chauffeur to bring him live rats, which were then beaten and pierced with hatpins until they died.

Oddly enough, Proust's vast novel was closer to Richardson than anything that had been published in the intervening century and a half. Like Richardson, he invites the reader inside his mind to listen to his ruminations and reflections. From the opening words – 'For a long time I used to go to bed early' – he is conducting the reader on a tour through the cosy Aladdin's cave of his feelings and memories. But the journey also makes us aware of the connection between Proust's enormous sensitivity and his morbid sexuality. In this twilit world of memory and imagination, there is no clear distinction between dream and reality, and therefore nothing to galvanise his vitality to real effort; so – as in de Sade – masochistic and sadistic fantasies become a substitute reality. Suddenly it becomes possible to see why Richardson was the father of sexual deviation as well as the modern novel. When he taught Europe to dream, he also taught European man to retreat into the Aladdin's cave of subjectivity. But nothing is easier than *to lose touch with reality*; every time we feel tired, every time we feel bored or guilty or upset, emotion, like a heavy sea, tries to break the rope that moors us to reality. At the present stage of his evolution, man's most urgent need is to discover some method by which he could instantly restore his contact with reality – it would be convenient if nature had created us with some button on the chest that could be pressed like a light-switch to flood us with instant vitality. But, to some extent, sexual desire *is* such a 'button' – hence modern man's increasing obsession with sexual fulfilment.

The critic Wladimir Weidlé remarked perceptively* that Proust was 'doomed to see nothing in the whole universe but the unattainable, slippery reality of his own ego'; and he adds that, like James Joyce, Proust had arrived at 'the negation of the novel as a spontaneous form of life transformed into art, of reality transfigured into poetry'. It seems strange to hear Proust classified with Joyce, the author of a novel that seems to be the ultimate extension of Zola's doctrine of realism. Yet Weidlé has an important point. Joyce, who did more than anyone else to undermine literary censorship in the twentieth century, was fundamentally a romantic dreamer who spent his life inside his own Aladdin's cave.

Joyce began as an admirer of Ibsen, but soon lost the ambition to follow in Ibsen's foosteps as a social critic. Instead, he began to write an immense novel about his own childhood and youth in Dublin. (Only a fragment of this novel – *Stephen Hero* – survives.) Later, he shortened and recast it as the autobiographical novel *A Portrait of the Artist as a Young Man*. So, from the beginning, Joyce had abandoned the Shakespearean attempt to make his work a 'mirror' of reality; it was simply a mirror that reflected his own face. But it was obviously impossible to go on writing autobiography – he had used most of it up in the *Portrait*. Joyce therefore decided to write a novel about a crucial moment in the life of his hero (he called such crucial moments 'epiphanies'): the day he decides that it is pointless to hope for recognition from the Dublin *literati*, and that he had better choose the lonely path of the artist-outsider. Since it would be necessary to portray his hero against the Dublin background, Joyce (who was now living in Trieste) began to research this background with unprecedented thoroughness, writing endless letters to Dublin relatives and acquaintances.

* in *Les Abeilles d'Aristée*

The 'photographic' method he had developed in *Portrait of the Artist* demanded a painstaking realism that sometimes jarred on the sensibilities of his Edwardian readers – as when he describes a character farting, or his hero itching owing to his unwashed state. In *Ulysses* he went further, and described his hero picking his nose, while the other main character, Mr Bloom, is shown relieving his bowels, masturbating as he watches a girl showing her knickers, and inserting his tongue into his wife's anus. Joyce seems to take a certain pleasure in describing smells and sights that would normally be regarded as disgusting: 'armpits' oniony sweat. Fishgluey slime'; 'an old woman's: the grey sunken cunt of the world'; 'He raked his throat rudely, spat phlegm on the floor. He put his boot on what he had spat, wiping his sole along it . . .' And the book finally explodes into a frenzy of obscenity and blasphemy in the brothel scene, which is written in the surrealistic form of a nightmare 'dream play'; here we see Bloom transformed into a woman and ridden like a horse, take part in a Black Mass, and witness the hero knocked unconscious by a drunken British soldier. Bloom is portrayed as an underwear fetishist with a powerful streak of masochism – both characteristics of Joyce himself (although the author prefers to attribute them to Bloom rather than to his artist-hero). It is probably no coincidence that the brothel chapter follows immediately on a chapter set in a maternity home, in which Joyce parodies every style in English literature from the *Anglo-Saxon Chronicle* to modern journalese. He seems to be trying to demonstrate that all previous writers have been inclined to evade the problem of capturing reality in language, and that he, Joyce, is the first who has really tried to 'tell it like it is'. So the Nighttown chapter that follows seems to be saying: 'No one ever dared to say *this* before.' But it does not take a great deal of penetration to see the fallacy in this argument. Joyce is not showing us reality; he is only showing us his own tormented ego. Even in the brutal realism of the earlier chapters we can sense an element of anger at a world that has ignored him and bestowed celebrity on writers like Yeats, Synge and 'AE'. *Ulysses* seems to be an attempt to shout so loud that no one could ever ignore him again.

In this, at least, he was successful. Within six months of its publication in February 1921, *Ulysses* had become the most talked-about book in Europe, although few people had read it. Influential critics like Middleton Murry, Arnold Bennett and Holbrook Jackson hailed Joyce as a man of genius; meanwhile, the poet Alfred Noyes called it 'simply the foulest book that has ever found its way into print', while James Douglas (of the *Sunday Express*) went further and described it as 'the most infamously obscene book in ancient or modern literature'. This clash of opinions naturally made everyone anxious to read *Ulysses*, and copies changed hands at enormous prices. (Noyes was later to throw J. B. Priestley out of his house for daring to defend *Ulysses*.) A copy was smuggled into Dublin in a Guinness stout barrel, while an American tore up the book and posted it to America a dozen pages at a time, hidden in French newspapers. Five hundred copies of the second printing were burnt by the New York Customs authorities in 1922, and 499 were seized by British Customs, early the following year. By 1930 it had gone into eleven printings. Finally, an American judge declared that *Ulysses* was not pornographic, and the book was finally published openly in America, greatly to Joyce's financial benefit.

The shock effect was produced by passages like the following, from Mrs Bloom's monologue as she lies on the point of sleep:

I took off all my things with the blinds down after all my hours dressing and perfuming and combing it like iron or some other kind of a thick crowbar standing all the time he must have eaten oysters I think a few dozen he was in great singing voice no I never in all my life felt anyone had one the size of that to make you feel full up he must have eaten a whole sheep after whats the idea of making us like that with a big hole in the middle of us like a Stallion driving it up into you because thats all they want out of you with that determined vicious look in his eye I had to halfshut my eyes still he hasnt such a tremendous amount of spunk in him when I made him pull it out and do it on me . . .

And the most striking thing about such a passage is that, while it is as specific as anything in *Fanny Hill*, it lacks the true element of the 'forbidden' that we associate with Victorian pornography. Like Proust, Joyce is turning back to the source of the novel in the eighteenth century.

Perhaps the ultimate condemnation of *Ulysses* lies in T. S. Eliot's remark that Joyce had destroyed his own future. It was true; after *Ulysses*, there was nowhere to go; its successor, *Finnegans Wake* – with its attempt to create a 'dream language' –

has hardly more significance than Lewis Carroll's 'Jabberwocky'. We can also see that Eliot's comment applies equally to Proust. Wladimir Weidlé pointed out that the trouble with Proust's 'subjective method' is that it is incapable of creating the 'second life which is the essence of the novel', that 'other world' inhabited by Tom Jones and Mr Pickwick and even Tolkien's Hobbits. It is as if Proust and Joyce preceded their work with the statement: 'This is how *I* see life.' And indeed, that is precisely what *Ulysses* and *À la recherche* tell us. But when they have finished telling us, they have no more to say. In Dickens or Balzac or Wells, also we are aware that this is how the writer sees life, but it would be quite unnecessary for him to tell us so – it is perfectly obvious. Instead, they get on with the important business of *telling us a story*. And that is why, when the story is over, they always have another story to tell, while Proust and Joyce have left themselves with nothing more to say.

This was also the problem encountered by D. H. Lawrence, and it explains why his last – and most notorious – work, *Lady Chatterley's Lover*, is so curiously unsatisfactory. As with Proust and Joyce, his work is basically autobiographical; he is anxious to make the reader understand his soul and his religion. And his religion, as he wrote in a letter of 1913, 'is a belief in the blood, the flesh, as being wiser than the intellect. We can go wrong in our minds. But what our blood feels, believes and says is always true.' Lawrence felt that his own elopement with Freda, the wife of his professor, was a marvellous release from all the problems of his adolescence and young manhood. And in all his subsequent novels, beginning with *The Rainbow*, he idealises the sheer magic of the relationship between a naked man and woman. What baffles him is that the relationships between men and women are so full of conflict. As he grew older, he entertained an increasingly strong 'male chauvinist' belief that the answer lay in the woman recognising the man as her master. But the man himself must recognise that 'the blood' is more important than the intellect. For Lawrence had an extremely negative attitude to the intellect. And this hatred of the intellect was also bound up with the feeling that modern civilisation condemns people to boredom and futility. The question Lawrence set himself was, 'How can man escape this boredom and futility?' His answer – as set forth in novels like *The Rainbow*, *Women in Love* and *The Plumed Serpent* – was his 'religion of the blood'. This meant that most of his novels are about the sexual relations between men and women – a topic many readers may find claustrophobic. But Lawrence obviously found it tiresome not to be able to speak straightforwardly about the very essence of the sexual relation – what happens when a man and woman take off their clothes. In *Lady Chatterley*, he decided to say precisely what he wanted, and accept that the book would be banned.

One of the discarded titles of the book was *John Thomas and Lady Jane*, referring to the male and female sexual organs, which Lawrence felt to be the heart of the matter. Lady Chatterley, whose husband is impotent, has a love-affair with her gamekeeper, Mellors, and in the sexual relationship with him finds a peace and tenderness that she has never experienced with her husband or other lovers. (Lawrence's original title was *Tenderness*.) Lawrence strains all his resources to try and convince us that Mellors and Lady Chatterley achieve a kind of mystical ecstasy:

> Then, as he began to move . . . there awoke in her new strange thrills rippling inside her. Rippling, rippling, rippling, like a flapping overlapping of soft flames, soft as feathers, running to points of brilliance, exquisite, exquisite and melting all her molten inside. It was like bells rippling up and up to a culmination. She lay unconscious of the wild little cries she uttered at the last.

Although more explicit, the language here is oddly reminiscent of Elinor Glyn's *Three Weeks*. And Mellors' last words to Lady Chatterley, in the final sentence of the novel, come very close to bathos: 'John Thomas says good night to Lady Jane, a little droopingly, but with a hopeful heart.'

As Lawrence anticipated, the book – which appeared in 1928 – was soon being seized by British and American Customs authorities; the ban was not lifted until 1960, when an English court judged that the book was not technically pornographic. This is undoubtedly true. Yet it shares with pornography that same obviously false assumption that sex is the be-all and end-all of life; and this may be identified as the reason why it leaves behind such a general sense of unsatisfactoriness. Sex is important, but it is not *that* important. What are Lady Chatterley and Mellors going to *do* when they are finally alone on their little farm? Will she, after a year or so, feel any less unfulfilled than she did with her husband? And what about Mellors? Lawrence has always emphasised that a man needs a purpose that transcends mere sexual fulfilment; in which case, Mellors is going to find life as 'Lady Chatterley's fucker' (as he calls himself) something of an anticlimax. It seems ironic that in Lawrence – the 'high priest of sex' – we should come upon all the false assumptions and intellectual confusions that we first encountered in de Sade.

These same confusions can be found in chaotic abundance in the work of that other great 'sexual liberator' of the twentieth century, Henry Valentine Miller. Miller was forty-three years old when his first book, *Tropic of Cancer*, was published in Paris in 1934. It was an exceptionally late start for a writer, and Miller's life had been, so far, exceptionally hard. Born in New York in 1891, the grandson of German immigrants, he spent much of his childhood and youth in Brooklyn. From a fairly early age he showed the same devotion to sex as the author of *My Secret Life* and, at the age of eighteen, took a mistress old enough to be his mother. By then his father had become an alcoholic. At the age of twenty, Miller was already convinced he was a failure. A first marriage soon turned sour, and ended in divorce five years later. A passionate relationship with a woman called June Mansfield was D. H. Lawrencian in its intensity, and made more so by her tendency to sleep with every other man she met. Another five years of drifting, and Miller decided to sail for France, hoping to begin a new life. During the next six years he starved, slept in empty houses, and borrowed money from acquaintances. June joined him in Paris, but they quarrelled incessantly. After years of trying to teach himself to write, Miller began a book about D. H. Lawrence, and a kind of autobiographical pot-pourri called *The Tropic of Cancer*. This, and its sequel, *The Tropic of Capricorn*, brought him a certain celebrity among English and American exiles in Paris. Little by little, he achieved the status of a legendary exile, like Joyce and Lawrence – a 'serious writer' whose freedom from sexual inhibition made him unacceptable to his own hypocritical countrymen.

In fact, this assessment is highly questionable. The first thing the reader of *The Tropic of Cancer* notices is that it is almost unreadable. It is a kind of journal, written entirely in the present tense, and makes very little attempt to 'tell a story'. Much of it consists of prose-poetry in the manner of Lautréamont or Rimbaud, and such passages are often excellent: 'Indigo sky swept clear of fleecy clouds, gaunt trees infinitely extended, their black boughs gesticulating like a sleep-walker. Sombre, spectral trees, their trunks pale as cigar ash. A silence supreme and altogether European.' And, immediately following this, the kind of passage that led to the book being 'banned'. 'The trouble with Irène is that she has a valise instead of a cunt. She wants fat letters to shove in her valise . . .' In a 1935 review of the book, George Orwell remarks: '[The sexual encounters] describe sexual life from the point of view of the man in the street – but, it must be admitted, rather a debased version of the man in the street. Nearly all the characters in the book are *habitués* of the brothel. They act and describe their actions with a callous coarseness which is unparalleled in fiction, though common enough in real life.' And he goes on to praise the book for trying to 'tell the truth' in a world increasingly full of sentimental evasions. 'Mr Miller is a discerning though hardboiled person giving his opinions about life.'

But when, in 1940, Orwell attempted a retrospective assessment of Miller (in an essay called 'Inside the Whale') he was more critical, for he can see that Miller's trouble is a certain head-in-the-sand attitude. 'In his books one gets right away from the "political animal" and back to a viewpoint not only individualistic but completely passive – the viewpoint of a man who believes the world-process to be outside his control and who in any case hardly wishes to control it.' Orwell goes on to describe how he met Miller in Paris when he (Orwell) was on his way to the Spanish Civil War. Miller told him that his ideas about fighting Fascism were 'all baloney'. 'Our civilisation was destined to be swept away and replaced by something so different that we should scarcely regard it as human – a prospect that did not bother him, he said.' Miller has, in fact, found a philosophy that suits his own sense of utter irresponsibility. It emerges in the first sentences of his next book, *Black Spring*. 'I am a patriot – of the 14th Ward Brooklyn where I was raised. The rest of the United States doesn't exist for me . . .' In fact, the title of Orwell's essay refers to Jonah and the Whale, and Miller's desire to find himself a 'womb big enough for an adult' where he can take refuge from the modern world, 'able to keep up an attitude of the completest indifference, no matter *what* happens'.

Since his books are little more than egoistic monologues, how does Miller succeed in holding the reader's attention? By talking engagingly about his many friends – Miller is a man whose life revolves around friends – and by throwing in the occasional 'quick poke.'

> . . . finally I lost my temper and I clouted her [his wife] and she fell on the floor and began to weep and sob . . . The girl upstairs came running down to see what was the matter. She was in her kimono and her hair was hanging down her back. In the excitement she got close to me and things happened without either of us intending anything to happen. We put the wife to bed with a wet towel around her forehead and while the girl upstairs was bending over her I stood behind her and lifting her kimono I got it into her and she stood there a long while talking a lot of foolish soothing nonsense. Finally I climbed into bed with the wife and to my utter amazement she began to cuddle up to me and without saying a word we locked horns and we stayed that way until dawn. (*Tropic of Capricorn*, p. 77)

The interesting thing about this account is that it is not in the least pornographic; there is none of the precise description of physical details that characterises pornography. This emerges even more clearly in the 'dirty book' that Miller wrote for a Los Angeles bookseller. *Opus Pistorum* (Latin for 'the work of the miller') was written in 1941 and finally published openly in 1983. It opens with a scene in which Miller sits with a naked thirteen-year-old girl on his knee while her father removes his trousers behind a screen. The girl performs fellatio on her father, then turns her attention to Miller. 'Marcelle stretches her tiny split fig, holds it open and pushes it down against my dong . . . the little monster gets it in somehow . . . I watch my dong stretch her to twice her size . . .'* And at this point, Miller pushes her away and calls her father a loony bastard. Then he goes outside with a prostitute who has also witnessed the scene, and he possesses her on a pile of boards.

> I dig John Thursday into her whiskers. He hadn't a brain in his bald head, but left alone he can fend for himself. He slips through her bush and butts her rectum. She has a flood coming down from her tail, this whore. There's no stopping it . . . you could

---

* Miller's own leader dots

stuff towels, blankets, mattresses between her legs, and it would still pour down to engulf you. I feel like the little boy who had to stop the break in the dike and had nothing but his finger. But I'll plug it, I'll fill it with my dong . . .

Gradually, it dawns on the reader that Miller is incapable of writing pornography. He is doing his best to sound 'dirty', but he cannot manage it for the life of him. He tries to disguise this by talking about mattresses and holes in dikes, but it is still perfectly obvious. In the next scene, he reads a letter from his girlfriend in which she describes sleeping three in a bed with her mother and her mother's lover, 'she makes me suck her off a lot. I don't care, I like to do it, but I wish that you were here so that I would be fucked more often . . .' It reads like a schoolboy exercise in pornography by a pupil who has no imagination. As the book goes on, we can almost sense Miller's desperation as he tries to think up 'something dirty'.

In the back of the taxi while we are being driven to my place, things become a great deal warmer. I pull Anna's dress up and take her pants off, and she brings Jean Jeudi out into the night air. She lets me tickle her crotch, but I mustn't try to play dirty finger with her . . . the driver would smell it. Shit, if he doesn't smell it already there's something wrong with him.

He seems to be totally unaware that, far from being sexually stimulating, this is all rather off-putting. It is as if he has arrived at his own working definition of 'dirty' as 'something that would shock a maiden aunt'; so references to shit and vaginal odours seem as good a way as any.

It may seem unfair to criticise a work that was written for a dollar a page. But then, *Opus Pistorum* tells us something about Miller that is not nearly so obvious in his more pretentious books; it might be described as Henry Miller with his hair down. An intelligent man who had been asked to write pornography at a dollar a page would at least try to make it sound plausible; the whole point of pornography is that the reader should be convinced by it. Miller cannot even be bothered with continuity; he incessantly mentions characters he has forgotten to introduce, so the reader ends in a state of utter confusion. But at this point it dawns on the reader that most of Miller's books produce this same effect. They all seem to be a series of *non sequiturs* laid end to end. And this is obviously an effect of the nihilism that Orwell criticises. In a 1946 review of *The Cosmological Eye*, Orwell objects to Miller's pretentiousness:

The arresting but almost meaningless phrase 'universe of death' strikes a characteristic note. One of Miller's tricks is to be constantly using apocalyptic language, to sprinkle every page with phrases like 'cosmological flux', 'lunar attraction' and 'interstellar spaces' or with sentences like 'The orbit over which I am travelling leads me further and further away from the dead sun which gave me birth.' . . . Even the title of this book, *The Cosmological Eye*, doesn't actually mean anything, but it sounds as though it *ought* to mean something.'

And when Miller drops these tricks and writes without artifice, as in *Opus Pistorum*, we suddenly become aware of his total intellectual bankruptcy. He pretends to be a life-affirmer, a kind of up-to-date Whitman, but in reality his philosophy is totally negative. 'I hope and believe that the whole civilised world will be wiped out in the next hundred years or so. I believe that man can exist, and in an infinitely better, larger way, without "civilisation".' Asked to defend this preposterous opinion, Miller would reply that he has no need to defend it because it is an 'intuition'. He wants to have the privilege of offering opinions, then of running away and hiding when asked to justify them.

This, of course, is precisely what D. H. Lawrence does. He explains that he detests intellect because its opinions are 'mere words' – but nevertheless explains his detestation in words that can be grasped only by the reader's intellect. So it is hardly surprising if the 'philosophy' he builds on these contradictions seems curiously futile and depressing.

It is no accident that Miller and Lawrence should end in the same anti-intellectual cul-de-sac. Their work is a logical development of the romantic tradition that we have traced from Samuel Richardson. Richardson said, in effect: 'Come with me into the world of imagination – forget your everyday life for a few hours.' And, like children following the Pied Piper, crowds of romantics danced in his footsteps. For what the Pied Piper seemed to be offering them was *freedom* – freedom from the burden of everyday life, with its paralysing triviality. Rousseau, Goethe, Schiller, Byron, Shelley, all preached this exhilarating doctrine of freedom – in *Frankenstein*, Mary Shelley even hinted that man might learn the secret of creating life itself. It was this 'smell of freedom' that made Byron and Swinburne the most popular poets of their day.

But the Victorians had common sense enough to recognise the dangers in this doctrine of freedom; John Morley, for example, recognised that Swinburne's anarchism was the anarchism of a naughty child, and that if we all obeyed his injunction to abandon the lilies and languors of virtue for the raptures and roses of vice, the result would be social chaos; he quite rightly compared Swinburne to a dirty-minded schoolboy. All the responsible Victorian thinkers – Carlyle, Mill, Arnold, Ruskin, Spencer – recognised the need for compromise. But the tide of 'reform' was too strong for them and, in the long run, it was Swinburne and his fellow rebels who won the day. So the great sexual revolution came about and, a century after *Poems and Ballads*, it was possible to print *My Secret Life* and the works of de Sade quite openly. And all the fallacies and confusions that vitiated the work of de Sade made their reappearance under a new guise. The generation of rebels insisted that man has the right to be totally 'selfish', to turn his back on all notions of public good, and to pursue his own visions and intuitions. Not merely, in fact, the right but the duty. *'Non serviam!'* cries Joyce's Stephen Dedalus, and Proust and Lawrence and Miller all murmur, 'Amen.'

It looks as if this romantic idea of freedom has resulted in the kind of intellectual anarchy that the Victorian moralists warned against. They always insisted that a philosophy of individualism and revolt would end in nihilism and futility. But it would be a pity to allow them to convince us that intellectual freedom is undesirable. For as soon as we look closely at the work of Proust, Joyce, Lawrence and Miller, we can see what went wrong. Like de Sade, they have simply gone too far. They all insist that man has no responsibility except to himself, and that the only part of himself that he needs to cultivate is his intuition. Because they distrust the intellect, they are forced to base their visionary philosophy on intuition. But it is impossible to build a philosophy, no matter how visionary, without a solid scaffolding of intellect. Their refusal to have any truck with intellect leaves them all in a hopelessly contradictory position – hence the pessimism and despair. If this obvious self-contradiction is avoided, the prospect begins to look altogether more promising.

NINE

Misfits or Mystics?

On a November afternoon in 1927, a beautiful Swedish girl walked into the music room of an ocean liner, and asked the man who was playing the piano if he would give her a lesson in playing the banjulele. The man explained courteously that he was busy at the moment, but offered to give her a lesson the following day – confirming her assumption that he was the ship's bandleader. It was not until several days later that Ella Strom learned that her music teacher was not an employee of the shipping line, but a famous concert pianist named Percy Grainger. Blushing with embarrassment, she hastened to offer her apologies. Grainger assured her that it was unnecessary, and they spent the next hour or so talking about themselves, and discovering that they had much in common. When the ship docked in Honolulu a few days later, she attended a recital given by Grainger, and sat watching with a 'pathetic, rapt expression'. It was only later that Grainger confessed to her that he had fallen in love with her at first sight.

It sounds like the beginning of a cheap romantic novelette. And indeed, Percy Grainger and Ella Strom were married two years later on the stage of the Hollywood Bowl, before an audience of about 20,000; many film stars and other celebrities were present. It was only after the wedding that Ella Grainger made the discovery that she had married a sexual deviate, a man whose demands struck her as horrifyingly abnormal. Grainger once confessed to a close friend:

> the fact is that I really worship evil and find everything else un-worth while. But it may (nay, must) be said that all my worship of cruelty cruises only around sex-instincts. Apart from sex I am not such a bad fellow. But as I am really not interested

in anything else but sex it just boils down to this: that I hardly think of anything but sex and that all my sex thoughts are full of evil and cruelty.*

But the talk of evil and cruelty is deceptive; Grainger was not possessed by an ambition to become another Jack the Ripper. The perversion he shared with Swinburne and Monckton Milnes was a fairly harmless fascination with the infliction and suffering of pain. He explained: 'Between seven and ten I read a lot of Homer & phrases like "The javelin crashed through the shield" were always on my lips. Later on when I was ten or twelve when I read the Icelandic Sagas the thought of the battleaxe hewing from the shoulder to the waist gave me the greatest mental delights . . . These passions were quite unconscious and I had no idea what caused me to shake with delight when I read such descriptions.' John Bird records that Grainger began auto-erotic experiments in flagellation at the age of sixteen; his mother was disturbed to find blood on his shirt. Grainger's sadism was probably hereditary; his father, John Grainger, had been at Westminster School, which had a reputation for flogging – so that many of its pupils remained flagellants for life. John Grainger had also been sexually hyperactive – he liked to boast that during the siege of Paris he had thought nothing of taking fourteen whores in one night. His wife, Rose, was a strong-minded woman who was basically puritanical, so she found his sexual demands tiresome – more so since he was a heavy drinker who had infected her with syphilis that he had picked up from a prostitute. When John Grainger fell into moods of drunken violence, Rose would control him – and often chase him out of the house – with a horsewhip. John and Rose Grainger separated in 1890, when Percy was eight.

Percy was born in Melbourne, Australia, on 8 July 1882; he remained an only child, and his mother's attitude towards him was fiercely and neurotically protective. She supported her son by giving piano lessons, and never had any doubt that he was a genius. The relationship between mother and son was so close and so intense that in later life there was gossip about incest – gossip which finally drove Rose to fling herself from an eighth-floor window.

* Letter to Cyril Scott, 23 July 1956, quoted in John Bird's *Percy Grainger*, P.51

Guilt may also have played a part in her suicide; her habit of chastising the young Percy with a whip undoubtedly played a major role in turning him into a sadist.

Percy was just twelve when he made his piano debut in Melbourne, and he was an instant success. Soon thereafter his mother took him to Frankfurt to study. By the age of seventeen, he was writing harmonies that are now reminiscent of Stravinsky – but a decade before Stravinsky achieved his first public performances. In London, at the age of nineteen, his recitals were a sensation. So was his way of climbing on to the platform – he would run down the aisle and leap on to the stage. Grainger was always obsessed with physical fitness; in later years, when staying with Delius, he liked to throw a ball over the roof of the house, then run through the house and catch it before it touched the ground. His music is full of springy, bouncing rhythms that reflect this athleticism.

Grainger thought his music grew out of his sadism. 'Out of this world of violence, war & tragedy, my longing to compose music arose. Many children are cruel to animals & many little boys harsh to little girls, but this fierceness wanes as they grow up. But I never grew up in this respect & fierceness is the keynote of my music . . .'

For the remainder of his life – he died of cancer in 1961 – Grainger was a famous pianist and a popular composer – his best-known composition being 'Country Gardens'. He was sadly underrated as a composer, and has received something of his due recognition only since his death.

Ella was deeply shocked to learn that her husband was obsessed by pain and flogging, and that he expected her to participate. His biographer, John Bird, records:

> But she loved him nonetheless, finding it 'hell to be with him and hell to be without him'. There were even periods when, because of his demands, she left him for a short time . . . Only she knew the full measure of his joys and frustrations, his saintliness and cruelty and his genius and aberrations. In the early 1930s he composed a letter which had instructions on the envelope that it was to be opened only in the event of his or Ella's death, or their both being found dead covered in whiplashes. It explained that no blame should be placed on either since flagellation was for him the greatest pleasure and the highest expression of his love.

In earlier days, he had persuaded one of his pupils, Karen Holten, to participate. While in the process of persuading her, he wrote: 'You shouldn't have a single stitch of clothing on your body, but I, "as man", must be allowed to wear a shield for the tediously easily destroyed parts of a man's body. I think it must be furiously painful for you to be whipped on your breasts, don't you think?' And he ends by mentioning that when, in his teens, he had a climax in his sleep, it was often while dreaming of being whipped by a woman. In another letter he describes his problems in forcing a needle through the flesh of his nipple; in yet another, he reproaches her for being poor at biting him, and urges her to practise on herself. 'It's good to roll or grind the teeth over already grasped flesh . . .'

Why did Grainger consider his fairly harmless obsession 'evil'? The reason that emerges clearly from his letters is that, unlike Swinburne, he was not merely excited by the idea of watching someone being birched on his (or her) bare behind; in his imagination he was an Ivan the Terrible, a Gilles de Rais. Thoughts of sex and cruelty dominated his whole life.

Everything that deals with sexual matters absolutely knocks me over. I love to simply wade and swim in a sea of overwrought, ceaseless sexual thought. I feel the hot parched wind from the Australian desert has entered into my soul, and with a fury of heat I must go through, burning up myself and others. This is how I live, following my lusts, and composing now and then on the side. And no sadist can call life poor or disappointing who can realise his cruellest, wildest dreams . . .

But, of course, Grainger never realised his cruellest, wildest dreams, except in auto-erotic fantasies, and flogging Karen Holten or his wife, Ella.

The phrase about the hot parched wind of the Australian desert offers the essential clue to Grainger: he somehow identifies his sadism with the forces of nature. Sadism produces the same wild, free sensation as a hurricane. Nietzsche had written: 'Lightning and tempest are different worlds, free powers, without morality. Pure Will, without the confusions of intellect – how happy, how free.' And when he was an orderly during the Franco-Prussian war, Nietzsche had seen his old regiment ride past him in the dusk and experienced an overwhelming exaltation: 'the strongest and highest

will to life does not lie in the puny struggle to exist, but in the
Will to war, the Will to Power'. Grainger was himself a kind of
proto-Nazi, at least in theory (in practice he had many Jewish
friends), who was obsessed by the idea of the superiority of blue-
eyed Nordic blonds. He even tried to write in a 'Nordic' English,
entirely free of 'Latin-begotten' words. (It is unnecessary to add
that Grainger himself was a typical example of the blue-eyed Nordic
blond.)

All these strands – the Nietzscheanism, the athleticism, the
'Nazism', the sadism – were not separate elements of Grainger's
character: they were essentially different facets of the same thing:
what Nietzsche called 'the Dionysian', the 'blissful ecstasy that
arises from the innermost depths of man, ay, of nature . . .' in
which our puny human individuality is swept away by a kind of
tempest of sheer power. 'I love being driven like a beaten slave to
sex, art, activity, sensuality. No freedom for me – give me the
brutal tyranny of some relentless blind urge, and I don't mind
being mashed up between two or three grinding away at once if I
get the chance.' So when Grainger thought of warriors charging
into battle, or of healthy bodies diving into cold water, or of
tremendous natural forces, he experienced what he valued above
all: the feeling of a vital current that raised him to a higher level of
vitality. His sadism was, in fact, a kind of mysticism. But this insight
makes us instantly aware that this is the essential key to *all* sexual
aberrations. They are all an attempt to achieve a higher level of
vitality. It is as if man felt like an underpowered electric light-bulb
that scarcely gives off enough light to read by; but then, in certain
moments, the bulb blazes with a radiance that lights the darkest
corners of the room. Understandably, those who have experienced
it feel it to be worth any sacrifice. In Grainger, the longing for the
'forbidden' had become a kind of mania; he admitted to Karen
Holten:

I wish to procreate independent children . . . I propose this:
Never to whip them till they are old enough to grasp the meaning
of lots of things, then say to them: Look here! I want to ask a
favor from you kids. I want to whip you, because it gives me
extraordinary pleasure. I don't know why it does, but it does . . .
Don't you think the children'd let me? I have hopes. Then
encourage them to whip each other . . . You know I long to flog

children. It must be wonderful to hurt this soft unspoiled skin
. . . & when my girls begin to awaken sexually I would gradually
like to have carnal knowledge with them . . . I have always
dreamed about having children & whipping them, & to have a
sensual life with my own daughters.

The negative side of this sexual obsession was a certain sense of
guilt; John Bird points out that in his letters he often refers to
himself as cowardly, sinful, weak, evil and wretched. He tells Karen
Holten that he regards himself as basically unlucky. This was partly,
as he admits, because he felt that he had never grown up, and that
his 'real self' was a naughty child waiting to be punished. The world
itself was to be the instrument of this punishment. In one of his
last letters, he signs himself: 'Your loving but defeated Percy'. This
was after he had discovered that he had an abdominal cancer.
Ironically, the last years of his life were haunted with pain – but
not of the kind he welcomed.

Among Grainger's contemporaries, there was only one, perhaps,
who could have fully understood his blend of sadism and mysticism,
and that was because he himself shared it. This was the novelist,
John Cowper Powys, who was ten years older than Grainger. Powys
was not interested in flagellation, but in cruelty and violence. In
his *Autobiography* he admits:

. . . from earliest childhood up to the present hour, my dominant
vice has been the most dangerous of all vices. I refer to Sadism.
I cannot remember a time – so early did this tendency show itself
– when sadistic thoughts and images did not disturb and intoxicate
me. One of my picture books, when I could not have been more
than three years old, contained a picture of an eagle seizing upon
a lamb, and from the age of three . . . this deadly vice transported
and obsessed me.

Every night when he went to bed, he indulged himself in sadistic
thoughts. Powys is deliberately vague about the nature of these
thoughts, but he offers a few clues. He describes how, as his father
was driving past a rural cottage, he (John) glanced in through the
window, and saw a momentary tableau of an old woman holding a
younger woman by the throat. This glimpse filled him with excitement, and was incorporated into the sadistic day-dreams. He de-

scribes minor acts of sadism committed as a child: pouring boiling water into a tin of live beetles, slicing up worms with a knife, tearing to pieces a nest full of young birds with his bare hands. But he insists that, beyond childhood, he has never committed a sadistic act; the indulgence was entirely mental.

In his greatest novel, A Glastonbury Romance (1932), Powys offers a full-length portrait of a 'mental sadist' in the person of the antiquary, Mr Evans. Evans is apparently a quiet, good-natured, bookish man, who is secretly obsessed by certain images of cruelty – for example, a passage in one of the Arthurian poems in which Merlin tears the antlers off a stag. Hidden in his basement, Evans keeps a book of sadistic pornography called The Unforgivable Sin, in which there is a passage 'so seductive that his knees grew weak' as he thought about it: an image about a man's skull and spine being shattered by a blow from an iron bar. In the novel, Evans learns that a half-insane alcoholic proposes to commit a murder by just such a means; instead of trying to prevent it, he finds it impossible to resist the temptation to allow it to happen, so that he can finally experience the pleasure of witnessing the act. But when he sees it happen, Evans vomits, and has a mental breakdown that leaves him little more than a vegetable.

Powys could not accept that his sadistic obsession could be explained in straightforward medical terms; he took the mystical view that 'such abominable wickedness came straight out of the evil in the heart of the First Cause, travelled through interlunar spaces, and entered the particular nerve in the erotic organ' that was 'predestined to respond to it'. This problem of 'fundamental evil' obsesses Powys, and runs throughout all his novels. Krafft-Ebing and Hirschfeld would obviously have regarded such a view as absurd romanticism. For them, sadism is a perfectly simple variation of the normal sex impulse. This impulse is fundamentally impersonal; a man does not have to be in love with a woman, or vice versa, to make love to her. In fact, he may even hate her. 'Walter' describes forcing his wife to have intercourse against her will: '. . . I jumped into bed, and forcing her on to her back, drove my prick up her. It must have been stiff, and I violent, for she cried out that I hurt her. "Don't do it so hard – what are you about?" But I felt that I could murder her with my prick, and drove, and drove, and spent up her cursing. While I fucked her I hated her, – she was my spunk-emptier . . .' Sadism is simply one stage beyond this – a 'Pavlovian' association of sexual satisfaction with aggression.

But although this may be 'scientifically' true, there is more to it than that. Grainger's sadism – and masochism – was an aspect of his 'Dionysianism' and his worship of physical fitness and Nordic 'purism'; it was a means to an end, and the end was a more *powerful* form of consciousness. Powys's sadism was connected with his peculiar nature-mysticism; he felt that hills, trees, grass, even rocks and crumbling old walls, possessed their own form of dim consciousness, which he was at times capable of sharing. Sexual desire, with its craving for intimacy with another being, was not so different from this craving for intimacy with the mysterious forces of nature.

Regarded in this light, all sexual perversion may be seen as having a 'mystical' aspect. The 'perverse' component is a deliberate attempt to raise normal sex to a higher level of intensity. Even D. H. Lawrence, usually regarded as the high priest of sexual normality, recorded this desire to go 'beyond normality'. In Chapter 16 of *Lady Chatterley's Lover* there is the following curious passage:

> It was a night of sensual passion, in which she was a little startled and almost unwilling; yet pierced again with piercing thrills and sensuality, different, sharper, more terrible than the thrills of tenderness, but, at the moment, more desirable. Though a little frightened, she let him have his way, and the reckless, shameless sensuality shook her to her foundations, stripped her to the very last, and made a different woman of her. It was not really love. It was not voluptuousness. It was sensuality sharp and searing as fire, burning the soul to tinder. Burning out the shames, the deepest, oldest shames, in the most secret places. It cost her an effort to let him have his way and his will of her. She had to be a passive, consenting thing like a slave, a physical slave. Yet the passion licked round her, consuming, and when the sensual flame of it pressed through her bowels and breast, she really thought she was dying; yet a poignant, marvellous death.

The word 'bowels' suddenly reveals that Lawrence is speaking about sodomy. And the phrase 'made a different woman of her' indicates that Lawrence feels it is more intense than normal sex. Chapter 23 of *Women in Love* contains a curious passage that seems to make the same point. Ursula kneels in front of Birkin on the hearthrug and puts her arms round his loins and her face against his thighs. A long description follows – too long to quote – in which she 'traces at the back of his thighs' with her 'sensitive finger tips', and discovers some 'mysterious life flow' there. 'It was here she discovered him one of the sons of God such as were in the beginning of the world, not a man, something other, something more.' 'She closed her hands over the full, rounded body of his loins, as he stooped over her, and she seemed to touch the quick of the mystery of darkness that was bodily him . . .' And both experience at the same time 'the marvellous fullness of immediate gratification, overwhelming, outflooding from the source of the deepest life-force, the darkest, deepest, strangest life source of the human body, at the back and base of the loins'. It finally becomes clear that what is being described is an act of fellatio during which Ursula inserts a finger in his anus. Similarly, in a poem, 'Manifesto', he writes:

> I want her to touch me at last, ah, on to the root and quick of
> my darkness . . .

If any further clarification is needed, it occurs in the section where Birkin commits an act of sodomy with Ursula, also described in terms of 'the root of her darkness'. That these acts of sodomy are touched with an element of sadism is revealed in the sentence about Lady Chatterley becoming 'a passive, consenting thing like a slave'.

We can trace this same element of perversion in Joyce – not simply in the underwear fetishism that made him carry a pair of doll's knickers in his pocket, but in the masochism that he attributes to Bloom, and which Joyce shared. In 1909, Joyce went back to Dublin and was told by an old friend, Cosgrave, that Joyce's wife Nora had often been unfaithful with another man – in fact, with Cosgrave himself. Joyce was shattered, and spent a sleepless night; he wrote Nora a letter ending: 'O, Nora, I am unhappy. I am crying for my poor unhappy love.' Yet, as Jeffrey Meyers comments in his study of Joyce's marriage,* 'Joyce used the fantasy of Nora's "betrayal" to revive his first passionate desires, and prolonged them in life so he could savour and record them in art.' Some element of masochism in him found the emotional upheaval so

* *Married to Genius*, 1977

exciting that he later tried to persuade Nora to sleep with another man – claiming that, for his portrait of Bloom in *Ulysses*, he needed to know what it was like to be a cuckold. It also seems to have triggered a flood of deviant sexual fantasies, expressed in a series of highly explicit letters to Nora. 'There is a place I would like to kiss you now, a *strange* place, Nora. *Not* on the lips, Nora . . .'

[I'd like to] fuck you up behind like a hog riding a sow, glorying in the very stink and sweat that rise from your arse . . . with you feeling your fingers fondling and tickling my ballocks or stuck up in me behind and your hot lips sucking off my cock while my head is wedged between your fat thighs, my hand clutching the round cushions of your bum and my tongue licking ravenously up your rank red cunt.

In another letter:

The smallest things give me a great cockstand – a whorish movement of your mouth, a little brown stain on the seat of your white drawers, a sudden dirty word spluttered out by your wet lips, a sudden immodest noise made by your behind and then a bad smell slowly curling up out of your backside. At such moments I feel made to do it in some filthy way, to feel your hot lecherous lips sucking away at me, to fuck between your two rosy-tipped bubbies, to come on your face and squirt it over your hot cheeks and eyes, to stick it up between the cheeks of your rump and bugger you.

A third letter rhapsodises about Nora's farts, and a time when, as they made love as she continually broke wind, 'a lot of tiny little naughty farties ending in a long gush from your hole. It is wonderful to fuck a farting woman.' In another letter – with odd overtones of Percy Grainger – he wishes she were strong, with a big bosom and fat thighs, so she could beat him. All this is closely linked to the desire to be cuckolded by her. In *Exiles*, the hero tells his best friend: 'In the very core of my ignoble heart I longed to be betrayed by you and by her . . . to be dishonoured for ever in love and lust, to be for ever a shameful creature and to build up my soul again out of the ruins of its shame.' But the proffered motivation is disingenuous; the reason the masochist wants to be betrayed is simply because the betrayal enables him to overcome 'the Coolidge effect' of taking her for granted; it intensifies his self-awareness of the act, exactly like 'Walter' looking at himself in a mirror.

Yet it must also be acknowledged that, biologically speaking, such perversions serve 'no useful purpose'. A male lion will, if given the opportunity, kill the cubs fathered on its mate by another lion; this is because it wants its own genes to survive, and 'rivals' are a threat. In the animal world, Joyce's masochism would operate against the survival of his genes. And this is also true, to a lesser extent, of Grainger's sadism and Lawrence's preference for sodomy. (It may be significant that neither Grainger nor Lawrence fathered children.) In the evolutionary balance-sheet, sexual perversion carries a minus sign.

Yet it also seems clear that there is one basic respect in which man differs from the other animals. He can deliberately use 'perverse' impulses to increase the intensity of the sexual urge. Animal sexuality is a straightforward desire to fertilise the female. But we only have to open *The Pearl* at any page to realise that human sexuality is far more complex. What biological impulse is served by flogging? Or by paedophilia? Or incest? The answer is, obviously, none. But the notion of 'the forbidden' has the power to intensify the human sexual urge, and to produce 'superheated sex'. Man has learned to intensify consciousness through the use of sexual imagination.

But how does the 'superheating mechanism' *work*? Grainger offers us the vital clue when he says: 'I love to simply wade and swim in a sea of overwrought, ceaseless sexual thought.' He clearly recognises that he is 'working himself up', just as a man might work himself up into a rage. It is as if there is an *aspect of himself* that can be made to respond to sexual imaginings just as another aspect might respond to music or poetry. It is as if this 'other self' was a good hypnotic subject, and can be made to respond to a snap of the hypnotist's fingers. Like Charcot's subjects at the Salpêtrière, he can be made to 'see' things that are not really there. In other words, he can be persuaded to respond to a *sexual illusion*. The sensible and rational part of him knows perfectly well that it is an illusion. When Swinburne went to the brothel in Circus Road and allowed beefy young women to flog him, he was pretending to be a naughty schoolboy being chastised by the schoolmarm. But when the women tried to *treat* him like a schoolboy and made exorbitant demands for payment, the rational part of him revolted and he marched out. 'It was one thing to be beaten like a child', says his biographer, Donald Thomas, 'but to be made a fool of over money by such creatures as these was quite intolerable.'

So the 'sexual illusion' depends on a *deliberately cultivated* self-division: a division between a 'childish' and a 'grown-up' aspect of the personality. The adult aspect knows that it is absurd to want to be flogged by a woman dressed in black leather, or to pretend to rape a prostitute dressed in a gym-slip and navy-blue knickers; but the child enjoys the fantasy – just as children enjoy tales about wicked giants, even though they know that giants do not exist. The adult justifies its surrender to the child by insisting that this is 'just a game' and that, in any case, sexual release is good for the health, like eating when you are hungry. To a certain extent, this is true. But it overlooks the fact that a starving man may die of hunger, while a sex-starved man is in no physical danger. The truth is that most of the justifications amount to self-deception. Swinburne and Grainger and Joyce and the rest – including Charlotte Bach – deliberately cultivate the child in themselves because it gives them so much pleasure. Like Barrie's Peter Pan, they have no intention of becoming grown ups.

But cultivating 'the hidden child' can be a dangerous game. The whole point about growing up is that we develop an increased *control* – over ourselves and the world around us. The more we achieve this control, the more we become 'individuals' instead of helpless bundles of fears and anxieties. This is why Jung calls the process 'individuation'. The man who cultivates his sexual deviations, as Swinburne and Grainger did, is resisting the process of individuation. He prefers to remain self-divided because, as William Blake said: 'stolen joys are sweet, and bread eaten in secret pleasant.'

Oddly enough, Jung was himself an example of this kind of resistance to individuation. Memoirs published since his death have revealed the extent to which he was thin-skinned, neurotic and unsure of himself. The world which had come to accept Jung as one of the great modern sages was startled to discover that his marriage had been undermined by a longstanding love-affair with one of his patients – Toni Wolff – and that there had been other infidelities. His later years, as described by Aniela Jaffé, his secretary, were clouded with pessimism, self-doubt and irritability, hardly the characteristics of a man who has achieved 'individuation'.

Even more curious is the case of the renowned Protestant theologian, Paul Tillich. Driven out of Germany because of his criticism of the Nazis (Tillich was a 'religious socialist'), he settled in New York and became perhaps the most famous of modern 'existential theologians'. In his three-volume *Systematic Theology*, Tillich developed what he called the 'method of correlation', which begins from the actual human situation. Man finds himself in a situation of suffering, doubt, meaninglessness and despair, and – like Byron's Manfred – he shakes his fist at God and asks questions. It is the business of theology to formulate these questions in precise language, and to attempt to answer them in terms of divine revelation. Tillich's critics protested that he had become too much of an existentialist, and that he paid too much attention to psychoanalysis, Marxist and other forms of modern materialist philosophy. But his emphasis on 'suffering man', trapped in the human situation, brought him wide influence; many still regard his *Systematic Theology* as the greatest modern work on the subject. He died in 1965, at the age of 79.

Eight years later, his wife Hannah published her autobiography *From Time to Time*, and revealed the great theologian had a more-than-human side: that, in fact, it would be no exaggeration to call him a sex maniac. He was a lifelong devotee of hard porn, which he read concealed inside the Bible or some theological book. He was also a 'satyr', a lifelong seducer of women, including his students – his wife found drawers-full of photographs of his girlfriends, and a pornographic letter under his blotting pad. She tells how, after their arrival in America, Tillich (whom she calls Paulus) began an affair with Hanna, the wife of one of his friends:

> On the day I arrived, after lunch and a quick game of pingpong with Gerhard [Hanna's husband], we went to find Paulus and Hanna. We found them together on the roof. Gerhard told me later that he had once found them on the roof, Hanna in the nude. I refused to let Paulus speak to me of his 'friendship' with her. I had had so much experience with his denying every fact until he made me believe him and not my own eyes, and I was sick of being betrayed. After dinner, when the children were in bed, Paulus, our friends, and I sat in the beautiful library of the

house and began to talk. He could not evade the facts with which I faced him. He threw himself on the floor, screaming and kicking, because this time there was no way out . . .

'Paulus' was inclined to behave like a small boy who eats sweets behind his mother's back. And this, of course, was part of the excitement. Hannah Tillich records that, after talking to a psychoanalyst about her husband's passion for pornography, she decided to accept it. 'I tried, then, to give Paulus pornography, which of course did not work, since the main appeal was its being kept secret from me . . .'

Does this mean that Tillich's religious belief was a fraud? No one who has read him could believe that. It means merely that he kept his religious belief and his sexual obsessions in separate compartments. The adult part of him wrote books to show how the existential miseries of fallen man can be abolished through 'Jesus as the Christ'; the childish part seduced his students and the wives of friends, and had screaming tantrums on the floor if he was found out. There was no real attempt at individuation, at growing up, because he found the two-compartment system pleasant and convenient. He was convinced that indulging the naughty child in himself made no difference to his philosophy – he probably told himself that he could think even better after a little adultery. Yet his attitude is bound to raise doubts in the minds of those who wish to assess his importance as a thinker. Is it not, for example, inevitable that a man who cannot keep his hands off his female students will emphasise human helplessness and man's inability to resist sin, and throw the whole burden of salvation on 'Jesus as the Christ'? Such reflections, at all events, raise doubts about Tillich's reliability as a spiritual guide and teacher . . .

Similar considerations would seem to apply to that other celebrated 'ethical teacher' of the twentieth century, Bertrand Russell: once again, the philosophy and the sex life seem to have been kept in watertight compartments; one biographer commented that his private life 'was a chaos of serious affairs, secret trysts and emotional tightrope acts that constantly threatened . . . ruinous scandal'. At the age of twenty – in 1892 – he fell in love with an American Quaker, Alys Pearsall Smith, but also engaged in an affair with her sister, Mary, who had just left her husband. After a year or two of marriage, Russell was out bicycling one day when it suddenly dawned on him that he no longer loved his wife, and he hastened home to break the news to her. Alys was shattered and did her best to persuade him not to leave her. But she was unsuccessful; Russell had made the discovery that he found seduction the most interesting game in the world. As with other obsessive Don Juans – Casanova and Frank Harris spring to mind– this seems to be less a question of boundless physical appetite than of a certain emotional immaturity and shallowness. In spite of his pre-eminence as a mathematical philosopher, he felt a lightweight as a human being, and sexual conquest flattered his ego. His life consisted of an endless series of affairs and several marriages, each of which ended in separation because he found the lure of infidelity too great. With his second wife, Dora, he launched an experimental school, and one of the things they advocated was free love. Russell had a regular affair with one female staff member, with whom he vanished for weekends to London, and he habitually propositioned any new female teacher. When the cook caught Russell in bed with the children's governess, she refused to let the governess near the children until Dora (who was spending the weekend with a boyfriend) returned home. Russell, 'who had an aristocratic attitude towards servants', sacked the cook.

That this lifelong Don Juanism was a psychological rather than a physical obsession seems to be proved by the case of a girl called Joan Folwell, whom Russell met when she was twenty-one and he was close on sixty. He had been addressing a political meeting in Salisbury, and stayed at the house of her parents. When he asked her to read aloud an essay she had written, it gradually dawned on her that 'he was more interested in me than in my writing'. He kept in touch by letter and was soon suggesting that they should sleep together. Eventually, after many delays and obstacles, they spent the night in a hotel. 'But the sleeping wasn't a success,' records Miss Folwell, 'so I gave him up.' Russell's three-year pursuit was evidently an attempt to prove something to himself rather than an overwhelming physical passion.

In later years, Russell embarrassed the philosopher Sidney Hook – who regarded him with reverence – with unsolicited advice on how to 'make' young girls, and what to do after having made them. He told Hook that if the hotel reception clerk seemed suspicious, the girl should complain loudly about the price of the room – that would convince anyone that they were really married. Hook commented (in an article in *Encounter*) that he regarded Russell as a brilliant mind allied to a curious emotional immaturity. (This may be a characteristic of 'logical' philosophers: the designer, Jocelyn Richards, has recorded in her autobiography *The Painted Banquet* that she broke off an affair with the logical positivist, A. J. Ayer, because of his obsessive promiscuity; she complained that he reduced her to one of a pack by picking up a different girl each night; but it was not out of pique that she left him, but simply because, when the number of his girlfriends exceeded seven, 'there weren't enough days in the week'.)

In the case of other influential figures of the twentieth century, the recognition of sexual self-division can produce a certain shift in perspective. When I wrote about T. E. Lawrence in *The Outsider*, I regarded him as being, like Nietzsche and Dostoevsky, a typical 'intellectual Outsider', deeply frustrated by the problem of what to *do* with his creative energies. This aspect of the problem was expressed perceptively by Edgar Lee Masters, in the poem 'Professor Newcomer', in *The Spoon River Anthology*:

> Everyone laughed at Col. Prichard
> For buying an engine so powerful
> That it wrecked itself, and wrecked the grinder
> He ran with it.
> But here is a joke of cosmic size:
> The urge of nature that made a man
> Evolve from his brain a spiritual life –
> Oh miracle of the world! –
> The very same brain with which the ape and wolf
> Get food and shelter and procreate themselves.
> Nature has made a man do this,
> In a world where she gives him nothing to do
> After all – (though the strength of the soul goes round
> In a futile waste of power,
> To gear itself to the mills of the gods) –
> But get food and shelter and procreate himself.

Here is the 'Outsider's' problem in a nutshell: man finds himself 'in a world where she gives him nothing to do'. So the fierce drive of a Nietzsche, a Tolstoy, a Lawrence of Arabia, finds itself revolving in a vacuum. Lawrence, like the ascetics of Thebaid, looked for his

answer in the desert. Before the First World War he went to Arabia
to study Crusaders' castles; during the War he found himself chosen
to lead the Arab revolt against the Turks. It gave him 'something
to do', yet at the same time made him more deeply aware of his
self-division. He wrote:

> Before me lay a vista of responsibility and command, which
> disgusted my thought-riddled nature. I felt mean, to fill the place
> of a man of action; for my standards of value were a wilful reaction
> against theirs, and I despised their happiness. Always my soul
> hungered for less than it had, since my senses, sluggish beyond
> the senses of most men, needed the immediacy of contact to
> achieve perception . . .

This sense of deep dissatisfaction became increasingly strong until it
finally drove Lawrence to apply for leave to return to England at
the moment of his supreme triumph – the conquest of Damascus.
After the War, he fought for Arab rights at the conference table
in Paris, but saw them betrayed by the Allies. Feeling himself
responsible, Lawrence returned to London, and declined the
honours with which the government tried to soothe his feelings. A
series of lectures about him by the journalist Lowell Thomas
brought him overnight fame; Thomas's book *With Lawrence in
Arabia* became a bestseller on both sides of the Atlantic. Predictably, his response was self-disgust and a powerful urge to escape
the limelight. Close to mental breakdown, he joined the Royal Air
Force as an ordinary aircraftman, under the name of Ross. But the
Daily Express revealed his identity, and he was discharged after
only four months. Within six weeks he had again enlisted, this time
as a private in the Tank Corps. Three years later, he was transferred
back to the RAF. He was still in the RAF when he was killed in a
motorcycle accident in May 1935.

As I wrote about Lawrence, it seemed to me that his response
to his feeling of alienation was unnecessarily violent. If he disliked
his notoriety so much, why did he not find himself a cheap cottage
somewhere – they could be bought for a few pounds in those days
– and live the life of a recluse? I could understand a desire to escape
'crowds' and live a life devoted to books and music; but entering
the RAF seemed – as I knew from personal experience – an obvious
recipe for boredom and frustration.

The answer, in fact, lay under my nose, in the eightieth chapter of *Seven Pillars of Wisdom*, which I had read again and again without grasping its full significance. It is the chapter in which Lawrence describes how he went on a spying expedition to the town of Deraa, which was occupied by the Turks, and was arrested under suspicion of being a deserter. He was taken before the Bey, who immediately grabbed him and threw him down on a bed. Lawrence fought back, so the Bey ordered soldiers to pinion his arms while his clothes were removed, then began to paw him. 'I bore it for a little, till he got too beastly; and then jerked my knee into him.' Lawrence was then stretched out on a wooden bench, and the corporal proceeded to lash him with a Circassian whip. After beating him unconscious, they threw him on the floor.

I remembered the corporal kicking with his nailed boot to get me up; and this was true, for the next day my right side was dark and lacerated, and a damaged rib made each breath stab me sharply. I remembered smiling idly at him, for a delicious warmth, probably sexual, was swelling through me; and then that he flung up his arm and hacked with the full length of his whip into my groin. This doubled me half-over, screaming . . .

In the midst of this long description of the flogging, most readers will understandably overlook those two words, 'probably sexual'. Besides, who can tell how any of us would react if subjected to such brutality? Yet if I had taken the trouble to think about it, I would have seen that there is something odd about a man who responds to a murderous beating with a sexual orgasm.

Probably aware that he had betrayed his lifelong secret – at least to those who share the deviation – Lawrence later made attempts to cover his tracks. He told Bernard Shaw that his account of what had happened at Deraa was untrue, but Shaw was too tactful to ask what really happened. But in a letter to Mrs Shaw of 26 March 1924, Lawrence finally admitted: 'For fear of being hurt, or rather, to earn five minutes' respite from a pain that drove me mad, I gave away the only possession we are born into the world with – our bodily integrity. It's an unforgivable matter, an irrecoverable position: and it's that which has made me forswear decent living . . .' So, according to Lawrence, it was guilt at having permitted the Bey to sodomise him that drove him to forswear public honours and enter the RAF. Yet this is flatly contradicted by another statement in *Seven Pillars*, in which he says that 'some part of me had gone dead that night in Deraa', then adds: 'It could not have been the defilement, for no one ever held the body in less honour than I did myself.' And he goes on to talk about the 'breaking of the spirit by that frenzied nerve-shattering pain . . . which had journeyed with me since, a fascination and terror and morbid desire, lascivious and vicious, perhaps, but like the striving of a moth towards its flame'. And so, according to Lawrence, the Deraa incident had created a taste for masochism . . .

In 1968, the Public Record Office in London began releasing documents about Lawrence – the period of official embargo on such documents had been changed from fifty to thirty years – and two investigative journalists, Philip Knightley and Colin Simpson, began to study them for the fresh light they threw on the 'Lawrence mystery'. The result was a series of articles which appeared in the *Sunday Times* and which were later expanded into a book, *The Secret Lives of Lawrence of Arabia*. And when they were unable to discover the truth about the Deraa incident from various documents, Knightley and Simpson decided to see if they could interview the man who was supposed to have sodomised Lawrence, Hacim Muhittin Bey. They were unlucky; the Bey had died in 1965. But it became clear that, far from being a homosexual, he was 'an aggressive heterosexual' with an immense sexual appetite. They interviewed many people who had known the Bey well, including some of his enemies, and all agreed that he had no homosexual tendencies. Whatever happened at Deraa, it seems clear that Lawrence was *not* sodomised by Hacim Bey.

Knightley and Simpson uncovered at least one revealing document; it was by a young Scot called John Bruce, who had met Lawrence early in 1922, at the time when Lawrence was working for Winston Churchill in the Colonial Office. Lawrence asked Bruce to become a kind of general factotum or valet. And one day Lawrence told him an extraordinary story. He had decided to join the RAF as an aircraftman – not as a matter of preference, but because he had been ordered to do so by some rich and influential relative called the 'Old Man'. The Old Man felt that Lawrence had disgraced the family honour and that he had to expiate his transgressions through pain and humiliation. Bruce was apparently taken in by this absurd story (although he sensibly suggested that Lawrence should tell the Old Man to go to hell), and agreed to join the army to 'look after' Lawrence. In 1923, Lawrence and Bruce did their army training at Bovington camp, in Dorset, and Lawrence rented a nearby cottage called Cloud's Hill. One day, Lawrence told Bruce that the Old Man was angry with him for failing to attend church parades, and had ordered that he should be punished. He showed Bruce a typed letter that threatened to publish Lawrence's illegitimacy to the world unless he agreed to be flogged with a birch. Bruce at first refused to have anything to do with it, but finally he agreed. Lawrence lay on the bed, and was thrashed with his trousers on. But later that day, he told Bruce that he had been to see the Old Man, and that his tormentor was not satisfied; Lawrence had to be thrashed on his bare buttocks. So this time Lawrence removed his trousers and lay on the bed while Bruce administered a dozen painful strokes of the birch, causing Lawrence to bleed. At the end, Lawrence asked Bruce to give him 'one more for luck' – which should have made Bruce suspicious. And from then on, this extraordinary charade continued, with Bruce receiving unsigned typed letters from the 'Old Man', asking if Lawrence's conduct had improved, and ordering more floggings. Bruce was not the only one – Lawrence apparently induced other soldiers to beat him by telling them the same cock-and-bull story. And when Bruce finally returned to Scotland, Lawrence often made the long journey to Aberdeen or Edinburgh on his motorbike to receive 'his usual dose'. After Lawrence's death, Mrs Shaw sent for Bruce and revealed that she knew about the floggings; she begged him to keep silent about them, knowing the harm they would do to Lawrence's reputation. Bruce agreed, and kept his promise for another three decades. And when he finally allowed Knightley and Simpson to publish his account in their book, it was clear that he still believed Lawrence's story about the 'Old Man'.

Knightley and Simpson conclude that, whatever really happened at Deraa, Lawrence continued to be oppressed by a sense of guilt, which led to the desire to be punished. Such a view is hardly consistent with their own new evidence. Masochists are born, not made; Lawrence's desire to be whipped probably dated from early childhood; but he was born into a 'manly' world, where healthy, muscular young males were supposed to administer the floggings, not receive them. It was the guilt about his 'perversion' that turned a brilliant and sensitive young intellectual into an ascetic 'Outsider' and which led, almost accidentally, to the production of one of the twentieth century's great works of literature. Auden once said that the aim of education was 'to create as much neurosis as the child can stand without cracking'. According to that definition, Lawrence's masochism must be regarded as one of the greatest formative influences on his genius.

If this statement seems to contradict the earlier conclusion that sexual perversions stand in the way of achieving 'individuation', the conflict is only apparent. It is important to remember the story about Negley Farson, cited in an earlier chapter: that when Farson went to see a doctor about his alcoholism, the doctor told him that he *could* cure it, but that he would probably cure him of his writing talent at the same time. In the case of Lawrence, the reader often suspects that he cultivates his self-division because it drives him to greater efforts of self-discipline. He seems to suspect that inner peace is a synonym of mediocrity. And the history of 'Outsiderism' in the past two centuries seems to bear out this uncomfortable conclusion.

Of all the major figures of the twentieth century, none illustrates the 'conflict mechanism' more clearly than the philosopher Ludwig Wittgenstein. I wrote about him in *Religion and the Rebel*, the sequel to *The Outsider*; but at that time (1957, only six years after his death) a heavy atmosphere of reverence surrounded his name, and no one had even hinted at his homosexuality. When it was finally revealed in print, I realised that it explained a great deal about Wittgenstein that had baffled me in 1957.

Wittgenstein was the youngest child of a wealthy Viennese family; all his brothers and sisters were gifted. Apparently determined to become an engineer like his father, he studied engineering in Berlin, aeronautics at Manchester, and mathematics at Cambridge under Bertrand Russell. He was deeply pessimistic by temperament, and as a young man was influenced by Schopenhauer's *World as Will and Idea*: like T. E. Lawrence, he seems to have had a lifelong day-dream of becoming a monk or religious ascetic. He was morbidly drawn to the idea of suicide – two of his brothers killed themselves before the First World War, and a third was to do so at the end of it. Wittgenstein later admitted that when he enlisted in the army in 1914, it was with a secret desire to be killed. In the event, he survived the War, carrying in his knapsack the manuscript of his most famous book, the *Tractatus Logico-Philosophicus* (which Wittgenstein called simply '*Der Satz*' – 'The Proposition').

At the end of the War, he was close to nervous breakdown. He had inherited a large part of the family wealth – in modern terms he was a millionaire – but one of the first things he did when he came out of the army was to give it away to the rest of his family. Then, for the next six years, he became a schoolmaster in a remote village in Lower Austria. Virtually driven out of it by resentful peasants, he spent two years designing and building a house for one of his sisters in Vienna, then returned to Cambridge, where he was made a Fellow of Trinity. In 1937 he succeeded G. E. Moore to the chair of philosophy, but he was a highly unorthodox professor. He tended to wear an old lumberjacket over an open-necked shirt, and avoided mixing with other dons. On the one occasion he dined at high table, he put his hands over his ears, groaning: 'But they don't even *enjoy* doing it.' During the Second World War, he went to London and became a hospital porter, then went to Newcastle and worked in a medical laboratory. In 1947 he moved to a cottage on the west coast of Ireland, and worked on his second philosophical book, *Philosophical Investigations*. He seemed to have some curious power over birds; when I was in Galway later, an old man told me of seeing Wittgenstein standing with his head and shoulders covered with birds. In 1949 he discovered that he was suffering from cancer, and died of it in 1951.

It was only in the 1970s that it became clear that the basic reason for Wittgenstein's gloomy asceticism was his guilt about his homosexuality. His brother, Hans, a musical genius who committed suicide at the age of twenty-four in 1902, was a homosexual; his brother, Rudolf, who committed suicide two years later, was probably so. From his mid-teens, Ludwig Wittgenstein also brooded on suicide; he was still talking about it when he first went to Cambridge in 1913. In a paradoxical sense, the Great War may have saved his life. And it was after the War that Wittgenstein finally gave way to his powerful compulsion, and began to haunt the Prater area, where he could pick up the kind of 'rough trade' he preferred. His own promiscuity horrified him, yet he felt unable to resist it. In November 1919, he fell in love with a heterosexual mechanic named Arvid Sjogren, and became a lodger in his home; he was forced to move out when Sjogren's mother fell in love with

224 · THE MISFITS

him. He went back to a life of promiscuity, writing gloomily to a friend: 'Things have gone utterly miserably for me lately. Of course, only because of my own baseness and rottenness. I have continually thought about taking my own life, and now too this thought still haunts me. *I have sunk to the bottom.* May you never be in this position.'* When I spoke to Dora Russell about Wittgenstein in 1975, she told me that she and Bertrand Russell had strongly disapproved of Wittgenstein's promiscuity, and that they had felt the need to keep a protective eye on some of their young male acquaintances.

William Warren Bartley observes penetratingly: 'When one is terrified, as was Wittgenstein, of what one might do, one may attempt to construct an environment that will help to protect one from doing what one in a sense wants but must not do. This Wittgenstein did; and in the pattern of his construction is to be found some explanation for some of his odder actions.' He goes on to say that Wittgenstein would try to stay away from large cities, where he was tempted to look for male prostitutes, and would form platonic relationships with young men like Arvid Sjogren, whom he could at once adore and dominate.

But Bartley's comment also helps us to understand Wittgenstein's attitude to philosophy. Wittgenstein possessed the disposition that is often to be found in saints and ascetics: a powerful craving for meaning and purpose, and immense self-disgust at his own failure to find them. He wrote to his friend, Engelmann, in 1921: 'I am one of those cases which perhaps are not all that rare today: I had a task, did not do it, and now the failure is wrecking my life . . . My life has really become meaningless and so it consists only of futile episodes.' In 1919 he had a dream which he considered of immense significance. He was looking in through the lighted window of a house, and saw a beautiful prayer rug. But when he tried to get into the house, a snake darted out of the door and blocked his way; other snakes blocked the windows. He interpreted the dream to mean that his sexual desires were blocking his 'religious' aspirations. After his period as a schoolmaster, he became a gardener in a monastery, and seriously considered becoming a monk. (His friend von Wright records that 'he could not muster enough religious faith'.)

* Quoted in *Wittgenstein*, by William Warren Bartley III, p. 25

It was this sense of failure, of living on the brink of an abyss, that produced in Wittgenstein the craving for certainty that led him to create the philosophical system of the *Tractatus*.

The *Tractatus* claims to be nothing less than the ultimate solution of all problems of philosophy. But this is less conceited than it sounds, since he begins by redefining the problems of philosophy, and restricting them to a compass that most philosophers would consider absurdly narrow. According to Wittgenstein, language is simply a picture of the real world, in the same way that a portrait is a picture of a real man. This world around us, says Wittgenstein, can be reduced to what he called 'atomic facts' or 'states of affairs' (in German, *Sachverhalten*). States of affairs consist, in turn, of simple objects, and these can be defined with names. These names can be combined into elementary propositions, and these in turn can be combined into more complex propositions, which Wittgenstein calls 'truth functions'. If the elementary proposition was 'I am here', then one of its truth functions would be 'I am not at the North Pole since I am here' (unless, of course, 'here' refers to the North Pole). And since it is perfectly obvious that I am not at the North Pole if I am here, Wittgenstein was led to define truth as tautology – a mere repetition of the same meaning.

This sounds like a thoroughly materialistic philosophy, almost as crude as Marxism. But Wittgenstein was not insisting, as Marx was, that all 'truth' can be defined in purely material terms. He agrees that there is such a thing as religious truth and ethical truth. But he insists that *it cannot be put into words*, and that any philosopher who thinks he is talking about these great universal truths is merely deceiving himself. And, according to Wittgenstein, it should be easy enough to show him that he is deceiving himself by getting him to read the *Tractatus* and demonstrating to him that he had simply failed to give meaning to certain signs in his propositions. In Wittgenstein's view, most of what has passed for philosophy since Plato is, quite literally, nonsense. 'Riddles do not exist.' The famous last sentence of the *Tractatus* states: 'Whereof one cannot speak, one must be silent.'

Such a philosophy obviously gave Wittgenstein a certain degree of comfort; he must have felt that he had created a firm foundation in a treacherously slippery world. Yet, in another sense, he is not much better off than before, for he has admitted that the realm that really interests him – the realm of religious (or, as Sartre would say, 'existential') meaning – really exists, although it is beyond the reach of words. To some extent, Wittgenstein concedes, it can be *shown*. For example, a friend sent him a poem by Uhland, 'Count Eberhard's Hawthorn', in which every stanza is concrete and informative, yet which succeeds in giving, in twenty-eight lines, the picture of a man's whole life. What Wittgenstein is really saying is that poetry somehow manages to say things in defiance of his logic of 'atomic facts' and tautologies. In which case, he has undermined his argument which asserts that such things cannot be said.

Wittgenstein's attempt to limit the scope of philosophy was inspired by the immense *Principia Mathematica* by Bertrand Russell and A. N. Whitehead, in which the authors attempted to demonstrate that mathematics is simply a branch of logic. One of the problems that arose was that of logical paradoxes, such as that of Epimenides: If I say I lie and I do lie, then I tell the truth; if I say I lie and I tell the truth, then I lie . . .The simplest form of such a paradox is: THIS SENTENCE IS UNTRUE. Is that true or not? If it is true, then it is untrue, and if it is untrue, then it is true. But a little thought shows us that, in fact, the sentence is meaningless; it cannot be true or untrue. To be true or untrue, it must *point to* another sentence whose truth *can* be determined, i.e. 'This sentence is untrue: it is snowing outside.' It is merely an *indicator sentence*, which serves the same function as a signpost. When it stands on its own, it is like a signpost with nothing written on it.

Wittgenstein took this kind of logic a step further, and declared that all 'metaphysical philosophy' is a signpost with nothing written on it. And he tried to do this by techniques similar to those used in *Principia Mathematica*. In fact, both the *Tractatus* and *Principia* were undermined at one blow in 1931 when Kurt Gödel produced his famous 'proof'. This states that, in any set of mathematical definitions or postulates (like that of *Principia Mathematica*), there will always be certain propositions that cannot be proved within the system. You have to construct a 'higher' kind of meta-system to prove them, and this system will also contain statements which cannot be proved . . . On the whole, then, we may regard the *Tractatus* as a mere dinosaur skeleton in the museum of philosophy.

In fact, by the early 1930s, Wittgenstein had reached the same conclusion. The legend has it that he was discussing the 'logical form' of propositions with the economist, Piero Sraffa, when Sraffa made a Neapolitan gesture – brushing underneath his chin with the fingertips of one hand, signifying contempt – and asked: 'What is the logical form of that?' It must have been some such experience that made Wittgenstein recognise that language is not an accurate *picture* of reality, but something much more complex. Words are tools, but tools are of many different kinds: hammers, screwdrivers, pincers, corkscrews . . . So the 'meaning' of a word is not rigidly defined – as in the *Tractatus* – but is something that varies according to the use we put it to. (The exclamation, 'Shit!', sounds like an order, yet we all know it is not.) The meaning is its *purpose in a particular context*, and we need to understand the context, just as, in order to understand what a chess player is doing, we need to understand the rules of chess. Wittgenstein says that language could be regarded as a vast game, in which there are thousands of smaller games. (For example, the language game played on a barrack square is quite different from the language game played in the pulpit or the philosopher's classroom.) It is useless to look for general 'overall' rules, says Wittgenstein, just as it is useless to look for some general definition of the word 'game'. (What have a game of chess, of charades, of patience and of clay-pigeon shooting in common?)

But if the arguments are more complex than in the *Tractatus*, the overall purpose of this 'linguistic analysis' is much the same. He regards most philosophy as a misunderstanding of language. The aim of philosophy is 'to prevent the bewitchment of our senses through language'. Some philosophers distort language to such an extent that the results are not so much philosophical systems that need refuting as illnesses that need treating. Wittgenstein saw himself as a kind of doctor.

Once again, we suspect that what Wittgenstein was trying to do was to avoid the slippery slope that led to brooding and insanity. He wanted philosophy to be something clear and concrete, like mathematics, with no 'riddles'. If he had lived on for another thirty years, one suspects he might have tried to invent computer programs to solve all philosophical problems. He wished to turn his back decisively on the kind of 'accursed questions' asked by the great novelists and moral philosophers; he would have liked to insist that Kierkegaard's question 'What am I doing here?' was simply a misunderstanding of language. He warns us against the method of introspection. If you want to know the significance of a word like 'pain' or 'memory' or 'feeling' or 'expectation', take a long, careful look at the way it is *used* in ordinary language . . . This, admittedly, is not intended as a general prohibition on introspection; yet this *is* very much in the spirit of Wittgenstein's later philosophy. To the question: 'What is the meaning of life?', he would answer: 'Explain precisely what you mean by life, and I think you will see that what you *imagined* to be a real question evaporates into thin air.'

To begin to see where Wittgenstein went wrong, we merely have to examine his statement that it is impossible to define the word 'game' in a way that covers *all* games. When children play Cowboys and Indians, we can see that their game is a kind of *rehearsal* for real life – for real combats and conflicts. And the same goes for chess and patience and charades and every other kind of game. A game is a rehearsal for reality; in that sense, day-dreaming is the archetypal game. This would have been obvious to Wittgenstein if he had tried introspection as a method of understanding what games are *for*. But introspection made him feel insecure; he preferred to consult a dictionary.

Wittgenstein once said that the aim of his philosophy was 'to show the fly the way out of the fly bottle'. Yet it is hard not to feel that the author of the *Philosophical Investigations* is himself trapped in his own home-made fly bottle. His philosophy gave him a means of criticising others, but offered him no clue to how to escape his own inner labyrinth. It is regrettable that he felt that it was a waste of time to read other philosophers; in the work of his contemporary, Edmund Husserl, he might have found a more fruitful method. Husserl's aim was also the creation of a purely scientific philosophy; but he recognised that the starting point must be a *precise and objective description of our own inner states*. On this foundation, Husserl succeeded in building at least the first storey of a 'system' which can ask questions about the meaning and purpose of human existence. (Heidegger and Sartre used it as the basis of their own forms of 'existentialism'.) Wittgenstein was obsessed by such questions but – on the evidence of his work – spent his lifetime evading them. It would not be too unfair to say that his philosophy was the philosophy of a child who is afraid of the dark.

Yet the same comments apply to Wittgenstein as to T. E. Lawrence: to recognise that his work was fuelled by a sense of guilt about his life does not invalidate the work or the life. What is significant about their lives is that both were driven by an

immense dissatisfaction with themselves. The source of this dissatisfaction is the conflict between their powerfully developed powers
of reason, and emotions and desires that seemed to mock them.
They epitomise again the problem stated by Fulke Greville:

> What meaneth nature by these diverse laws,
> Passion and reason, self-division's cause?

And behind this lies the greatest and most irritating problem of
human existence: the fact that, when confronted by crisis, we
suddenly understand the meaning of freedom, and then grasp how
easy it would be to live on a far more intense level of vitality and
purpose. Yet almost as soon as the crisis vanishes, we sink back
into the 'triviality of everydayness' (Heidegger's phrase), and find
ourselves totally unable to galvanise ourselves back into a state of
purpose. The problem lies in our slavery to habit, in our 'mechan-
icalness'. All men of genius glimpse these higher levels of drive
and purpose, and recognise that *lack of challenge* causes most of
us to waste our lives. We need to discover some higher level of
motivation that will enable us to make proper use of these powers
that slumber inside us.

This was obviously the basic motivation that drove Lawrence to
his remarkable feats of endurance in the desert, and that led
Wittgenstein to become a hospital porter in London, then a recluse
in a hut in Galway. Their sense of guilt also undoubtedly contributed, but readers of the *Seven Pillars* or of Wittgenstein's letters
may often find themselves wondering how far both men cultivated
a sense of guilt in order to galvanise themselves to greater efforts.
What is quite apparent is that, in both of them, it was the genius
rather than the guilt that led to those frantic efforts to escape the
'triviality of everydayness'.

This is not, of course, a problem that is confined to 'Outsiders' and
men of genius. Every human being on the surface of the planet
experiences the same compulsion to avoid boredom, to escape
triviality. We instinctively seek out anything that induces a sense
of meaning and purpose. What most people require is to see their
own personal cravings and longings projected on to a large screen.
This explains the rise of political movements like Nazism, as well
as of absurd religious cults whose beliefs apparently require a total

suspension of sanity. Intelligent individuals find such a suspension of common sense impossible: hence 'Outsiderism'. Yet even the most intelligent experience the desire to seek out – or create – a system of belief that can unite them with other people and rescue them from the sense of isolation. Hence Byron's Greek adventure, Swinburne's Italian patriotism, Gogol's religious obsession, Grainger's Nordic mysticism, D. H. Lawrence's borderline fascism. All reveal the craving to escape the burden of individualism and merge into some form of 'collective' effort.

In the postwar years, perhaps the most spectacular example of this compulsion is provided by the Japanese novelist, Yukio Mishima. His public suicide in 1970 was a shock from which the Japanese psyche is still recovering, almost two decades later. (One interesting consequence is that, at the time of writing, there is still no Japanese biography of the novelist.)

On 25 November 1970, the forty-five-year-old novelist – perhaps the most successful Japanese writer of all time – drove to the Eastern Army headquarters in Tokyo with four other men, one of them his lover, and seized the commander, General Mashita. Mishima then explained that his condition for sparing the general's life was that all the garrison should be assembled in the courtyard to listen in silence to a speech he had prepared. He had also notified the media, and when he stepped out on to the balcony at midday, television cameras were focused on him. But the soldiers refused to listen in silence; there were hoots, jeers and shouts of 'Arsehole!' Mishima's exhortation to the army to rise up and throw off the democracy that had deprived Japan of her soul was unheard in the racket; after seven minutes he gave up and went in again. Inside, he knelt on the floor, unbuttoned his trousers, and held a dagger against his abdomen. Then he drove it in, and tore it sideways to disembowel himself. His lover, Morita, tried to cut off Mishima's head with a sword, but his hands were shaking, and he only succeeded in cutting his back. A second blow made a deep wound on the body. Only with the third blow did he succeed in partially severing the neck. Another of the group seized the sword and chopped off the head with one blow. Then Morita tried to disembowel himself, but failed to drive the dagger home; as he nodded his head, the sword descended again and decapitated him. General Mashita was then released. The great romantic revolt against the modern world was over.

Yukio Mishima was the pen-name of Kimitaké Hiraoka, the son of a government official. He was born in 1925 in the home of his grandparents, with whom his parents lived. His grandfather, Jotaro Hiraoka, had once been governor of the island of Sakhalin, but a financial scandal had forced his resignation; after this, he had become a businessman, and had taken about ten years to plunge into bankruptcy. His wife, Natsuko, was an unstable and neurotic woman with a strong hysterical streak; when her grandson – born 14 January 1925 – was only seven weeks old, she literally snatched him from his mother's arms and installed his crib in her own sickroom. The baby's mother did not dare to object. For the next twelve years, Natsuko guarded her grandson with total possessiveness. He was not allowed to play with other children, hardly allowed to see his parents. His grandmother brought him up as a girl rather than a boy. He grew into a weak, sickly child, totally dominated by Natsuko; even his play was rationed. The only pleasure in which he was allowed unlimited indulgence was reading. His grandmother's library included the fairy tales of Hans Andersen and Oscar Wilde. The Andersen story called 'The Rose Elf' seems to have awakened Mishima's latent sadism, the story of 'that beautiful youth who, while kissing the rose given him as a token by his sweetheart, was stabbed to death and decapitated by a villain with a big knife . . . My heart's leaning towards Death and Night and Blood would not be denied.' Tales like this became the material of his sadistic day-dreams. (As with Grainger and Powys, Mishima's sadism seemed to be inborn.) In the autobiographical novel, *Confessions of a Mask*, he describes how he had his first orgasm when looking at a picture of Saint Sebastian pierced with arrows. His biographer Henry Scott Stokes recorded: 'he dreamt of bloodshed, he dreamt of massacring youths, preferably Circassian [i.e. white youths] on large marble tables and eating parts of their bodies'. And so, like John Cowper Powys and Percy Grainger, Mishima fed this insatiable cannibalistic worm with horrible dreams of torture and murder. As he became aware of his homosexuality – experiencing erections at the sight of men in bathing trunks – dreams of young *samurai* cutting open their bellies mingled with images of muscular *sumo* wrestlers, not yet grown fat . . . He fell in love with a boy at school, and envied his powerful body, and the hair under his armpits. He began to write a story called 'Mansion' (*Yakata*) about a satanic aristocrat whose sole pleasure is murder. In

Confessions of a Mask he describes how, at the age of fourteen, he devised a 'theatre of murder' in which young gladiators wallowed in blood. He was not interested in gallows or instruments of torture, for they would not produce the blood that gave him such sexual excitement.

He began publishing in the school magazine when he was eleven; at sixteen, he wrote a short novel called *The Forest in Full Bloom*, to be published in instalments in a literary magazine; it was a historical fantasy, covering several periods of Japanese history, and was remarkable for a controlled richness of language – possibly learned from Oscar Wilde. Throughout his life, Mishima was basically an aesthete, and most of his work is about violent – and negative – emotions. Because he was only sixteen when this first work was published, his teacher suggested that he should use a *nom de plume*. 'Yukio Mishima' was chosen for its aesthetic qualities, *yuki* meaning 'snow', and Mishima being a town at the foot of Mount Fuji.

When war began, Mishima, like all other Japanese, became an ardent patriot. He took part in military training, served in a naval dockyard, and dreamed of dying in battle. In 1944, he passed out of the Gakushuin school at the top of his class, and he was presented with a gold watch by the emperor in person. His father insisted that he study law at Tokyo University, and he agreed without enthusiasm. But soon after entering the University, he was drafted to work in a factory devoted to manufacturing kamikaze aircraft – Japan was now obviously losing the war, and the notion of trying to reverse the position by using pilots as human bombs was typical of the Japanese military tradition. For someone so obsessed with the idea of blood, working in such a factory was almost like a religious initiation. 'I have never seen such a strange factory. In it, all the techniques of modern science and management . . . were dedicated to a single end – Death.'

By now his first book – *The Forest in Full Bloom* – had appeared, and an edition of 4,000 sold out within a week. In the following year, 1945, he was called up. He succeeded in convincing the army doctor that he was tubercular – declaring that he suffered from night sweats and spat blood – and was rejected as medically unfit. It was a lie that haunted him for the rest of his life. Yet the motive was not so much cowardice as masochism. He wanted to become a soldier because it might 'provide me at last with an opportunity for gratifying those strange sensual desires of mine' – that is, to see blood and agony. He liked to think of himself as a person who wanted to die but had been refused death; evading military service allowed him to wallow in a kind of self-laceration.

Early in 1946, Mishima showed a short story about homosexuality at the Gakushuin school to the famous writer, Yasunari Kawabata, who recommended it to a magazine editor. Kawabata quickly became Mishima's patron and sponsor – a role that is more important in Japan than in the West. Mishima also had one single meeting with Osamu Dazai, a writer whose pessimistic romanticism was to culminate in suicide in 1948; because he felt threatened by the similarities between them, Mishima did his best to insult him – without success. It was as if Dazai's suicide – by drowning – freed Mishima to express his own romantic pessimism; in November 1948, he began *Confessions of a Mask*. When it appeared in the following year, it brought the twenty-four-year-old Mishima instant fame, and critics acclaimed him as a genius. It is a largely autobiographical account of Mishima's childhood and youth, as egoistic – and as compellingly frank – as Rousseau's *Confessions*. But the central episode of the novel – the narrator's abortive love-affair with a young girl called Sonoko – was pure fiction. On the whole, Mishima detested and mistrusted women. In a typical last scene, the narrator and Sonoko sit in a cheap dance-hall, and the narrator is suddenly convulsed with violent sexual desire at the sight of a young gangster (*yakuza*) who sits stripped to the waist, with tufts of hair sticking out of his armpits – typically, the narrator derives additional satisfaction from imagining someone driving a knife into the youth's belly. It is as if the ending of the book is a calculated – and slightly sadistic – rejection of women.

In *Confessions of a Mask* we can see the elements that gave Mishima's work its immense appeal – the intense romanticism of the subject-matter, and the cool classicism of the style; these were the elements that would bring success to Françoise Sagan six years later with *Bonjour Tristesse*, and which had brought fame to Raymond Radiguet a quarter of a century earlier with his autobiographical *Devil in the Flesh*. (Mishima admitted to being strongly influenced by Radiguet, who had died at the age of twenty.) Sagan's range was to prove limited; so was Mishima's – but this was, to some extent, disguised by his fascination with style for its own sake, and with precise physical detail. (A character in the novel *Temple of the Golden Pavilion* remarks: 'The special quality of hell is to describe everything down to its last detail.')

In spite of his overnight fame, and the adulation that went with it, Mishima was not a happy man; he was subject to violent changes of mood – one of the penalties of his intense subjectivity. His work continued to be obsessed by a morbid sexuality. *Thirst for Love* (1950) is about a widow in her thirties who falls violently in love with a handsome young farm boy, and adores him from a distance; but when he shows signs of being interested in her, she kills him by driving a mattock through his neck. The reader senses that Mishima's attitude to this murder is as unwholesome as that of Powys's Mr Evans towards the idea of 'a killing blow with an iron bar'. The book is transparently a sexual fantasy in which Mishima kills the youth who attracts him. *Forbidden Colours*, which appeared in the following year, is an equally unpleasant study of an ageing homosexual novelist who takes his revenge on women by persuading a highly attractive young homosexual to marry them. Mishima's portraits of women often have some of the bitter, sadistic flavour that is reminiscent of Somerset Maugham in his most acidulous moods. To 'gather material' for the novel, Mishima began to spend a great deal of time in Tokyo's gay bars, although his attitude to homosexuals was ambivalent, and he also liked to cultivate intelligent woman friends.

On Christmas Day 1951, Mishima set off on his first round-the-world voyage – America, Brazil, Paris and Greece. The latter impressed him deeply, as it had impressed the young Oscar Wilde (another of Mishima's literary heroes), and he began to develop a cult of beautiful bodies, and of a Nietzschean 'will to health'. His own body was still, at this time, pitifully thin and unbeautiful. Back in Japan, he continued to enjoy fame and success – as early as 1953, his publishers issued his 'collected works' in six volumes. And in 1954, he achieved bestsellerdom with a novel, *The Sound of Waves*, an innocent story of love between a fisherman and a fishergirl that was based on Longus's *Daphnis and Chloe*, and which seemed to suggest that Mishima had turned his back on 'unwholesome' themes and was writing with a new classical purity.

In fact, Mishima's period of classicism was coming to an end; he was to write later: 'I don't believe in the classicism for which I had such a passion at the age of twenty-six . . . I exploited and used up my sensitivity completely.' He went on: 'At the same time I feel no attachment towards age and experience. Thus, in a sudden flash, is born within me the idea of Death. This is, for me, the only truly vivid and erotic idea . . . In a sense I may have suffered from an incurable romantic illness since birth.' This illness was his sadism and his obsession with blood.

In a gay bar, he had met a young homosexual named Akihiro Maruyama, who later became a distinguished actor and female impersonator. It was when he was dancing with Maruyama one day that Mishima suddenly decided that he was sick of his unhealthy body. Maruyama described it later in a television programme.

> When he got to know me first he was ugly and thin. Once we were dancing together in a night club, and I said to him jokingly: 'Where are you? I can't find you, you're so small. All I can feel is the padding.' . . . Straightaway he lost his temper, saying, 'I find this most unpleasant,' and flounced out.

He took up body building with typical obsessional passion: swimming, boxing, weight-lifting. It was a long, slow business – in 1958, after three years, a weight-lifter described him as looking 'too anaemic to go on'. But eventually he developed magnificent muscles. It underscored his exhibitionist qualities. 'When, at last, I came to own such a body, I wanted to display it to everyone, to show it off and let it move in front of every eye, just like a child with a new toy. My body became for me just like a new sports car for its proud owner. In it I drove on many highways to new places. Views I had never seen before opened up for me and enriched my experience.' Now he had physical attraction as well as fame to recommend him to those who appealed to him physically. He was fascinated by *onnagata* – male actors who play female roles in the Kabuki theatre – and he had affairs with many of them.

Financially he was immensely successful. His books were often filmed, his plays received lavish productions, his novels seldom sold fewer than 100,000 in the 1950s. And when, in 1956, his novel *The Temple of the Golden Pavilion* appeared, even formerly hostile critics hailed it as a masterpiece. It is the story of a Buddhist acolyte who burns down the temple because he is obsessed by its beauty; and it has many touches of Mishima's typical misogyny – like the club-footed monk who likes to seduce virgins, then abandons them. Its discussions of Zen Buddhism lend the book a specious kind of depth. In fact, Mishima was not a writer of ideas, and this was his greatest weakness; as with D. H. Lawrence and Henry Miller, his anti-intellectualism and distaste for thinking left him trapped in a world of mainly negative emotions.

In 1957, Mishima made a lengthy trip to America – he was obsessed by a craving for fame in the West. With typical will-power, he learned English in a few weeks from recorded tapes. It was a disappointing trip; he was hoping to see his modernised versions of *No* plays produced, but finally only a single one was given a private performance. Back in Japan, he learned with dismay that his mother – whom he adored more than anyone in the world – was seriously ill, probably with cancer; he decided to please her by getting married. It was an arranged marriage – as is still common in Japan – and he specified that his wife should be shorter than he was (he was only a little over five feet tall) and that she should not be interested in his work; he married Yoko Sugiyama, the daughter of a painter, in 1958, and they were to have two children. Mishima built himself a western-style house, with a statue of Apollo in the garden, and a home for his parents immediately next door (for in fact, his mother's health improved).

His next novel, *Kyoko's House*, was a critical failure; it was a 'study in nihilism' in which the four main characters are all aspects of Mishima; one of them, a narcissistic actor, commits a bloody suicide with his mistress. Another, a boxer, dies in a street brawl. Violence and blood continued to dominate his work. The attacks on the novel shook Mishima's confidence – it was his first taste of real failure; it seemed a bad omen for the Sixties – when, in fact, his popularity waned in Japan. *After the Banquet* (1960), a political novel, was a welcome success, but his satirical portrait of a real politician led to a court case (for 'invasion of privacy') which Mishima eventually lost. At about this time, he horrified his friends and supporters by acting in a film – not an 'artistic' film, which would have been perfectly acceptable, but a cheap gangster movie; Mishima not only played the part of a gangster, but sang the title music. (His friend and biographer, Henry Scott Stokes, remarked that Mishima was 'part gentleman and part gangster'.) It seemed to be a piece of pointless exhibitionism.

But 1960 was also the year that saw a fundamental change in his outlook – or at least, in his opinions. There is evidence that Mishima was feeling increasingly lost and directionless. In 1960, there were riots when the right-wing government revised its treaty with America, making its ties stronger than ever. The leftists and the students were outraged, and there were violent demonstrations. Mishima had never been much interested in politics – except as an ironic spectator – but now his craving for a direction began to take shape in a kind of reactionary idealism. It was in many ways reminiscent of the sort of religious idealism of T. S. Eliot and T. E. Hulme: a longing for medievalism and simplicity. In Mishima, this took the form of a powerful nostalgia for the days of the *samurai* – the warrior class who had lost power a century before, when Japan decided – or was forced – to open its doors to the West. Mishima was a descendant of the *samurai* (on his grandmother's side of the family) and he felt that he was one of the last great representatives of its noble traditions. There can be no doubt that one of the most powerful motives behind this conversion to militaristic romanticism was his fascination with the tradition of ritual suicide, *seppuku*. One of his favourite erotic images was a knife entering the belly. He made powerful use of it in a short story, 'Patriotism' (1961), which describes the ritual suicide of a young lieutenant involved in the abortive right-wing rebellion of 1936. Twenty-one officers had attempted to assassinate various army commanders whom they regarded as responsible for liberalising the army; they wanted the emperor restored to supreme command. When the emperor declared them to be traitors, the officers were captured by assault; two committed suicide, the rest were executed. Mishima's young lieutenant decides to kill himself because, although he had no part in the plot, he cannot bear to take part in the attempt to capture the rebels. The story is a lengthy and gruesome description of the ritual preparations of the officer and his wife, then of their suicide – with the graphic (and inevitable) description of the sword plunging into the abdomen. Mishima was later to direct and star in a film based on the story, in which he commits *seppuku* to the music of Wagner's '*Liebestod*'; it had an immense success in Japan.

The story of Mishima in the Sixties is basically the story of an actor who feels he has found an ideal role and is determined to play it to the end. His aim was – he wrote in 1968 – 'to revive the soul of the *samurai* within myself'. This was, in itself, a kind of suicide – in fact, precisely the kind of suicide embraced by so many of the nineteenth-century romantics: a rejection of reality in favour of a dream. In Mishima's case, the dream-like quality of these new political beliefs was underlined by his cult of devotion to the emperor-as-god. In 1946, Hirohito had announced that he was not a god and had never been a god. To Mishima, this meant that the millions of Japanese soldiers who died for the emperor-god had died in vain. He expresses his criticism of the emperor in the short poem, 'Voices of the Heroic Dead':

Noble and courageous souls are ignored; blood is defiled.
Everywhere apathy – pure blood dries up.
The wing of idealism is clipped.
If you talk of glory, the white ants laugh at you.
In such days, how can the emperor lower himself to be merely human?

And the souls of dead kamikaze pilots repeat in chorus:

How can the emperor lower himself to be merely human?

But in explaining his film *Patriotism* in a television interview, Mishima offered the vital clue to his imperialism: 'Such a way of very extreme eroticism, and such a bloody eroticism . . . maybe it was born in my mind from my birth. On the other hand, I don't want to show it as a private confession. I want to combine it with the public situation.' The 'public situation' was a reference to the status of the emperor as an ordinary human being. In short, Mishima's 'return to medievalism' was a method of expressing his sadistic eroticism.

That he was still in the grip of this eroticism becomes clear from the 1963 novel, *The Sailor Who Fell from Grace with the Sea*, one of his most 'unwholesome' pieces of writing. A thirteen-year-old boy discovers a hole through which he can look into his mother's bedroom and spy on her as she undresses. When she takes a lover – a sailor – he spies on their love-making. But when she announces that she intends to marry her lover, he determines on revenge. He is number three in a gang of precocious schoolboys. They decide that, since they are not punishable by law while they are under fourteen, they will kill the sailor before any of them reach that age. Their plan is to drug him, then to vivisect his body with a scalpel. The story ends as the sailor accepts a glass of drugged tea, and drinks it down. In her book on Mishima, Margaret Yourcenar describes the novel as 'icy like the thin blade of a scalpel', and praises its 'unbearable tragic beauty'. Most readers will simply find it unbearably sick.

The Sailor Who Fell from Grace with the Sea had relatively poor sales in Japan, and this seemed to be part of a general decline in Mishima's reputation in the Sixties. The Japanese are inclined to take their writers seriously – far more so than in England or America – but Mishima was beginning to acquire for himself a reputation as an exhibitionist, and something of a buffoon. And even before his rightist sympathies became obvious in the mid-Sixties, a leftist younger generation found his romantic egoism irresponsible. In 1963, Mishima had quarrelled with the theatre group, the *Bungakuza*, that presented his plays; they objected to certain 'rightist' speeches in his play *The Harp of Joy* – although at that time Mishima insisted that his political stance was neither rightist nor leftist. In the same year, he posed for an album of photographs, *Torture by Roses*; nude pictures of Mishima lying on the seashore, or posing in his garden with a white rose in his mouth, seemed to justify accusations of narcissism. In 1966, he posed for an even more extraordinary series of photographs by Kishin Shinoyama; one showed him as Saint Sebastian shot full of arrows, another as a leather-jacketed thug wearing a jock-strap and leaning against a motorcycle; in Japan – a country that prefers understatement – their theatricality was received with raised eyebrows. In a less restrained country, there would have been hoots of derision.

In 1965, Mishima began to write a book that he conceived as his masterpiece, a vast tetralogy called *The Sea of Fertility*; it would cover sixty years of modern Japanese history, and the central character would die at the end of each volume and be reincarnated in the next. The first volume, *Spring Snow*, was based on an eleventh-century romance describing the love-affair between Kiyoaki and the Lady Satoko. Kiyoaki is – typically – unsure whether he loves her or not until she gets engaged to someone else; then he seduces her and gets her pregnant. She has an abortion and enters a nunnery, where he is not allowed to see her. Now sure that he loves her – at last – he makes desperate and futile attempts to regain her, and finally dies at the age of twenty. The story is beautifully written, but seems oddly pointless. The second volume, *Runaway Horses*, is about a young right-wing terrorist – the reincarnation of Kiyoaki – who assassinates a businessman, then commits *seppuku*. In the third volume, *The Temple of Dawn*, the hero's friend, Honda, becomes convinced that Kiyoaki has been reincarnated as a Thai princess, and spends most of the book trying to confirm this. By the end of the novel, Honda has become a peeping Tom, and the princess dies from a snake-bite. In the fourth volume, *Decay of the Angel*, Honda adopts a beautiful boy called Toru, believing that he is the latest incarnation of Kiyoaki; but the boy becomes his tormentor. When Toru lives on beyond his twentieth year, Honda begins to doubt whether he is indeed his dead friend. He decides to visit the Lady Satoko, now the abbess of a nunnery. But although she grants him an interview, she flatly denies having ever heard of Kiyoaki. At the end of the novel, Honda finds himself doubting everything, even his own identity. And so *The Sea of Fertility* ends on a note of ambiguity. This may be intended as a reminder of the religious teaching of the Buddhist *Hosso* sect, which forms the philosophical background of the novel and which affirms that all experience is purely subjective and that existence cannot be verified. Mishima had stated that his title, *The Sea of Fertility*, indicated some kind of conversion from the nihilism that runs through so many of his books, but this is hardly supported by the ending of the final volume.

When the first two volumes appeared in 1969, the critics ignored them: Mishima's criticism of the emperor had made him virtually an untouchable. And by this time, Mishima's political activities seemed to confirm charges of exhibitionism and narcissism. He had by now formed his own private army or militia, the 'Shield Society' *(Tatenokai)* from right-wing students. At their inauguration, each dripped blood from a cut finger into a cup; then Mishima flavoured it with salt and they all drank from it while swearing loyalty to Imperial Japan. Some of them had to rush out to vomit. Mishima laughed at the sight of their red mouths and teeth and commented: 'What a fine lot of Draculas!'

Because of Mishima's reputation, the Shield Society was allowed to train with the army. Mishima's closest associate was a twenty-one-year-old youth named Masakatsu Morita, who became his lover. When Mishima showed the recruits their gaudy new uniforms, many of them left, confirmed in their opinion that this was exhibitionism rather than serious politics. The title of one of Mishima's last plays, *My Friend Hitler*, may have added to their doubts. (The English initials of the Shield Society are, of course,

SS.) Few people took the organisation seriously, and the newspapers which, a mere twenty years ago, had hailed Mishima as a writer of genius studiously ignored this latest lapse from good taste. But Mishima declared defiantly: 'Some people mockingly refer to us as toy soldiers. Let us see . . . Until the last desperate moment we shall refuse to commit ourselves to action.'

And so, on that morning of 25 November 1970, when Japanese television showed pictures of Mishima addressing – or trying to address – the assembled soldiers in the courtyard at Ichigaya base, the general reaction was one of blank astonishment. They found it impossible to take this 'stunt' seriously. And even the announcement of Mishima's suicide made little difference; the reaction to it was a kind of embarrassment. The 'buffoon' was trying to blackmail them into taking him seriously by driving a sword into his intestines; but after ten years of enduring his exhibitionism and sensationalism, the Japanese public was in no mood to be blackmailed. Many people suggested that Mishima had been insane; others thought that the double hara-kiri was merely a suicide pact beween homosexual lovers. And the same attitude persisted for more than a decade after his death. No Japanese biography of Mishima appeared (although there were two in English); his posthumous books were ignored. After attending the trial of Mishima's three accomplices – who received four-year sentences – his friend Henry Scott Stokes commented: 'It seemed as ironic an ending to the life-story of Yukio Mishima as *The Sea of Fertility* had been to his writing.'

Looking back over Mishima's career, it seems clear that the Japanese attitude towards his suicide is fundamentally sound. It was not, as he wanted the world to believe, a political gesture, but a sexual one: the outcome of a lifetime's fascination with blood and violence. So, as an attempt to prove his political sincerity, it was a total failure. In fact, as we study Mishima's works, and the events that led up to his suicide, we can see that he is a perfect example of what Sartre labelled 'magical thinking'. Magic, in this sense, has nothing to do with 'the occult'. It means simply a tendency to impose one's emotions on the real world – like a man who, seeing his wife in the arms of a lover, tells himself that she is being raped. Logically speaking, Mishima knew perfectly well that the emperor was not a god, and he would have resented any attempt to convince him otherwise. But his emotions – and his sexual obsessions – demanded a world of *samurai* ethics in which noble-hearted warriors disembowelled themselves in the name of the emperor. Translated into the world of literature, this attitude had a certain romantic authenticity – not unlike Tolkien's mythical sagas. In the world of modern actuality, it became an absurdity, rather as if Tolkien had organised a plot to overthrow Queen Elizabeth and put Gandalf on the throne of England. This is why the Japanese found Mishima's suicide embarrassing rather than inspiring; it was less of a noble gesture than a social *gaffe*.

Mishima's problem was that he was in the grip of the great romantic obsession; it had him by the throat and refused to let go. In that sense he was an archetypal 'Outsider', living in his subjective world like a baby in the womb, detesting the external reality that compelled him to acknowledge its existence. 'The body is doomed to decay, just like the complicated motor of a car. I for one will not accept such a doom. This means that I do not accept the course of nature. I know I am going against nature. I know I have forced my body on to the most destructive path of all.' There is an extremism about this logic that reminds us of de Sade. If Mishima had been a westerner he would have said, 'I do not accept God.' Like de Sade, and like some of Dostoevsky's heroes, he refused to accept that he himself was not the ultimate moral authority in the universe, the final arbiter of good and evil. But this placed him in a position that was basically solipsistic – which assumed, in theory at any rate, that he was the only person in the universe.

In that sense, Mishima could be regarded as one of the most symbolic figures in this book. As such, he enables us to understand the essence of romanticism. To put it crudely, we might say that before Richardson set the romantic revolt in motion, man took it for granted that he was a creature of his environment, ultimately dependent on the world around him; it would have struck him as insane to quarrel with the world. The novel was literally a *new invention*, like the automobile or the aeroplane, which brought him a new kind of freedom; it could carry him off to places that had formerly been inaccessible. Intelligent men began to catch a glimpse of an intoxicating but frightening idea: that man may be the *master* of the world, not its servant. In their moments of greatest confidence, poets like Byron and Lautréamont and Swinburne experienced a sudden conviction that they were 'monarchs of all they surveyed' – that, in some paradoxical sense, man is a god.

Now one of man's most basic problems is his desire to have his own way, to behave with total selfishness. But in the days before romanticism, there were certain natural limits to human selfishness. The most imperious and egocentric lord of the manor could only waste his days in hunting or seducing the daughters of his peasants. He thought of himself as a king, not as a god. Whether he liked it or not, he had to stay in touch with reality. But after Richardson, such a man could allow his egoism to carry him into a new dimension of selfishness; like de Sade, he could convince himself that he had no responsibility whatever towards other people.

Such an attitude raises a serious problem. Cutting adrift from reality may be exhilarating for the first hour or so, like an astronaut's sensation of weightlessness. But because our minds are so feeble, this soon degenerates into a sense of futility, a loss of direction. De Sade begins to suffer from the law of diminishing returns. Seduction is not enough; only torture and murder can satisfy the craving for the forbidden. This increasing demand for strong sensation is a natural result of the feeling of weightlessness, which deprives us of our sense of reality. The truly logical romantic, the romantic who refuses to accept half-measures, finds himself caught in the trap of solipsism, the terrifying sense that, in the last analysis, there is no such thing as reality.

This, as we can see, is what happened to Mishima; the last volume of *The Sea of Fertility* shows the result. Mishima announces that this tetralogy will be his definitive statement, his ultimate achievement; he sets to work as never before to convince us with the power of his realism. Yet in the final pages, the abbess announces that she has never heard of Kiyoaki, and Honda suddenly finds himself doubting his own sanity. And at this point, we seem to be able to hear the novelist saying: 'But you and I already knew there was no Kiyoaki – he was an invention of my mind.' We are trapped in a hall of mirrors, with its illusion of infinite regress. For the obvious corollary is: 'And you and I are also illusions . . .' And the novelist's 'ultimate statement' turns out to be a confession of his own insecure grip on reality. He reminds us of a man shouting, 'Listen to me!' and then, when he has obtained silence, announcing: 'I have nothing to say.'

POSTSCRIPT

The Fifth Window

How far does this study of 'sexual Outsiders' tend to confirm or support Charlotte Bach's theory of evolution? On the whole, the answer would seem to be that it does not. We have encountered no evidence whatever that transsexuality has some special status among sexual deviations and that all the other deviations spring from it. In fact, the greatest weakness of her theory is her failure to explain how sadism, masochism, necrophilia, exhibitionism and the rest arise out of the urge to transvestism.

Let us recall again the basic outlines of her theory. According to Charlotte, every man and woman has a powerful unconscious desire to *become* a member of the opposite sex. To remain 'sexually normal', each of us has to resist this urge, and the resistance generates a certain creative tension which is the driving force behind evolution. On a smaller scale we can see the workings of this creative tension in men of genius; it turns them into 'Outsiders', and drives them to 'objectify' their tensions in the form of works of art. But again, there seems to be little or no evidence for her theory. A few men of genius – Michelangelo, Leonardo, Tchaikovsky – have been homosexual, but homosexuality seems to have a hormonal basis; and in any case, it is not the same thing as transvestism; I cannot recall a single man of genius who was a transvestite. As to Shakespeare, Beethoven, Rembrandt, Goethe, Balzac, Hegel, it is quite impossible to see the slightest trace of transvestism in their work. Charlotte would reply: 'Precisely – they were men of genius because they repressed their transvestism.' But in that case, the onus is on her to demonstrate that what they are repressing *is* transvestism, and not – say – a Freudian Oedipus complex.

As to Charlotte herself, it seems clear that her own transvestism was a form of fetishism; dressing up in silk stockings sexually excited her. And if this study has demonstrated one thing, it is that sexual deviations are Pavlovian in nature, an *association of ideas*. A dog salivates when it hears a bell that it associates with food; a man salivates when he catches a glimpse of something he associates with sexual excitement. A single image can 'fix' the association – Swinburne's image of bare buttocks reddening under blows, Ellis's image of his mother urinating. Charlotte's image of sexual excitement was apparently feminine underwear, particularly silk stockings.

Charlotte's novel *Fiona* suggests another interesting possibility. The author attached great importance to the notion of the ten-spined stickleback performing the female courting dance when its male sexuality was frustrated. It is as if the stickleback is trying to supply the missing element – the missing vitamin, so to speak – from *inside* itself, just as the sexually frustrated adolescent tries to conjure up a naked girl in his bed. Fiona, Charlotte's image of the ultimately desirable female, is gentle, yielding, adoring, entirely uncritical. If he had encountered such a girl – or perhaps a series of them – it seems possible that he would never have developed the urge to transvestism; as it was, he tried to supply the missing vitamin from inside himself, and 'became' Fiona. This, at all events, seems to be an interpretation that fits the facts.

If this interpretation is correct, it suggests a view of evolution that has something in common with Charlotte's, but with an important change of emphasis. *If* the ten-spined stickleback is attempting to supply the missing stimulus from inside itself, then it is attempting to counter its frustration by a *rudimentary use of the imagination*. For what is the imagination? It is basically the ability to create 'substitute realities'. It seems clear that, by performing the female's courting dance, the male stickleback or zebra finch somehow assuages its frustration – and if this is not imagination, it seems remarkably close to it.

A dog responds to the smell of the bitch on heat. In human beings, the sexual response has been 'psychologised'; it is the human *imagination* that responds to a sexual stimulus. And it is possible to see human evolution as the development of imagination – our power to conjure up 'substitute realities'. Our ancestors invented tales of battle – and memorised thousands of lines of verse – so they could sit by the fire and experience some of the excitement of confronting the enemy. The Greeks invented the drama because the sight of actors *reinforced* the stimulus, and made the Trojan War or the story of Oedipus twice as real. By the time northern Europe invented the novel, the imagination had developed enough for a man to be able to sit alone with a book on his knee and share the moral dilemmas of Pamela and Julie and Werther.

But it is the next step in this story that is in some ways the most interesting. The Marquis de Sade whiled away his time in jail by trying to use his imagination as a substitute for the orgies he had been forced to forgo. But the imagination was still not strong enough to bear such a burden. One of his libertines admits that 'the imagination becomes vexed, and the slenderness of our means, the weakness of our faculties . . . leads to these abominations'. De Sade's mental orgies *weakened* his imagination – his sense of reality – so that he had to conjure up more and more nauseating forms of violation. He became subject to the law of diminishing returns. Quite clearly, the human imagination was not yet strong enough to meet the demands de Sade placed upon it. Victorian pornography, and the deviations described by Krafft-Ebing and Hirschfeld, could be regarded as a deliberate attempt to reinforce the imagination, as the Greeks had reinforced it by inventing the drama. By conjuring up images of the 'forbidden' – of incest, seduction of children, forcible violation and flogging – the Victorians transformed sex from a pleasant physical activity into a kind of intoxicating wickedness, the nineteenth-century equivalent of diabolism. They had invented 'superheated sex'.

But, like romanticism itself, superheated sex had one immense disadvantage. It condemned its devotees to a world of *unreality*. It opened up a gap between the world of feverish day-dreams and the world of common-sense actuality: a gap symbolised by that absurd picture of Swinburne standing beside Adah Mencken – gazing into her eyes, and looking crumpled, unwashed and unshaven. This is the gap that Mishima tried to bridge by hurling himself into political activity and body-building. Yet the gap remains ultimately unbridgeable because there is something inherently absurd in the idea of superheated sex, just as there is something unintentionally comic in de Sade's descriptions of sexual orgies. Grainger talked about his devotion to evil, but the standard reaction of those who have seen photographs of him trussed up in ropes is to murmur, 'Poor old Percy.' We feel that an adult who remains obsessed by this kind of thing has condemned a part of himself to perpetual adolescence. Most deviants seem to invite the comment, 'Poor old Percy.'

What is at issue here is the recognition – noted in an earlier chapter – that sex is important, but not *that* important. The psychologist Abraham Maslow expressed the same insight in his theory of the hierarchy of needs or values. Maslow suggested that the most basic human need is for food and drink; a starving man can think of nothing but food, and imagines that if he could have three large meals a day, he would be blissfully happy. If, in fact, he achieves this goal, then the next level of need emerges: for a home, a roof over his head, even if it is a cottage without running water or sanitation. If that need is satisfied, then the next level emerges: for sex, for love and human warmth. Every frustrated spinster imagines that she would be perfectly happy if she could find Mr Right. If this level is satisfied, then the next emerges: for self-esteem, for recognition by one's neighbours, for fame. And if all these levels are satisfied, then a fifth level may emerge: for what Maslow calls 'self-actualisation', for some kind of satisfying creative activity. This need not be artistic creation but any form of activity that we enjoy doing – and doing well – for its own sake.

We can see that, according to Maslow, sex is halfway down this hierarchy of needs; the natural course of human development is to satisfy the need and to pass on to the next level, the social level. Abnormal needs – like the desire to see a man killed with a blow of an iron bar, or to father children for the purpose of committing incest – may create an unusual intensity of imagination, but they also obstruct the normal course of an individual's evolution. Charlotte Bach contends that these abnormal needs create an intensity that drives us 'upward and on'. But every case in this book seems to prove the opposite. 'Perverse' drives create a certain feverish intensity, but they always seem to have disastrous side-effects that end up by dragging the individual to a lower level. And this – as we can see in de Sade – is because 'superheated sex' is subject to the law of diminishing returns.

All this is not to say that Charlotte was entirely wrong. There has undoubtedly been an evolution of human consciousness since the days of Samuel Richardson, and this evolution has been accompanied by a rise in 'sexual deviancy'. But if our analysis is correct, the deviancy is only a by-product of this evolution, not the cause of it; Charlotte was putting the cart before the horse.

To understand what has happened, we need to take a wider view of human evolution. H. G. Wells points out in his autobiography that, since the beginning of time, all living creatures have been 'up against it', so life is a perpetual struggle. It is this struggle, as Darwin recognised, that has been the basic driving force behind the evolution of species.

Yet it would not be true to say that living creatures are merely slaves of their environment. We fight the environment, and often win the struggle. Life is an active, not a passive, force.

The real problem of living creatures is that for most of the time they *are not aware* that they are an active force. They become aware of it briefly – as the lion tracks its prey, as the warrior gallops into battle – but, for the most part, they feel as helpless as leaves carried on the wind. When we look back on our struggles, we often become aware of how much we have achieved. Meanwhile, as we plod along in the present moment, trying to anticipate the next problem, life seems a long uphill grind.

Yet man has always had these moments in which he sees that things are not as bad as they appear – those moments of exaltation or deep relaxation, when he suddenly becomes aware of the powers of his own mind. It is in these moments that he suddenly grasps the basic nature of his problem: that he is stifled and blinded by 'close-upness' – by the sheer pressure of the world against his senses. The moments of insight permit him a bird's-eye view of his own life, and make him aware that his everyday consciousness amounts to a worm's-eye view.

His problem is simple, yet oddly baffling. He achieves the bird's-eye view through excitement, determination, response to crisis; *then* he grasps the extent of his own hidden powers. If he could somehow *maintain* this sense of awareness, then his problem would be solved. But the moment life is 'back to normal' – the everyday struggle with trivialities – he sinks back into the worm's-eye view, with its tendency to exaggerate problems and waste energy on pointless worries.

Man finds himself caught in a particularly insidious trap because his basic aim is to overcome long-term problems and enjoy a relatively crisis-free existence. But it is mainly through crisis that he achieves the bird's-eye view that liberates him from boredom. Crises make him feel more alive. So, in a paradoxical sense, the greatest obstacle to his long-term happiness is this civilisation that has cost him so much effort. He seems to be trapped in a kind of vicious circle.

Yet there *is* an obvious solution. A man appreciates a peaceful life for just as long as he can remember the inconveniences of a more unsettled existence. Another name for this memory of past inconveniences could be the 'sense of reality'. And human beings have a far more powerful sense of reality than any other living creature. We have more foresight than other creatures, more power to lay long-term plans and anticipate long-term problems. If a man knows that he must maintain a high level of vigilance to avoid disaster, then he will maintain it without any difficulty for as long as necessary. He does this by somehow 'programming' his unconscious mind to a high level of vigilance. Surely, in that case, man could overcome the 'worm's-eye view' problem by the use of his imagination, his 'reality function'?

And this, in theory, is indeed the solution. But there is a purely practical problem. Man has reached his present stage of evolution after about fifteen million years of struggle. It is only during the past few thousand years that, with the aid of his imagination, he has succeeded in creating this remarkable civilisation. It is hard to break the habit of fifteen million years and to recognise that he is not really the slave of his environment. And his habit of passivity is reinforced by the marvellous skill with which he has adapted to his environment. This has become so much a part of him that he is not even aware of it.

A simple mechanical analogy will clarify the point. If I drive a car with an automatic gearbox, the car appears to do most of the work for me. I approach a hill and the car slows down. I automatically depress the accelerator, and the engine goes into a lower gear, and sails up the hill without any difficulty. Once on the flat again, I ease my foot off the accelerator, and the engine slips into another gear.

If I drive a car with an ordinary four-speed gearbox, I am far more aware of my control over the vehicle. In fact, I may, like James Bond, prefer a car with an ordinary gearbox, because I enjoy this sense of control. An automatic gearbox *does too much for me*, and makes me feel as automatic as the car.

The human mind is like an automatic gearbox. When confronted by crisis, we slip into a more powerful gear without even noticing it. As a result, we tend to assume that *it is the crisis* that has galvanised us into effort; we fail to notice that *we* depressed the accelerator that caused us to change gear.

This may seem unimportant, but it has one immense disadvantage. When I am driving on the flat or downhill, the car slips automatically into fourth gear, and *I* drift into a state of bored indifference. And if I happen to detest boredom, my response is to *go and look for another hill.* In other words, when human beings find themselves slipping into the 'worm's-eye view', they do their best to create crises.

Now, as any driver knows, this is absurd; for even an automatic car has three manual gears in addition to its automatic mode. If I want to achieve a sense of greater control, I can use one of these.

Now we can begin to grasp the significance of the 'imaginative revolution' that has taken place over the past three thousand years. At the same time that man was building civilisation, he was also trying – dimly and instinctively – to create a 'manual gearbox' that would prevent him from becoming the victim of his own success. Henry V urges his men to:

> . . . imitate the action of a tiger;
> Stiffen the sinews, summon up the blood,
> Disguise fair nature with hard-favour'd rage . . .
> Now set the teeth and stretch the nostril wide,
> Hold hard the breath and bend up every spirit
> To his full height . . .

But by making use of his imagination, man learned to achieve these effects without the need to risk his life in battle; he could bend up his spirit 'to its full height' while sitting round a camp fire and listening to a bard reciting the story of the fall of Troy. And by the end of the nineteenth century, any imaginative child could achieve the same effect merely by reading the battle scene in *King Solomon's Mines.*

In other words, what man is attempting to develop is the power to summon the 'sense of reality' – and the energy and vitality that go with it – by a mere act of intense concentration, a deliberate 'change of gear'. I can, if necessary, hurl myself out of my armchair and across the room with a single bound. But I find it hard to perform the equivalent act of imagination: to hurl myself out of a condition of boredom and indifference into a state of total 'wide-awakeness'. Yet it *can* be done – particularly if we can begin to grasp the urgent necessity of learning how to do it.

In 1794, William Blake wrote:

Five windows light the cavern'd Man; through one he breathes
    the air;
Through one hears music of the spheres; through one the
    eternal vine
Flourishes, that he may receive the grapes; through one can
    look
And see small portions of the eternal world that ever groweth;
Through one himself pass out what time he please; but he will
    not,
For stolen joys are sweet and bread eaten in secret pleasant.

This 'fifth window', through which man can 'pass out what time he please' is the imagination. Before Richardson, each man was imprisoned in his 'cavern', with only his own life to live. After Richardson, he could slip out through his fifth window and live other people's lives.

But, as Blake notes, 'stolen joys are sweet, and bread eaten in secret pleasant'. One of the first uses to which man put this new faculty was sexual day-dreaming. So Clarissa is raped and Julie seduced, and 'Monk' Lewis's Antonia loses her virginity in a dungeon among rotting corpses. De Sade contented himself with murderous day-dreams; but two centuries later, killers like Ian Brady, Dean Corll and Ted Bundy put them into practice. The late twentieth century has seen the emergence of a horrifying new phenomenon: the 'serial killer', who wanders from place to place and kills – and rapes – women as casually as a cat kills mice. All this is the negative side of the imaginative revolution that began with *Pamela*. But this is no reason for condemning the revolution. Every major invention of the past three thousand years has been used for evil as well as for good; the 'fifth window' is no exception.

It is important to try and grasp the precise nature of this revolution. First of all, we need to recognise how far our senses – and their responses – are tied to the external world. From the moment I get up in the morning I am moving in a world of objects, and my life consists of continual manipulation of various objects. I may go through the whole day feeling like a slave of the material world around me. But if I suddenly begin to see an interesting way of solving some irritating problem, my mind seems to concentrate; I experience a curious flow of power, and a sense of *control*. Suddenly, I am no longer the slave of reality, but its master. It is as if I have pushed the material world to arm's length, so it no longer has any power over my emotions. It is then that I suddenly glimpse my human birthright: the power of my mind to control the world. *This* is the feeling that Homeric man experienced as he charged into battle; but Homeric man *needed* battles to experience this sense of control over the body and the emotions, just as a child needs to stand on a chair to reach the food cupboard. As I experience this sense of control, I realise that I am now sufficiently grown up to dispense with the chair. Homeric man was basically a child, and when a child is tired, he puts his thumb in his mouth and closes his eyes. But an adult can *summon* energy by awakening a sense of urgency. Moreover, when he has summoned the sense of urgency, he can see that it should be perfectly easy to do this at any time; he merely has to overcome that childish laziness, the tendency to surrender to the first wave of fatigue.

The real difference between Homeric man and modern man is that Homeric man had very little inside his head. If he sat alone, with nothing to do, he became bored. The rooms of his 'interior castle' (as St Teresa called it) were all bare and empty. But ever since then, man has been making furniture. The descendants of Homeric man created the *Iliad* and the *Odyssey*; Pythagoras and Socrates and Plato created philosophy; Euclid created geometry; Aeschylus and Euripides and Sophocles created the drama; Aristarchus and Eratosthenes laid the foundations of astronomy. And by the end of the Middle Ages, most of the rooms in the castle had *some* kind of furniture, so that no intelligent man need ever be bored. By the beginning of the twentieth century, most of the rooms were luxuriously furnished, even if some of the furniture was a little old-fashioned. By that time, man had made an interesting discovery: that he could spend days wandering around his castle without giving more than a passing thought to the external world. Chekhov has a story about a man who bets a millionaire that he can spend fifteen years in solitary confinement, provided he is allowed all the books he wants. At the end of the fifteen years, he leaves the millionaire a note saying that he wouldn't dream of taking his money, because he is too grateful for this opportunity to explore his own inner world: 'Your books have given me all wisdom. All that unwearying human thought has created through the ages is compressed into a little lump in my skull . . .'

This is the fundamental difference between Homeric man and modern man. When we experience that strange feeling of patience and inner control, we suddenly know that we are no longer children, that some great change is taking place inside us and that we are on the verge of adulthood. We can glimpse the meaning of that change in some of the great creators of the nineteenth century, men like Beethoven and Balzac and Dickens and Hegel and Wagner, who were inspired by the recognition that they had the power to create a whole world. Compared to Hector and Achilles, they were virtually gods. The Greeks would have felt that the creation of the *Comédie Humaine* or the 'Ring' cycle was an insane kind of *hubris*.

This is the real significance of the imaginative revolution that is the subject of this book, and of the lives of the 'misfits' who played such a central part in it. In sexual ecstasy, these men caught glimpses of a 'godlike' state of consciousness. They made the simple and obvious mistake of thinking that the key to such states lay in the sexual urge. But even before the age of romanticism, the work of de Sade had made it clear that this is not so. The sexual urge derives its strength from the body and the emotions, and is not powerful enough to lift us to a new level of conscious awareness. This can be achieved only with the aid of the intellect. Those who have attempted to use sex as a rocket fuel to escape the body's gravitational field have always come crashing back to earth. *This* is the real objection to the Charlotte Bach theory of evolution. Even allowing for the 'ritualisation' of deviations, it still seems an inadequate mechanism for evolution.

When, on the other hand, we grasp the full significance of the imaginative revolution, it becomes clear that *this* provides a basic mechanism for evolution. If, for example, we regard the peculiar behaviour of the ten-spined stickleback – the male performing the female courting dance – as a crude attempt to use imagination to overcome frustration, then we can also see that such an ability has an evolutionary value; a creature that can 'let off steam' in this way is fitter to survive than a creature that goes half mad with frustration.

One obvious objection is that it is hard to believe that a stickleback possesses any kind of imagination, no matter how crude. But this

254 · THE MISFITS

could be a mistake. I have cited elsewhere* the strange experiment performed in 1958 by Irvin Rubinstein and J. B. Best, in which they demonstrated that one of the most primitive of all creatures, the flatworm, can become bored if subjected repeatedly to the same crisis. Rubinstein and Best kept depriving the worms of the water they needed to live, and eventually the worms became so bored that they preferred to lie there and die rather than make yet another effort to locate water. Boredom ranks next to predators as one of the most dangerous challenges to life. But boredom is inconceivable without imagination. If my heart sinks at the thought of some 'boring' task, it is because I am already performing it in imagination. So even the flatworm – whose brain is so primordial as to be almost non-existent – must have some primitive form of imagination.

We can interpret the stickleback's courting dance as an attempt to *reinforce* its feeble imagination – that is, as a form of 'support'. We can also see that the same thing is true of the *Iliad* and *Agamemnon* and *Hamlet* and *Don Quixote*: they all serve as 'crutches' for the human imagination. The troubadours made the interesting discovery that romantic love makes a far more effective crutch than mere heroic adventure. Richardson made the even more interesting discovery that primitive sex is still more effective. While the romantics used imagination to create ethereal dream-worlds, the Victorian pornographers used it to conjure up bizarre sexual escapades. Both may have had disastrous side-effects (suicide and sex crime), but they undoubtedly taught human beings something of the proper use of imagination. Its purpose is not to conjure up dream-worlds, but to enable us to grasp the reality of other times and places, instead of being the slaves of the present moment. And since the sense of reality enables us to 'summon' our vital energies, we could say that the real purpose of imagination is to enable us to call upon our hidden powers. We are speaking, in fact, of the development of a new human faculty.

I have elsewhere† spoken of this 'latent sense' as 'Faculty X'. It is, quite simply, that curious ability that we all possess to suddenly grasp the reality of some other time and place. The simplest example occurs in *Swann's Way*, when Proust describes how, coming home one day feeling tired and discouraged, he tasted a

* *Mysteries*, pp. 327–8
† *The Occult*, Chapter 1, 'Magic – the Science of the Future'

small cake dipped in tea, and was vividly reminded of his childhood in Combray – so vividly that it was as though, for a moment, he became a child again. He writes: 'An exquisite pleasure had invaded my senses . . . At once the vicissitudes of life had become indifferent to me, its disasters innocuous, its brevity illusory . . . I had now ceased to feel mediocre, accidental, mortal . . .' The historian Arnold Toynbee described a similar event when he was sitting in the ruined citadel of Mistrà, in Greece, meditating on the invasion of 1821 that had turned the place into a ruin. Quite suddenly, it was as if he could *see* the barbarians pouring into the fortress, as if time had been obliterated.

We can see that in both these experiences, it is as if the imagination has been suddenly galvanised so that, instead of presenting a dim picture of the past, like a faded old photograph, it presents a kind of technicolor hologram that is indistinguishable from the real thing. We can also see that it does this by a kind of 'leap' of energy, a sudden *reinforcement*. This, quite plainly, is the end-product of three thousand years of 'reinforcement'. We are beginning to understand *why* life regards imagination as its most powerful instrument.

But Faculty X need not involve some specific time and place. Toynbee has also recorded how he once experienced a sudden flash of the whole of history, 'all that had been, and was, and was to come'. And Arthur Koestler has described how, sentenced to death in a Spanish jail, he tried to work out Euclid's proof that there is no ultimate prime number, and, as he succeeded, was swept into a kind of mystical ecstasy, a sense of floating on his back 'in a river of peace, under bridges of silence', at the thought that man has succeeded in saying something concrete about the infinite. Troubled by some faint sense of annoyance at the back of his mind, he remembered suddenly that he was due to be shot the next day, then brushed it aside with the thought: 'So what? Have you nothing more serious to worry about?' Here, we can see, he experienced Proust's feeling that 'the disasters of life' were innocuous. It is as if Faculty X involved the recognition that our apparent entrapment in time is an illusion.

But this 'mystical' aspect of it is unimportant. What matters is that curious feeling of power that enables us to overcome the sense of imminent defeat that dogs most of us throughout our lives. Because we lack imagination – the sense of reality – we exaggerate

the power that the material world has over our essential being. Like
children, we exaggerate our helplessness. The slow development of
the power of imagination is to enable us to realise that the helplessness is an illusion.

Compared to Darwin, such a theory may sound unscientific. In
fact, it was first propounded by that arch-Darwinian, Sir Julian
Huxley, in an essay called 'Transhumanism' (in *New Bottles for
New Wine*). Huxley argues that 'as a result of a thousand million
years of evolution, the universe is becoming conscious of itself . . .
This cosmic self-awareness is being realised in one tiny fragment
of the universe – in a few of us human beings . . . It is as if man
had suddenly been appointed managing director of the biggest
business of all, the business of evolution.' So far, says Huxley,
evolution has been mechanical and Darwinian, a matter of the
survival of the fittest. But human culture has given it a new
dimension. By means of art and literature and philosophy, man can
now pass on his mental evolution directly to his contemporaries
and descendants, without bothering with the biological mechanisms
of DNA. He has found a quicker and more direct method of
evolution.

Sir Julian Huxley died in 1975. Six years later, a young biologist
named Rupert Sheldrake propounded a theory that, at the very
least, added a new dimension to Huxley's 'transhumanist' view of
evolution. *A New Science of Life* is subtitled: 'The Hypothesis of
Formative Causation'. Sheldrake points out that heredity cannot
be explained entirely in chemical terms: DNA and so on. Something
else is needed, and embryologists have concluded that the 'something else' is a factor called 'morphogenetic fields'. The wing of a
bird or the tentacle of an octopus is shaped by a kind of electrical
'mould' – just like the moulds into which we pour jellies – which
is why many creatures can re-grow a limb that has been cut off.
These 'moulds' seem to be magnetic fields, which shape the living
molecules just as a magnet can 'shape' iron filings into a pattern.
Sheldrake suggests that these 'fields' can be used to explain some
rather odd observations made by biologists.

For example, in 1920 the psychologist William McDougal performed an experiment at Harvard to see if baby rats could inherit
abilities developed by their parents (the 'inheritance of acquired
characteristics' that Darwinists regard as such a fearful heresy). He
put white rats into a tank of water from which they could escape

up one of two gangplanks. One gangplank had an electric current running through it, and the first generation of rats soon learned to choose the other one. Then McDougal tried the same experiment on their children, and then on *their* children, and so on. And he found that each generation learned more quickly than its parents – he had proved that the inheritance of acquired characteristics *does* occur.

Now when a scientist performs an experiment on a group of animals, he always keeps an exactly similar group who are *not* subjected to experiments; these are called the 'control group' – the purpose being to have a ready standard of comparison. When a colleague of McDougal's – W. E. Agar of Melbourne – repeated his experiment, he also decided to test the control group at the end of several generations. To his baffled astonishment, these *also* showed the same ability to learn more quickly. And that was impossible, for they had merely been sitting passively in cages. It looked as if the control rats had learned by some kind of telepathy.

Not telepathy, says Sheldrake, but by 'morphic resonance'. The control group of rats 'picked up' the morphogenetic field of the trained rats in the same way that an iron bar can pick up the electrical field of a coil of wire and turn into a magnet. Simple induction.

Incredibly, this seems to work not only with living creatures but with crystals. New chemicals, when synthesised for the first time, are often extremely difficult to crystallise. But as soon as one of them has been crystallised in any laboratory in the world, it becomes easier to crystallise in all the others. At first, it was suspected that scientists travelling from one laboratory to another might be carrying fragments of crystals in their clothes or beards – or even that tiny quantities are carried in the atmosphere. Both explanations seem highly unlikely. The likeliest, Sheldrake suggests, is a process of 'induction' through morphogenetic fields.

A series of experiments has been performed to test the Sheldrake hypothesis and has produced positive results. At Yale, Professor Gary Schwartz found that people who do not know Hebrew were able to distinguish between real words in Hebrew and false words – because Jews all over the world already know the genuine words. Alan Pickering of Hatfield Polytechnic obtained the same result using Persian script. In another experiment, English-speaking people were asked to memorise two rhymes in a foreign language – one a well-known nursery rhyme, one a newly composed rhyme. The result – as the hypothesis of formative causation predicts – is that they learned the nursery rhyme more easily than the newly composed rhyme.

If Sheldrake is correct, then it becomes altogether easier to understand what has been happening since the time of Richardson. The obvious objection to the 'imagination' theory suggested in this book is that the majority of the inhabitants of Europe were illiterate, even in the nineteenth century, so that even the spread of circulating libraries could hardly explain the enormous influence of romanticism and of the 'sexual revolution'. Could a mere change in literary fashion explain why, by the time Krafft-Ebing came to write *Psychopathia Sexualis*, the capital cities of Europe seemed to have an astonishingly high level of sexual perversion? Is it not more likely, for example, that the explanation lies in the increasing stresses of industrial society? (One answer to that objection is that cases of sex crime in the nineteenth century occurred in rural areas as frequently as in cities.) The hypothesis of morphic resonance suggests an altogether more satisfying explanation. If Sheldrake is correct, we would expect the 'imaginative revolution' to spread to every class of society, so that it would affect illiterate working men like Bichel and Pieydagnelle and Verzeni as much as aristocrats like de Sade and Byron and Swinburne. It is true that, according to Huxley's 'transhumanist' theory, it *should* have been possible for the imaginative revolution to have reached every level of society by 'cultural osmosis'. But Sheldrake's morphic resonance certainly offers a more interesting and exciting interpretation of the facts.

It also suggests, of course, a more optimistic intepretation of human history. Darwin's theory of evolution by murderous conflict is, by general consent, one of the gloomiest ever advanced. Sheldrake's theory suggests that advances in the level of human consciousness can be passed on by a kind of magnetic induction; so that if one single human being could learn to achieve Faculty X at will, this ability would soon spread to every member of the species. Sheldrake's theory suggests a simple *mechanism* by which man could become the 'managing director of evolution' on this planet.

Having said which, it also becomes possible to see that there is a great deal more to be said for Charlotte Bach's theory of evolution than appeared at first sight. Like Huxley, Charlotte believed that man is at last in a position to take charge of his own evolution. He will do this by learning to understand his own dual nature, and then making conscious use of it to achieve higher levels of intensity: that is to say, he will learn to achieve consciously the same effect that the shaman and the man of genius achieve unconsciously. He will learn that his inner conflicts are not a misfortune but a source of power, like a dynamo.

We have seen that Hajdu's obsession with his own transvestism led him to overestimate the 'transsexual' element in the evolutionary process. But there *is*, undoubtedly, a transsexual element. All human beings contain male and female components, the 'animus' and the 'anima'. The great artist seems to be distinguished by his ability to understand and make use of his 'opposite'. We regard Tolstoy as a greater artist than, say, Hemingway, because he shows deeper understanding of women; and he does this by 'projecting' the feminine within himself. Hemingway remains trapped in his own masculinity, and seems insensitive and superficial compared to Tolstoy. Goethe recognised that it is this ability to enter into our own femininity – or masculinity – that 'draws us upward and on' – that is, that it is the driving force behind the evolution of the individual. It is also self-evident that the essence of artistic creation is a certain self-conflict or inner tension. When any human being decides to become an artist, he is offering himself as a hostage to his own inner conflicts.

When Julian Huxley talked about man taking control of his own evolution, he did not specify the exact nature of the process. But he *did* emphasise the immense importance of art in human cultural evolution. So it would be fair to say that Huxley's 'transhumanist' view of evolution could also be regarded as a theory in which human 'bisexuality' plays a central part. We may reject Charlotte's obsessive overemphasis on transsexuality while recognising the vital importance of her insight into the evolutionary process. She was fundamentally correct when she leapt to her feet shouting: 'That's what it's about – evolution!'

Where (it seems in retrospect) she went most wrong was in her theory of the mechanism of evolution: sexual deviations are displacement activities; displacement activities become sexual releasers; sexual releasers become social releasers; social releasers are passed on – through Darwinian mechanisms – to produce a

260 · THE MISFITS

more evolved species . . . But this may be less important than it seems. For the real core of Charlotte's theory is that the 'Philosopher's Stone' is another name for 'the eight-hour orgasm' – that is, for some level of consciousness that is far higher than the normal. And the 'romantic' theory of evolution that has been argued in this book suggests that man has evolved through the development of his imagination, and that this in turn aims at a revelation of *hidden powers*. The most important of these hidden powers is the function I have labelled Faculty X: the ability to suddenly *grasp* the reality of other times and places. At present, our experiences of Faculty X last for a fairly brief period – a minute or so at most. But if we could achieve control over them and learn to sustain them, then the result would be indistinguishable from Charlotte's eight-hour orgasm.

In that case, the vital question concerns the mechanism of Faculty X; *this* is what concerns the individual who is driven by an evolutionary compulsion. What actually *happened* when Proust tasted the madeleine dipped in tea, or Toynbee had his moment of 'time travel' in Mistrà? We can see that the stimulus acted like a coin dropped into a slot machine; there was a whir of mechanism and a sudden overwhelming sense of hidden powers. The reality function suddenly roared into life, bringing a sense of *mastery over time*.

Now if there is one thing that seems self-evident to human beings, it is that they do *not* have much power over time. 'Time like an ever-rolling stream/Bears all its sons away . . .' But this, as we have seen, is actually an illusion due to our 'worm's-eye view'. We are not helpless and passive. Human beings put up an extremely creditable fight, and some reach astonishing heights of achievement. Then why do we fail to grasp this? Because most of our time is spent in a dreary struggle against triviality and 'repetition'. We are trapped in the 'worm's-eye view', and the one thing we need above all else is to develop a 'bird's-eye view'. And that, of course, is another name for the reality function, imagination.

All this enables us to state the basic grounds for optimism about human evolution. Whenever men briefly achieve a 'bird's-eye view' of their lives, they are overwhelmed by a delighted feeling that 'all is well', and that their miseries and agonies were childish miscalculations. It suddenly becomes obvious that the philosophers who think that life is futile and that 'man is a useless passion' are mistaken, having allowed themselves to be hoodwinked by the 'worm's-eye view', which they assume to be more important than it is. (Sartre is even on record as saying that 'nausea' – the worm's-eye view – is the real foundation of human existence.) Since it is obvious that a bird sees more than a worm, then it follows that 'absurd good news' refers to an objective reality, and that the objective truth is that life is fundamentally good.

Now if it is true that all evolution has been a movement in the direction of the 'bird's-eye view', then 'glimpses' like those recorded by Proust and Toynbee may be seen as more than mere flashes of optimism. They suggest that human beings are getting very close to a turning point in their history – and in the history of life. They indicate that we are getting close to the truth that has been concealed from us by the 'worm's-eye view' and the sheer gravitational pull of the material world. Our senses may be dull and stupid, but once we have seen something at the end of our noses, it becomes impossible to doubt its reality. And when this happens, we have a stage in our development that could be labelled 'the feedback point'. The feedback point is that stage at which the pleasure – or profit – from any activity is greater than the effort we put into it. A simple example is what happens when a child learns to read; to begin with, it strikes him as a boring effort, then at a certain point he realises that books are full of things he wants to know, and reading becomes a pleasure. If I start a business, the feedback point is that stage at which I begin making enough profit to begin expanding.

Life has so far been forced to evolve through pain and inconvenience; living creatures have been goaded up the evolutionary ladder by discomfort. Yet, in the past few thousand years, man has begun to realise that the pursuit of knowledge can be enjoyed for its own sake, and that knowledge brings him a new sense of control, so that being alive becomes a pleasure in itself. He can still be undermined by fatigue and discouragement; yet in his moments of insight, he recognises that these miseries are largely self-inflicted. They are the result of confusion and short-sightedness; that is to say, they are subjective rather than objective. The moment we clearly recognise this, we have come close to the feedback point at which we would become 'undiscourageable'. A study of the history of the past few centuries suggests that we are now close to the feedback point in the history of consciousness – that man is on the point of achieving full consciousness of his evolutionary purpose, and ceasing to be the slave of mechanisms that confuse his sense of direction.

It is because Charlotte Bach – in spite of her conceit, in spite of her muddle-headedness, in spite, even, of her criminality – had caught a glimpse of this insight that I regard her as one of the most rewarding thinkers of the late twentieth century.

BIBLIOGRAPHY

Bartley III, William Warren. *Wittgenstein*. Quartet Books, London, 1974.

Bird, John. *Percy Grainger*. Elek Books Ltd, London, 1976.

Bloch, Dr Ivan. *Marquis de Sade. His Life and Works*. Brittany Press Inc., New York, 1931.

Crompton Louis. *Byron and Greek Love*. Faber & Faber, London, 1985; University of California Press, U.S.A., 1985.

Daniels, Guy. *A Lermontov Reader*. The Macmillan Company, New York, 1965.

De Sade, The Marquis. *The Complete Justine. Philosophy in the Bedroom and other Writings*. Grove Press Inc., New York, 1965.

——*The 120 Days of Sodom and other Writings*. Grove Press Inc., New York, 1966.

——*Juliette. 6 Volumes in One*. Grove Press Inc., New York, 1968.

Eaves, T. C. Duncan and Ben D. Kimpel. *Samuel Richardson: A Biography*. Oxford University Press, London, 1971.

Grosskurth, Phyllis. *Havelock Ellis. A Biography*. Penguin Books, London, 1980; Alfred A. Knopf Inc., U.S.A., 1980.

Haire, Dr Norman Ch.M., M.B. *Sexual Anomalies and Perversions. A Summary of the Works of the Late Professor Magnus Hirschfeld*. Encyclopaedic Press, London, 1938.

Hartnack, Justus. *Wittgenstein and Modern Philosophy*. Methuen & Co. Ltd, London, 1965.

Hayman, Ronald. *De Sade: A Critical Biography*. Constable & Co. Ltd, London, 1978.

Kelly, Laurence. *Lermontov: Tragedy in the Caucasus*. Constable and Co., London, 1977.

Knight, G. Wilson. *The Saturian Quest. A Study of the Prose Work of John Cowper Powys*. Methuen & Co. Ltd, London, 1964.

Knightley, Phillip and Colin Simpson. *The Secret Lives of Lawrence of Arabia*. Thomas Nelson & Sons Ltd, London, 1969.

Krafft-Ebing, Dr R. von *Psychopathia Sexualis*. Rebman Ltd, London, 1899.

Lely, Gilbert. *The Marquis de Sade. A Biography*. Elek Books, London, 1961.

Magarshack, David. *Gogol. A Life*. Faber & Faber, London, 1957.

Marchand, Henry L. *The Sexual History of France*. Tower Publications Inc. New York, 1968.

Marcus, Steven. *The Other Victorians*. Bantam Books, London and New York, 1966.

Martin, Jay. *Always Merry and Bright. The Life of Henry Miller*. Sheldon Press, London, 1979; Capra Press, Santa Barbara, U.S.A., 1978.

Moore, Harry T. *The Intelligent Heart. The Story of D. H. Lawrence*. Penguin Books, London, 1960.

Nabokov, Vladimir. *Nikolai Gogol*. Editions Poetry, London, 1947.

Nathan, John. *Mishima. A Biography*. Hamish Hamilton, London, 1975.

Powys, John Cowper. *Autobiography*. John Lane (The Bodley Head), London, 1934.

Raphael, Frederic. *Byron*. Thames & Hudson, London, 1982.

Ruggiero, Guido. *The Boundaries of Eros*. Oxford University Press, Oxford and New York, 1985.

Stokes, Henry Scott. *The Life and Death of Yukio Mishima*. Peter Owen Ltd, London, 1975.

Sulloway, Frank J. *Freud, Biologist of the Mind. Beyond the Psychoanalytic Legend*. Burnett Books, London, 1979.

Symons, Donald. *The Evolution of Human Sexuality*. Oxford University Press, Oxford and New York, 1979.

Thomas, Donald. *Swinburne. The Poet in his World*. Weidenfeld & Nicolson, London, 1979.

Troyat, Henri. *Pushkin. A Biography*. Victor Gollancz Ltd, London, 1951.

'Walter'. *My Secret Life*. 2 Vols: I–VI and VII–XI. Grove Press Inc., New York, 1966.

Wolff. M.D., Charlotte. *Magnus Hirschfeld. A Portrait of a Pioneer in Sexology*. Quartet Books, London, 1986.

Wolff, Tatiana. *Pushkin on Literature*. Methuen & Co. Ltd, London, 1971.

Yardley, Michael. *Backing Into the Limelight. A Biography of T. E. Lawrence*. Harrap Ltd, London, 1985.

INDEX

A

After the Banquet (Mishima) 236
Alastor (Shelley) 79–80
alchemy 36
Aleksander, Della 32, 41, 42, 44, *see also*
  Alexander, Derrick
Alexander, Derrick 30–32, *see also*
  Aleksander, Della
Aline and Valcour (Sade) 56, 61
animus and anima 24
Ann Veronica (Wells) 188
Apollinaire, Guillaume 66
Arnold, Matthew 115
Ashbee, Spencer 132, 161
asseverationists 24, 25
Atalanta in Corydon (Swinburne) 148
Austen, Jane 134
axolotls 35
Ayer, Sir Alfred Jules 217

B

Bach, Dr Charlotte Maria Beatrix Augusta
  19–46, 185, 213
  evolutionary theories 33–46, 244–6, 247,
  253, 258–62
  life story according to herself 21, 22
  life story, true 26–32
  personality 29–32, 39–46
  Homo Mutans, Homo Luminens 19–21
  Man and/or Woman 30, 33
  see also Hajdu, Carl; Karoly, Michael
Baker, Frederick 140
Balzac, Honoré de 131–2
Barbusse 87, 112
  Hell 17–18, 69, 169

Barbusse phenomenon 87–9, 138
Barrin, Abbé 81
Bedfellows, The 132
Bertrand, Sergeant 154–6
Best, J. B. 254
Bibliography of Prohibited Books (Ashbee)
  132, 161
Bichel, Andrew 139–40
Binet, Alfred 175
Bird, John 203, 204, 207
Black Spring (Miller) 197
Blake, William 124, 137–8, 213, 251
blasphemy 49–50
Bloch, Dr Ivan
  Marquis de Sade 72–5
  Sexual Life in England 48
Bolk, Ludwig 35
Borel, Petrus 80–81
Boris Godunov (Pushkin) 120
Boundaries of Eros, The (Ruggiero) 71–2
Breuer, Josef 173, 174, 180
Bride of Abydos, The (Byron) 103
Brothers Karamazov, The (Dostoevsky)
  43–4
Bruce, John 220–21
Burton, Sir Richard 147
butch lesbians 24, 26
Byron, Annabella Milbanke, Lady 104–5,
  110, 111
Byron, Catherine Gordon of Gight 94, 95,
  100
Byron, George Gordon, Lord 92–114,
  115–18, 123, 124
  life story 94–109
  Bride of Abydos, The 103
  Cain 104, 107

Childe Harold 92–4, 96, 99, 100–101, 103, 106, 107, 109–10, 120, 121, 124
Corsair, The 103, 116
Don Juan 107, 109, 117, 120
Giaour, The 103, 106
Hours of Idleness 96, 97
Lara 103, 104, 106, 116
Manfred 107, 116, 124
Byron, "Mad Jack" 94, 96
Byron, "Wicked Lord" 95

C

Cain (Byron) 104, 107
Captain's Daughter, The (Pushkin) 120
Casablanca 93
Castle of Otranto (Walpole) 80
Champavert: Immoral Tales (Borel) 80–81
Charcot, Dr Jean-Martin 172–3
Childe Harold (Byron) 92–4, 96, 99, 100–101, 103, 106, 107, 109–10, 120, 121, 124
childishness 35
Claremont, Claire 105, 107, 108, 109, 111
Clarissa (Richardson) 76, 77, 78, 84, 90
Cleland, John 81, 82–5, 132, 133, 137, 177
clothes fetishism 38
Confessions of a Mask (Mishima) 231–2, 233
Coolidge effect 87–9, 108, 111, 112, 212
Corsair, The (Byron) 103, 116
Corydon (Gide) 19
Cosmological Eye, The (Miller) 200
Count Oxtiern (Sade) 60
creativity and sexual perversion 20–21, 25
Crime and Punishment (Dostoevsky) 43
Crimes d'Amour (Sade) 67
criminality 41–4, 46, 63
Culwick, Hannah 157–8, 160
Cyon, Françoise 180, 181

D

Dagger, The (Pushkin) 119
Darwin, Charles 21, 39, 256, 258
Days of Sodom, The 120 (Sade) 47, 54, 58, 74
De Sade *see* Sade, Marquis de
Dead Souls (Gogol) 127–8, 129, 130, 131
Death of a Poet (Lermontov) 121–2
Decay of the Angel (Mishima) 240

definition of sexual perversion 18–19
denialists 24, 25
Dialogue between a Priest and a Dying Man (Sade) 53
displacement activity 34–5, 36, 38
Don Juan-ism 28, 29, 41, 216
Don Juan (Byron) 107, 108, 109, 117, 120, 122
Dorner, Dr Gunter 184, 185
Dostoevsky, Fyodor Mikhailovich 43–4, 120, 121
drag queens 24, 25
drama 91
Ducasse, Isidore 153–4

E

Earth, The (Zola) 187
Edleston, John 96, 98, 99–100
eight sexual types 24
eight-hour orgasm 25, 36
Eliade, Mircea 25
Ellis, Edith 179, 180
Ellis, Havelock 74, 178–83, 186
New Spirit, The 179
Sexual Inversion 179, 180, 182, 184
Studies in the Psychology of Sex 180
Eugene Onegin (Pushkin) 119, 120–21, 122
Eugénie de Franval (Sade) 57, 67
Eugénie de Mistival (Sade) 67
Evenings on a Farm near Didanka (Gogol) 125
evolution
a wider view 248–62
and sexual perversion 20–21, 25, 33–46, 244–6, 247, 253, 258–62
and social sensitivity 159

F

Fanny Hill (Cleland) 81, 82–4, 132, 177, 193
Faust (Goethe) 116
femme lesbians 24
fetishism 75, 175–6, 177–8
Fielding, Henry 85, 86, 133, 137
fifth window 251
Finnegans Wake (Joyce) 193–4
Fiona (Hajdu) 27, 29, 39–42, 45, 245
Fitzgerald, Scott 168–9
flagellation 48–9, 59, 72, 145, 150, 152, 156, 203, 205, 212, 219–22, 246

flogging *see* flagellation
Folwell, Joan 216
Forbidden Colours (Mishima) 234
forbiddenness 67, 69, 110, 112–13, 134,
  137, 246
Forest in Full Bloom, The (Mishima) 232
Frankenstein (Shelley) 107, 201
French Revolution 59, 77, 78, 149
Freud, Sigmund 172–5, 179, 180
From Time to Time (Tillich) 214–15

G

Gavriliad, The (Pushkin) 119
Ghosts (Ibsen) 187
Giaour, The (Byron) 103, 106
Gide, André
  Corydon 19
Giraud, Nicolo 99, 105, 117
Glastonbury Romance, A (Powys) 208
Glyn, Elinor 188, 195
Godwin, Mary 107, 108
Goethe, Johann Wolfgang von 78, 100,
  116–17
  Faust 116
  Sorrows of Young Werther, The 78, 100,
  116
Gogol, Nikolai Vasilevich 124–31
  Dead Souls 127–8, 129, 130, 131
  Evenings on a Farm near Didanka 125
  Government Inspector, The 127, 128
  Hans Kuchelgarten 125
  Marriage, The 129
  Nose, The 126–7
  Overcoat, The 120, 127
  *Selected Passages from Correspondence
  with Friends* 128
  Shponka and his Aunt 129
  Sorochintsky Fair 125
  Taras Bulba 126, 129
  Terrible Revenge, The 126
  Woman 128
Gordon, Mary 145, 147
gorillas 159
Gosse, Edmund 145, 150
Government Inspector, The (Gogol) 127, 128
Grainger, Ella 202–5
Grainger, Percy 202–7, 209, 211, 212, 246
Guiccioli, Countess Teresa 108, 109, 111
Gurdjieff, Georgei Ivanovich 136

H

Hajdu, Carl Michael Blaise Augustine
  26–32, 33–4, 39–46, 177, 181
  theory of sexual deviation 68–70
  Fiona 27, 29, 39–42, 45, 245
  see also Bach, Dr Charlotte; Karoly,
  Michael
Hajdu, Phyllis 28, 30
Hans Kuchelgarten (Gogol) 125
Harp of Joy, The (Mishima) 239
Heine, Maurice 55, 66
Hell (Barbusse) 17–18, 69, 169
Hero of Our Time, A (Lermontov) 122
Hiraoka, Kimitaké 231, *see* Mishima, Yukio
Hirschfeld, Dr Magnus 49, 70, 74, 90, 176,
  179, 183–7, 208, 246
  Sexual Anomalies and Perversions 15–17
  Sexual Disasters 185
  Sexual Pathology 186
Hobhouse, John Cam 97, 98, 99, 100, 108,
  115
Hoffmann, Ernst Theodor Amadeus 131,
  133
Holten, Karen 205, 206, 207
Homo Mutans, Homo Luminens (Bach)
  19–21
homosexuality 19, 22, 24, 25, 34, 179,
  182–5, 223–4, 244
Hook, Sidney 216–17
Houghton, Lord 147, 152
Hours of Idleness (Byron) 96, 97
Humphrey, Nicholas 158–9
Huxley, Sir Julian 256, 259

I

Ibsen, Henrik 187
Idiot, The (Dostoevsky) 43
imagination 70, 86, 88, 90, 250–53
incest 102, 105, 106, 135, 146, 147, 246
Industrial Revolution 77
Institute of Human Ethology 37

J

Jack the Ripper 170–71
Johnson, Dr Samuel 38, 45, 84
Josephine Mutzenbacher 136
Jowett, Benjamin 146–7, 150, 151

Joyce, James 89, 169, 191–4, 210–11
  Finnegans Wake 193–4
  Portrait of the Artist as a Young Man, A
    191, 192
  Ulysses 169, 192–3, 194
Joyce, Nora 210–11
Julie, or the New Héloïse (Rousseau) 77, 78,
  101
Juliette (Sade) 47, 64, 73–4, 113, 117
Jung, Dr Carl Gustav 24, 174, 213
Justine (Sade) 60, 66
Justine and Juliette (Sade) 63, 66, 67

K

Karoly, Michael 30–32, *see also* Bach, Dr
  Charlotte; Hajdu, Carl
Keller, Rose 51
Kipp's Apparatus 177
kleptomania 41–2, 46
Knightley, Philip 220–22
Koestler, Arthur 15, 255
Krafft-Ebing, Richard von 71, 75, 90, 140,
  174, 176, 179, 182, 185, 208, 246
Kreutzer Sonata, The (Tolstoy) 18
Kyoko's House (Mishima) 236

L

Ladies' Telltale, The 132–3, 135, 137
Lady Chatterley's Lover (Lawrence) 194–6
Lamb, Lady Caroline 98, 100, 101, 102,
  106, 110, 116, 117
Lara (Byron) 103, 104, 106, 116
Latouche, Charles Gervais de 81–2
Latour 51–2
Lautréamont, Comte de 153–4
Lawrence, David Herbert 64, 188–9,
  194–6, 200, 209–10
  Lady Chatterley's Lover 194–6, 209–10
  Plumed Serpent, The 194
  Rainbow, The 188
  Women in Love 194, 209
Lawrence, Thomas Edward 217–22
  Seven Pillars of Wisdom 123, 219–20
Leigh, Augusta 96, 102–3, 105, 106, 111,
  114, 115
Lermontov, Mikhail Yurevich 121–3, 124
  Death of a Poet 121–2
  Hero of Our Time, A 122

Tambov Treasurer's Wife, The 122
Lesbia Brandon (Swinburne) 147–8
lesbianism 22, 24, 148, 149, 179, 184
Lewis, Matthew 80, 101, 133
Louis XIV, King 81
Louis XV, King 50, 72
Louis XVI, King 52, 59, 72

M

McDougal, William 256–7
Maldoror (Ducasse/Lautréamont) 153–4
Man and/or Woman (Bach) 30, 33
Manfred (Byron) 107, 116, 124
Marat 60
Marquis de Grange, The (Sade) 67
Marquis de Sade *see* Sade, Marquis de
Marriage, The (Gogol) 129
Maruyama, Akihiro 235
Maslow, Abraham 247
masochism 49, 71
Masse, Nicolas 66
masturbation 90
Matthews, Charles 97, 99, 100
Maupassant, Guy de 149–50
Melbourne, Lady 99, 102, 106
Mellors, Bob 27
Memoirs of a Woman of Pleasure (Cleland)
  81, 82–4
Memoirs of Émilie, The (Sade) 67
Memoirs of the Devil (Soulie) 80
Mencken, Adah (Dolores) 150, 246
Milbanke, Annabella *see* Byron, Lady
Miller, Henry Valentine 196–200
  Black Spring 197
  Cosmological Eye, The 200
  Opus Pistorum 198–9, 200
  Tropic of Cancer 196
  Tropic of Capricorn 196, 198
Milnes, Richard Monckton, Lord Houghton
  147, 152
Misfortunes of Incest, The (Sade) 57, 67
Misfortunes of Virtue, The (Sade) 56, 60
Mishima, Yukio 230–43, 246
  After the Banquet 236
  Confessions of a Mask 231–2, 233
  Forbidden Colours 234
  Forest in Full Bloom, The 232
  Harp of Joy, The 239
  Kyoko's House 236

Mishima, Yukio (*cont.*)
  My Friend Hitler 240–41
  Patriotism 237, 238
  Sailor who Fell from Grace with the Sea,
    The 238–9
  Sea of Fertility, The 239–40, 241
  Sound of Waves, The 234
  Temple of the Golden Pavilion, The
    233–4, 235
  Thirst for Love 234
Moll, Albert 175, 176
Monastery Gate, The (Latouche) 81–2
Monk, The (Lewis) 80, 101, 133
Montreuil, Anne de 51, 52, 53
Montreuil, Mme Marie-Madeleine de
  50–51, 52, 60
Moore, Tom 102, 104
Morita, Masakatsu 230, 240
Morley, John 143–5, 147, 148, 149, 201
Morris, Dr Desmond 23, 34
Mrs Warren's Profession (Shaw) 187
Munby, Arthur Joseph 156–8, 160
My Friend Hitler (Mishima) 240–41
My Secret Life 160–68, 196, 201
Mysteries (Wilson) 44–5

N

Nabokov, Vladimir Vladimirovich 125
Nana (Zola) 187
necrophilia 17, 154–6
neoteny 35, 36, 43
New Bottles for New Wine (Huxley) 256
New Science of Life, A (Sheldrake) 256–8
New Spirit, The (Ellis) 179
Nicholas I, Tsar 119–20
Nietzsche, Friedrich Wilhelm 205–6
Nose, The (Gogol) 126–7
Notes from the Underground (Dostoevsky)
  43

O

Opus Pistorum (Miller) 198–9, 200
Origins of the Sexual Impulse (Wilson)
  18–19, 21
Orwell, George 197–8, 200
Outsider, The (Wilson) 17–18, 20, 46, 222
Overcoat, The (Gogol) 120, 127
Oxford, Lady 102, 117

P

paedophilia 15, 43, 97–9, 106, 246
Painted Banquet, The (Richards) 217
Pamela (Richardson) 75–6, 77, 78, 81, 84,
  90, 116
Patriotism (Mishima) 237, 238
Payne, James Bertrand 143
Pearl, The 134–5, 137, 138, 139, 152, 212
pederasty *see* paedophilia
perversion, definition of 18
Peter Pan-ism 35, 213
Philosophical Investigations (Wittgenstein)
  223, 228
Philosophy in the Bedroom (Sade) 61, 113,
  149
Pieydagnelle, Eusebius 140–41
Piping Hot (Zola) 187
Plato 38
Plumed Serpent, The (Lawrence) 194
Poems and Ballads (Swinburne) 143–5,
  148–9, 151, 153, 201
Pomeroy, Jesse 141
pornography 67–9, 81, 85, 86–91, 132–3,
  134–7, 147, 198–9
Portrait of the Artist as a Young Man, A
  (Joyce) 191, 192
Possessed, The (Dostoevsky) 43
Power of Mesmerism, The 135
Powys, John Cowper 207–9
  Glastonbury Romance, A 208
Principia Mathematica (Russell) 226
Prisoner of the Caucasus, The (Pushkin)
  118–19
Pritchett, Sir Victor Sawdon 76, 90, 132
Proposition, The [Tractatus
  Logico-Philosophicus] (Wittgenstein)
  223, 225, 226, 227
Proust, Marcel 84, 189–91, 254, 260, 261
  Remembrance of Things Past 189–90, 194
Psychopathia Sexualis (Krafft-Ebing) 71, 176
Pushkin, Alexander Sergeevich 118–21,
  123, 124, 125, 127
  Boris Godunov 120
  Captain's Daughter, The 120
  Dagger, The 119
  Eugene Onegin 119, 120–21, 122
  Gavriliad, The 119
  Prisoner of the Caucasus, The 118–19
  Ruslan and Liudmilla 118, 119

R

Rainbow, The (Lawrence) 188, 194
Rayevsky, Alexander 118
Reich, Wilhelm 64
Religion and the Rebel (Wilson) 222
religious obsession 49–50, 73
Remembrance of Things Past (Proust)
   189–90, 194
Renelle, Marie-Constance 60, 65
Richards, Jocelyn 217
Richardson, Samuel 75–7, 79, 81, 100, 101,
   132, 254
   Clarissa 76, 77, 78, 84, 90
   Pamela 75, 76, 77, 78, 81, 84, 90, 116
Ritual in the Dark (Wilson) 37–8
Rogers, Samuel 92, 101
Rossetti, Dante Gabriel 146, 147, 150, 156,
   158
Rousseau, Jean-Jacques 77–8, 100
   Julie, or the New Héloïse 77, 78, 101
   Social Contract, The 78
Rubinstein, Irvin 254
Ruggiero, Guido 71–2
Runaway Horses (Mishima) 239
Ruslan and Liudmilla (Pushkin) 118, 119
Russell, Alys 215–17
Russell, Bertrand Arthur William, Lord
   215–17, 224
   Principia Mathematica 226
Russell, Dora 216, 224

S

Sade, Donatien Alphonse François,
   Marquis de 46, 47–70, 73–5, 113, 147,
   152, 160, 169, 246
   philosophy of sex 64–70
   Aline and Valcour 56, 61
   Count Oxtiern 60
   Days of Sodom, The 120 47, 54, 58, 74
   *Dialogue between a Priest and a Dying
   Man* 53
   Eugénie de Franval 57, 67
   Juliette 73–4, 113, 117, 47, 64
   Justine 60, 66
   Justine and Juliette 63, 66, 67
   Marquis de Grange, The 67
   Memoirs of Émilie, The 67
   Misfortunes of Incest, The 57, 67
   Misfortunes of Virtue, The 56, 60
   Philosophy in the Bedroom 61, 113, 149
Sade, Renée-Pelagie, Comtesse de 50, 52,
   54, 59
sadism 47, 49, 71, 153, 156, 202–3, 207–9,
   235
*Sailor who Fell from Grace with the Sea,
   The* (Mishima) 238–9
salamanders 35
Sanger, Margaret 180
Schwartz, Prof Gary 257–8
science according to Charlotte Bach 36–7
Scott, Sir Walter 100, 103, 131, 132
Sea of Fertility, The (Mishima) 239–40, 241,
   243
Secret Lives of Lawrence of Arabia, The
   (Knightley & Simpson) 220–22
Segati, Marianna 108, 111
*Selected Passages from Correspondence
   with Friends* (Gogol) 128
Selincourt, Hugh de 181
Selwyn, George 17
Seven Pillars of Wisdom (Lawrence) 123,
   219–20
sex crimes 138–42, 169–71
Sexual Anomalies and Perversions
   (Hirschfeld) 15–17
Sexual Disasters (Hirschfeld) 185
Sexual Inversion (Ellis & Symonds) 179,
   180, 182, 184
Sexual Life in England (Bloch) 48
Sexual Pathology (Hirschfeld) 186
shamanism 25
Shaw, George Bernard 187, 219
Sheldrake, Rupert 256–8
Shelley, Mary 107, 108, 124
   Frankenstein 107, 201
Shelley, Percy Bysshe 79–80, 107, 108, 109,
   124
Shponka and his Aunt (Gogol) 129
Simpson, Colin 220–22
Sitwell, Sir Osbert 146
Smith, Alys Pearsall 215–16
Smollett, Tobias 85, 86, 133, 137
Social Contract, The (Rousseau) 78
Sodom, The 120 Days of (Sade) 47, 54, 58,
   74
sodomy 49, 50, 59
Sodomy Simplified (Hobhouse) 97
Song of Songs, The (Sudermann) 188

Songs Before Sunrise (Swinburne) 151, 152, 153
Sorochintsky Fair (Gogol) 125
Sorrows of Young Werther, The (Goethe) 78, 100, 116
Soulie, Frederic 80
Sound of Waves, The (Mishima) 234
Spring Snow (Mishima) 239
Sterne, Laurence 85–6, 137
sticklebacks 23, 34, 70, 253–4
Story of Dom Bugger, The (Latouche) 81–2
Strom, Ella 202–5
Studies in the Psychology of Sex (Ellis) 180
Study of Human Sexuality, The (Symons) 87–9
Study of Instinct, The (Tinbergen) 34
Sudermann, Hermann 188
Swinburne, Algernon Charles 143–53, 154, 156, 160, 201, 213, 246
   Atalanta in Corydon 148
   Lesbia Brandon 147–8
   Poems and Ballads 143–5, 148–9, 151, 153, 201
   Songs Before Sunrise 151, 152, 153
Symonds, John Addington 179, 183
Symons, Donald 87–9
Symposium (Plato) 38
Systematic Theology (Tillich) 214

T

Tambov Treasurer's Wife, The (Lermontov) 122
Taras Bulba (Gogol) 126, 129
Tchaikovsky, Pyotr Ilyich 183
Temple of Dawn, The (Mishima) 240
Temple of the Golden Pavilion, The (Mishima) 233–4, 235
Terrible Revenge, The (Gogol) 126
Thirst for Love (Mishima) 234
This Side of Paradise (Fitzgerald) 168–9
Thomas, Lowell 218
Three Weeks (Glyn) 188, 195
Tillich, Dr Paul 214–15
   Systematic Theology 214
Tillich, Hannah
   From Time to Time 214–15
Tinbergen
   Study of Instinct, The 34

Tolstoy, Count Lev Nikolaevich
   Kreutzer Sonata, The 18
Toynbee, Arnold Joseph 255, 260, 261
Tractatus Logico-Philosophicus (Wittgenstein) 223, 225, 226, 227
transvestism 21–2, 23, 24, 25, 26, 28, 30–32, 34, 37, 42, 43, 185, 244
Tristram Shandy (Sterne) 85–6
Tropic of Cancer (Miller) 196–7
Tropic of Capricorn (Miller) 196, 198
TV *see* transvestism

U

Ulysses (Joyce) 169, 192–3, 194
urolagnia 178, 180–81, 186

V

Venus in the Cloister (Barrin) 81
Verzeni, Vincent 141
voyeurism 17

W

Wainhouse, Austryn 66
Walpole, Horace 80
Watts-Dunton, Theodore 151–2
Wells, Herbert George 188, 248
Wilde, Oscar 182, 183
Wilson, Colin
   Mysteries 44–5
   Origins of the Sexual Impulse 18–19, 21
   Outsider, The 17–18, 20, 46, 222
   Religion and the Rebel 222
   Ritual in the Dark 37–8
With Lawrence in Arabia (Thomas) 218
Wittgenstein, Ludwig Josef Johann 222–9
   Philosophical Investigations 223, 228
   Tractatus Logico-Philosophicus 223, 225, 226, 227
Woman (Gogol) 128
Women in Love (Lawrence) 194, 209–10
Wordsworth, William 124

Z

zebra finches 23, 34, 39
Zola, Émile 187

DATE DUE

HIGHSMITH   #LO-45220